Proverbs

A Devotional Commentary
Volume Two

Chapters 7-12

PTLB
PRINCIPLES
TO LIVE BY
LIFE IS RELATIONSHIPS

Gil Stieglitz

Proverbs: A Devotional Commentary

Volume Two

Chapters 7-12

© Gil Stieglitz 2015

Published by Principles to Live By, Roseville CA 95661

www.ptlb.com

Cover by John Chase

All Scripture verses are from the New American Standard Bible unless otherwise indicated.

New American Standard Bible: 1995 update.

1995 La Habra, CA: The Lockman Foundation.

ISBN 978-0-9909641-5-5

Commentary

Printed in the United States of America

Dedication

This book is dedicated

to the *Stieglitz* family

and to those who are

or will be a part of my family

through faith.

Table of Contents

Preface

This small little project which was originally meant to help my girls – Jenessa, Abbey, and Grace as they grew up and raised families of their own – has turned into a 2400+ page behemoth which just scratches the surface of God's wisdom through the pen of Solomon. I feel very privileged that these devotional thoughts on God's wisdom through Solomon have been spread around the world through email. I have received many encouragements to collect these thoughts into a commentary so people can easily go to any verse in the Proverbs and understand the depth of what Solomon is saying. The fact that many have been filled with God's wisdom to act differently than they would in themselves means that my comments have helped Solomon achieve the original purpose for the Proverbs.

I must give thanks to a number of crucial people who without their efforts these volumes would not exist. Sandy Johnson who has read these comments over and over to edit them, you are invaluable. Debbie Purvis is a true God-send as she has seamlessly made the material in this book ready for publication and arranged with all the appropriate people to make these volumes happen.

I must give thanks to my Hebrew professor Dr. Tom Finley from Talbot School of Theology who made me memorize many sections of Scripture in Hebrew and understand the Hebrew grammatical structures until I grasped at least some level of Hebraic thinking. What you taught gave me the opportunity to dig deeper than the average reader of the proverbs.

I must also give thanks to Richard K. Hum who was at one time my youth pastor and instilled in me a deep love of the Scriptures. He put into me the incredible value of digging deep in Scripture in order to understand it and then the value of meditating upon it to initiate a more lasting change. I can remember countless times when he initiated my memorizing Scripture and quizzed me about the lessons that that Scripture should have on my life if I really took it seriously.

How can I not thank my wonderful wife, Dana? Every day she asks me what God said in my quiet time. What verses from the Proverbs did God highlight to you last night? What insights did God give you about our situation through the Scriptures? What do you think God wants you to do? Her rapt attention and desire to live in the will of God completely is another constant joy to me.

I must thank the Lord God Almighty who is willing to meet with me about my petty issues and pour out wisdom to me personally so that I will be wiser. It is a wonderful grace that He gives. The wonder of my interaction with God through the pages of the Scriptures and often through Proverbs is my daily highlight. Almost every night I enjoy a deep interaction with God about my day, the state of our world, my concerns, meetings I have planned in the future, and things I hope to accomplish. I am thrilled to say that the answers to my questions to God pour out from the Scriptures. It is wonderful to know that I can ask God a question and He will answer. More often than not His answers to my personal questions come through the proverbs. He explains how my natural reaction is not correct and that there is a better way to handle the situation. He helps me dig for a higher level of wisdom than I would pursue on my own. He helps me classify a person's tendency and understand how to treat that type of behavior.

Prepare to be amazed by the insights from a man who lived 1,000 years before Jesus Christ. What you wanted to know about how to handle the people in your life is in this book; don't miss it.

Introduction

King David kept saying to his young son Solomon that the key to life was to *Acquiring Wisdom* and *Acquiring Understanding*. In other words if Solomon was going to be successful in life, he was going to need both of these crucial qualities in increasing amounts: Wisdom and Understanding. David boiled success in life down to these two things for his young son, Solomon: If you get these, my son, then you will be guaranteed a great life. What was David trying to pound into Solomon's head as the keys to a great life? Wisdom in the proverbs means to know how to find and make the triple-win choice. Wisdom is the choice that would honor God, benefit others, and be a win for the individual. Wisdom is the practical application of information and people in such a way as God is glorified, righteous people are benefited, and the individual also wins. Understanding in the book of Proverbs means that the individual sees the connections between people, events, situations, and reactions. Seeing both the public and hidden connections changes how one acts, speaks, and plans. We see in the book of Proverbs that Solomon got his father's message – even more than David could have imagined.

God inspired Solomon, the King of Israel, to record incredibly insightful wisdom on human relations. This book was penned 3,000 years ago, and it is still weighty, profound, and insightful about making our way through life. Let me give you an abbreviated list of the wisdom in this book. There are in this book the secrets of leadership. There are comparisons throughout this book that bring us to our senses before we get lost in a stupid pursuit or perspective. There is in this book the ways to deal with 63 different kinds of fools that will come into your life at various times. There are in these pithy sayings the rules of money that will allow you to gain all you need without being corrupted by it. There are crucial insights for marriage. This book contains the answers on how to conduct your life so you stop yourself from being stupid or destructive. In reality, the secrets of having a great relational life are recorded in the powerful statements in the book of Proverbs. It is amazing. Too often a person waits till they have experience before they know what to do. The Book of Proverbs is God's way of saying: here is wisdom so you don't have to learn the hard way what is the wise path. There is not a day that goes by that I do not consult the book of Proverbs for God's answers to the specific issues and problems I am facing. This book is a collection of my comments about Solomon's insights into life and people.

Take a look at the genesis of the book of Proverbs. Solomon did not start out as the smartest man to ever walk the planet (just like all of us). He started as an overwhelmed, young man who inherited a job that was too big for him. He knew it and the people knew it. He cried out to God for wisdom and insight to be able to rule the people he had been put over. God's answer to Solomon's prayer clearly came true.

> 1 Kings 1:3:5 - *In Gibeon the Lord appeared to Solomon in a dream at night; and God said, "Ask what you wish Me to give you." Then Solomon said, "You have shown great loving kindness to your servant David my father according as he walked before you in truth and righteousness and uprightness of heart toward You; and you have reserved for him this great loving kindness that You have given him a son to sit on his throne, as it is this day. Now, O Lord my God, You have made Your servant king in place of my father David, yet I am but a little child; I do not know how to go out or come in. Your servant is in the midst of Your people which You have chosen, a great people who are too many to be numbered or counted. So give your Servant an understanding heart to judge Your people to discern between good and evil. For who is able to judge this great people of Yours?"*

It was pleasing in the sight of the Lord that Solomon had asked this thing. God said to him, "Because you have asked this thing and have not asked for yourself long life, nor have asked riches for yourself, nor have you asked for the life of your enemies, but have asked for yourself discernment to understand justice, behold, I have done according to your words. Behold, I have given you a wise and discerning heart, so that there has been no one like you before you, nor shall one like you arise after you. I have also given you what you have not asked, both riches and honor, so that there will not be any among the kings like you all your days. If you walk in My ways, keeping My statutes and commandments as your father David walked, then I will prolong your days."

Aren't you glad that Solomon wrote down some of the insights that God gave him so that we could benefit from the wisdom that he received? I believe that if you cry out to God for wisdom rather than riches and power, God will give you wisdom. I believe He will direct you to the book of Proverbs and the wisdom He gave Solomon. My prayer is that you will grow and behave differently because of the explanations and understandings that come from this devotional commentary on Proverbs.

Proverbs 7

Chapter 7

PROVERBS 7:1 · *My son, keep my words and treasure my commandments within you.*

This is the thirteenth group of instructions to the young learner of wisdom in the book of Proverbs. The master pauses and instructs his pupils in the ways of wisdom in short little groupings.

This is the second packet of instruction on the problem of adultery and how to avoid it. The last packet of information on this subject was in what we call chapter 5 but what was the 7th packet of wisdom information.

This particular pathway of foolishness called adultery is so tempting and such a sure way to be diverted from a fruitful and productive life that Solomon spends a lengthy period of time to give an example of a person he has seen be sucked into this errant path. This type of example or actual story is unique in the book of Proverbs, suggesting that this diversion from the path of wisdom is the most common or the most powerful. Those who would learn wisdom or live wisdom must be aware of the power and the danger of this foolish direction.

The point of this section of the proverb is to show the results of those who go down this path. Solomon even shares the nature of the conversation and the look of the woman. We are taken inside the foolishness so that its powerful, seductive energy will be known to us and thereby not as intoxicating. Solomon is saying: watch for this; watch for that; this is what it will feel like; don't get fooled by this. It is all the same and has been that way since the time of Solomon and before.

The young learner is to observe the interaction of adultery from a safer emotional distance. They are to see the trap being sprung and the effect in the individual. He wishes that he had not done it even though he wanted with all his being to do it before he did it.

treasure my commandments within you

The things I am saying are so valuable – is what Solomon is saying. You have to realize how valuable and to embrace their value. This is not relative value; this is absolute value. If you want to have a life filled with riches, honor, and life, then do not go down this path. The seductions of the adulterous and adulterer are strong and seem incredibly valuable, but they are fake pearls and cosmetic jewelry. They have no real value compared to wisdom.

Remember these lessons and do not give in to the pull of illicit sexual behavior.

In our day and age this type of lesson needs to be taught to young men from 11 to 65 years of age and maybe beyond. The spread of pornography and a loose culture adds to the acceptance of this wisdom-destroying action. Realize that if one is to make something of one's life and not get shoved into a dead end cul-de-sac in life, one has to practice self-limiting behavior. Only when we practice self-control and stop ourselves short of all we could do, do we prepare ourselves for great relationships and have the control and energy to excel at what is really important.

PROVERBS 7:2 - Keep my commandments and live, and my teaching as the apple of your eye.

What commandments are being mentioned? Clearly the whole, but specifically a group of commandments that are the capsulated summary of what will be said in the whole of the book – Prov. 3:3-11.

> **Do not let kindness and truth leave you**
>
> **Trust in the LORD with all your heart**
>
> **Do not lean on your own understanding**
>
> **In all your ways acknowledge Him**
>
> **Do not be wise in your own eyes**
>
> **Fear the LORD and turn away from evil**
>
> **Honor the LORD from your wealth**
>
> **My son, do not reject the discipline of the LORD**

These commandments form the core of what God is trying to get people to do in life. These are simple rules, but many get sucked aside from the paths of life by violations of these simple rules – adultery, pride, get-rich-quick schemes, hoarding, greed. The next few verses will detail the problems of adultery. It looks like it is all sweetness and light, but instead it is a narrow well.

PROVERBS 7:3 - *Bind them on your fingers; write them on the tablet of your heart.*

bind them on your fingers

This seems to refer to a physical way of reminding. It could have been how our culture got the idea of tying a string around your finger to remind you of something. The idea is that every day one needs physical reminders to prod us to remember the biblical truth that will be the focus of the day. The soul needs training and a template for the day. Give it Scripture. Each day write down a verse, phrase, or word from Scripture that God can use to direct your actions, speech, and thoughts that day.

write them on the tablet of your heart

The word *heart* expresses the deepest inner recesses of a person – both the material and immaterial aspects of a man's being. This is the soul and the mind.

What is interesting here is that the soul is open to new programming. Humanity is not just the result of random chemicals or the reactions to those who act upon it. God declares that a person can program his/her soul to follow a righteous set of instructions. In our day of evolution and naturalism we have almost completely ignored the soul as an aspect of mankind. We believe that there is nothing beyond the brain and the firing of the nerves in it. This, however, is not true. Mankind has a soul – an immaterial part of their being that is not dependent upon the physical. Studies done on those who have gone through various surgical procedures and have been pronounced brain-dead have been able to recount memories of the time during which they were brain-dead. This suggests that those memories were stored in something beyond the brain. It is the strongest purely physical evidence of the existence of the soul.

We must be roused from our naturalistic stupor and re-embrace the fullness of what we were created to be – mankind body, soul, and spirit. It is in the soul that the programming for the life you live will take place. We are not only the product of our environment, our genes, and the universe as a whole. God declares that we can be different than the flow around us. We can program the soul to respond to different stimulus than the natural.

We don't have to be proud, selfish, greedy, power hungry, immoral, and lazy beings; but instead we can take the Word of God internally and use it as an operating system for our lives to orient us to God and run the hardware of our body.

We have largely given up on moral training because we have bought the lie of being only physical chemical beings. Moral training is essential to have a civilized society. Instead of moral training, we have substituted advertising and have bombarded our body and soul with messages of materialism, lust, selfishness, greed, and envy until it is these messages that form the dominant operating system for our lives.

This is tragic because we already had an orientation toward these things in our fleshly nature anyway. Since the fall of Adam, mankind has been oriented to selfishness and rebellion. And added on top of that is the orientation toward activities that will destroy relationships with God and others – further immoral training is tragic.

This is a long way of saying that what we think about and repeat over and over again programs us. What we hear repeatedly, sing, or watch in the movie theater of our mind creates an orientation to the world. If that orientation is not godly, then we will go in that direction. Jesus stated this when He said: *If your eye be single then your whole body is full of light... but if the light that is in you is darkness... how great is the darkness.* If the internal messages that are guiding your life are all materialistic, sexual, selfish, haughty, and angry, then your life will be constantly directed toward destruction.

God's way is different; it orients us toward relationships, not against them. It guides us to submission to God rather than rebellion. We have a constant need to hear again these counter-intuitive messages or we will never make the right choices.

Let's get practical. This proverb would suggest that one needs to have a phrase or verse that you are repeating over and over again that day which will be your moral prod that day. It could be one of the two great commandments. It could be one of the Ten Commandments. It could be one of the Proverbs. It could be the fruit of the spirit. It could be a particular word from Scripture that you are focusing on that day.

If you don't have a verse or phrase of Scripture to ruminate on, then most likely you will be left with some advertising slogan you hear or a song on the radio you like or a phrase from a character on TV. These are rarely, if ever, moral training. These phrases will not keep you out of trouble. In fact, the phrases from advertising, music, and TV often encourage impulsive, selfish, and rebellious behavior.

What is your godly phrase today? Write down your phrase each day at the beginning of the day in a conspicuous place so that you will see it throughout the day. You might want to put in on a card or a Post-it note. If you don't have a phrase for today, use a major theme command of Proverbs and wisdom. Do not let loving-kindness and truth leave you. Listen for the guidance of the Holy Spirit moving you toward living out these ideas.

PROVERBS 7:4 - *Say to wisdom, "You are my sister," and call understanding your intimate friend;*

Notice that there are two separate items that a person needs to draw close to in this proverb – both wisdom and understanding.

Wisdom is the ability to choose the triple-win choice and to take the triple-win action: the one by which God is glorified, others are benefited, and you are profited. All three sighting mechanisms must be lined up, not just one or two.

Understanding is the connection between things. What happens to others if I do this? What happens in the future if I do this? What do others do if I do this? What happens in me spiritually, emotionally, mentally, physically if I do this?

Notice that the next proverb ties this need for wisdom and understanding to keeping a young man from pre-marital and extra-marital sexual activity. When one is under the pull and possibility of sexual involvement, one does not consider wisdom and understanding. It is imperative that one has thought through these types of scenarios before they come up. What will you do? How will you respond? How will you ensure that you do not go down that road? Why shouldn't you go down that road?

Too often, in our age, people just feel that if it is available then it is okay or they had no choice. No, they had a choice way before they got in that situation. They needed to embrace wisdom and understanding at a much earlier place like they want to embrace the illicit love now.

It is usually too late to think clearly when one is faced with the pull of temptation or with a willing paramour right in front of you. So the time to think about what you will do is now. The time to decide that you will not do this is now, not then.

This is the time to realize that there are permanent incurable diseases that come from this. That one of the reasons for infertility in women is premarital involvement and its disease involvements. That one will forever remember these involvements and they will have echoes into your future. That do you really want to be comparing your future spouse with this person? Do you really want this person to program how you will respond to intimacy? Those deep emotional wounds come from implicit promises that are not kept. That spiritual agreements and power are transferred in the act of intimacy; is this really the person that you want that to take place with? That lust tasted is hard, if not impossible, to satisfy and that ultimate sexual satisfaction does not come on the road of illicit romance and involvement. That this is a selfish act and will strengthen selfishness, not love, in both parties.

your sister... intimate friend

Solomon tells the young man to cling to wisdom and understanding. There is a suggestion that Solomon is saying something very unusual and involving a thought rhyme with the ideas that are coming. He may be saying, by using sister and intimate friend as the relationship connections, that he is encouraging an affair with wisdom and understanding rather than with this illicit individual. Solomon used very similar wording in the Song of Solomon 4:9,10 to describe his love for his fiancée.

It is entirely possible that Solomon is saying that before you get married, and even afterward, have an affair with wisdom and understanding. Make these two qualities of a wise life the means of deep satisfaction and pleasure. Don't try and find pleasure and satisfaction in the arms of a person who is not your lawful spouse. Find those pleasures in wisdom and understanding.

It is entirely consistent for Solomon to see – in wisdom and understanding – an endless source of joy, pleasure, and satisfaction. It is almost like he is saying to play a chess game with yourself about what happens if you do this and all the things that flow from that? And what happens if you do this and all the things that flow from that? Think through the various paths that your life can take. Be so enraptured with the possibilities and actions of wisdom that you are too busy to suck into the temporary pleasure of lust.

In other words, have your affair with wisdom and understanding rather than one with some loose individual who will destroy and disappoint. Wisdom and understanding do not disappoint but allow you to build a great life. Get real close with them.

Think through your life from all the various angles. Before you actually make a decision, think about it and look at all sides. Don't act impulsively or because of peer pressure. Will this decision still seem like a good one twenty years from now? Does this action actually move me towards my goals or away from it?

Since I have only girls in my home, let me say a word specifically to young women. I cannot tell you how many women have derailed their noble gifts and aspirations because they wanted to please a special boyfriend. Do not let a young man sidetrack what you know God is calling you to. The pressure of the moment and the "need" to have him like you should not be enough to throw away your future. Be strong. Do not give in. Even if the moment is passionate, do not sell yourself cheaply. If he is willing to make a permanent commitment to you through marriage, then you will think about whether he is the one and whether you are ready for that commitment and you will have other men you trust examine him also so that you are not fooled by a smooth talker. Sexual fulfillment requires a down payment upfront of lifetime commitment and examination by your physical and spiritual family. Anything less is a fool's choice.

Don't end up pregnant, diseased, or brokenhearted. Demand the down payment in full before any sexual involvement: lifetime commitment called marriage and examination by your physical and spiritual family.

PROVERBS 7:5 ~ *That they may keep you from an adulteress, from the foreigner who flatters with her words.*

The word *foreigner* is the Hebrew word *nokri* which means that which is foreign or strange. The word translated *adulteress* is the Hebrew word *zur* which is stranger. This is clearly a reference to the practice of allowing foreign women to ply their trade as prostitutes within a Jewish city. It also would suggest that everyone except the person you are to marry is strange or a foreigner to you.

Many times young people in a search for love will take any kind of love just to have some comfort. This is unfortunately a misguided action and only results in difficulty and pain. The proverb here reminds us yet again that wisdom and understanding will keep you from the person who is foreign to you. Seek the Lord and His choices for you

The idea of a strange man or woman has considerable potency for singles. I have asked men and women whether they feel that the person they are presently dating is really the right person for them. Countless numbers will say no; they are just right for right now. In other words, this is a person they are putting up with so they can get some love and companionship while they are waiting for Mr. or Ms. Right. Often this Mr. or Ms. Right now becomes their life companion because they did not use wisdom and understanding to distance themselves from a person who was not really the right mate for them.

PROVERBS 7:6 - *For at the window of my house I looked out through my lattice,*

This simple statement reminds us of so much about sin. Notice that Solomon was looking out of the lattice of his house. His house would have been one of the biggest houses of the city. It would have been on one of the highest points of the city -- God's house being the highest and then the king's house. He could literally look out over the whole city just as his father David had done when he spied Solomon's mother, Bathsheba, taking a bath on the roof which led to their adultery, Uriah's murder, and David's eventual marriage of Bathsheba, the baby's death, and then Solomon's birth.

Solomon could see the whole city through his lattice which meant that the young man could not see him. Solomon probably knew who the man was and that he did not belong in that part of the city and that the woman who came to see him was not his wife. There is always someone watching. Sin seems private and hidden, but there are people who are watching. God is watching and someone else is aware.

What you are doing will come out. We have blinders on when we are in the pursuit of sin which makes it seem as though our sin is more private than it is. I know a man who was having an affair that he thought no one could know about. He was proud of how he had deceived everyone, and yet it became known and his denials and deception just broke trust to a deeper level. Realize that your sin will find you out.

Solomon is introducing a real life story to describe the deceptiveness of sin and the naiveté of the sinner. He goes on in this section to describe the actions, words, and even thoughts of adulterer and adulteress. He also does something that few do in these kinds of detailed descriptions of the course of sin. He gives the consequences of following this course of action in verses 23, 26, and 27.

PROVERBS 7:7 ~ And I saw among the naive, and discerned among the youths, a young man lacking sense,

The whole of the book of Proverbs is written to be a training manual for people just like the one that Solomon sees out of his window.

Remember that Solomon lives in the home that has the highest vantage point in the town other than God's Temple. He, like David his father before him, can watch the activities of the town going on below him.

Solomon spots a young man going toward a home that he has no business approaching. He knows that this young man is not sophisticated enough to really understand what he is doing; he is just following a lustful impulse. He is following through on a glance or word or brief encounter in the market earlier. He believes that a beautiful woman wants him, and he is about to be gripped by lust and crushed for his naiveté.

Solomon cannot rush out of his palace and save this young man, but he can write down exactly why this happened and the insights that will be needed for other young men not to take the path that this young man has taken.

It is for the naive, the young, the person who can't see how what they are doing right now affects the whole of their future.

naive

This is the Hebrew word *pethi* which means simple, open-minded, naive. It is interesting that this word which means lacking experience; lacking knowledge has a meaning of open-mindedness. This person is open to too much. This person is looking for experiences and information and is not discerning enough as to what to refuse to be exposed to.

In our culture we keep pleading with people to be open-minded. That is good up to a point, but there are a whole lot of things that we should not be open-minded about. We should be closed toward sin; not open-minded. We should be closed toward violence and dishonesty. We should be closed to blasphemy and demonic spiritual power. And yet in our day and age, these are just the things that our society is saying we should be open-minded about. The naive youth are being sucked into the vortex of these experiences and many will never recover from the exposure. Their whole lives will be changed and the direction of their lives will be altered.

As you are growing up you do not want to understand sin and perversion by experience. Listen to Solomon and do not go outside the Ten Commandments to try and get smarter; you will be warped and twisted by the experience. The future that you had as your potential will forever be changed by your embrace of iniquity and wickedness. It is not harmless.

It is like Solomon is screaming out of his window: "STOP DON'T MESS UP YOUR LIFE"! It may seem like those who break all the rules in high school are having all the fun but watch their lives for a longer time and you will see that they are paying a heavy price for their education in sin.

youths

This is the Hebrew word *ben* which means sons. It seems in this context to mean someone who is not completely out from under his parents' shadow. He may be past the age of 13 and be a son of the Law; but he is not really independent, married, and existing as a separate family unit. He is in that period where many want to experiment with life. This is what we call the teen years, and now it extends through the mid-twenties. The person doesn't yet have all the responsibilities of a full-blown adult even though they want all the respect of an adult.

It is during this period that a young man or young woman can make choices that can destroy their life. Often those choices involve romantic relationships. Young girls can give too much to a man who is not committed and get pregnant. Young men can be ensnared by sexually experienced or emotionally needy women. It is a period of time that parents need to prepare for much earlier as the child is growing up. Help them understand what not to be open to. Help them realize that there are temptations that will seem like a great deal – like everything they have ever wanted – but will destroy them if they give in.

lacking sense

This is the Hebrew word *leb* which means heart. It is translated sense but the word is the word for heart or soul. Solomon is saying that this young man is becoming an animal with no soul. He is just becoming a stimulus-response animal. There is no contemplation of the future. There is no realization of judgment day. There are no evaluations of the consequences. There is just a desire to fulfill a physical want. When you just do what the flesh impulses – whether that is sex, drink, food, hatred, bitterness, coarse laughter and jokes, violence, etc. – then you become more animal than man and you lose your soul. You just begin going through life waiting to be stimulated by the next impulse. You allow that to stimulate you until you are satisfied. But you give little or no thought to the meaning of life; your contribution to society; your reason for existence; a higher calling beyond your own gratification.

This brings up an important point. The cultivation of a soul takes work. To build an inner life which contemplates life – meaning God and others – is a process. We come equipped with the ability to develop a deep and rich soul life; but, alas, many do not ever develop it because they are too busy chasing after the next impulse in their life. Jesus says, "What does it profit a man if he gains the whole world and yet loses his soul?"

Many people will never have a deep relationship with God or hear His gentle whisper in their spirit because they are too busy paying attention to the fleshly impulses that scream at them. Many people will never enjoy a deep and satisfying relational connection with another person – soul-to-soul contact – because they have never developed their own soul enough to connect with another.

The soul is the inner life. It is the development of what is called the soul and spirit of the person. It is the mind, will, emotions, creativity, connection to God, personality, conscience, meaning. To have an abundant life, one must have a rich inner life. Solomon points out that this young man that he is watching must have little or no inner life to just blindly go to a woman who is not his wife for physical relations just because she is pretty. He is allowing his fleshly impulses to rule his life.

PROVERBS 7:8,9 - *Passing through the street near her corner; and he takes the way to her house, in the twilight, in the evening, in the middle of the night and in the darkness.*

This verse suggests that he is coming past her house or near her house repeatedly; he wants to be caught. He is being carried away by lust and enticed, and it will bring forth sin. Notice that he is passing through the street near her house – in the twilight – in the evening – in the middle of the night – in the darkness. Four different times he goes that way and then all of a sudden, BEHOLD a woman comes out to meet him. She knows that he has been coming by and then moves her sexual aggressiveness into high gear and she gets him.

You cannot take trips to be near sin and expect that you will not be caught by your own sin. It is not wise to see how close you can get to sinning. The proverb was written to wake you up to this natural tendency in all of us to try and get as close as we can to sin and then pull away. It won't happen. Give sin a wide berth; do not move into the path of sin at all.

The concluding advice from God on this proverb-parable is that we should not let our minds fantasize about what she will do for us and to us or any sin. If you mentally fantasize about doing it, you are over halfway to sinning. Also, the proverb says do not actually physically move into the paths that she treads. Don't go near her house. Don't be around where she is.

PROVERBS 7:10 - *And behold, a woman comes to meet him, dressed as a harlot and cunning of heart.*

Solomon describes the woman for the first time here. There are three things that he wants you to know. She comes to meet him. She is dressed as a harlot. She is cunning of heart.

a woman comes to meet him

woman

This is the Hebrew word *ishshah* which means woman, female, wife. If the verse had been translated *a wife comes to meet him,* it would be more powerful and possibly convey the shock in the verse. A woman who is pledged to another man comes to meet this guy who is wandering by. She is pledged; her husband is counting on her trustworthiness as he is away on business trying to earn enough for the family.

meet

This is the Hebrew word *qara* which means encounter, engage, befall, meet. The idea is that this man has taken enough steps toward her that she is ready to spring the trap and to make sure that he does not get away. She goes out to meet him. She is aggressive sexually, and he is captivated by her aggressiveness. He is pulled in the last part of this seduction to his destruction by her aggressiveness, her dress, and her cunning soul.

If she had greeted him as she greets her husband, he would not have been interested. She does not go out to meet her husband before he makes it home. She does not dress up in a sexy way to greet her husband. She does not use all her mental and emotional smarts to meet her husband's needs. No, this is saved for the new man. Her husband gets the tired, wore-out housewife presenting him a list of honey-do chores and a disinterested approach to his interest in her.

If she put the same energy into her marriage that she is putting into capturing this new young man, her marriage would take fifty steps forward. But her energy is wasted on that which will cause her and her husband and this new man's destruction. She does not even realize that she is doing all this work on something that cannot last and will ultimately prove devastating to her emotional and mental health.

she is dressed as a harlot

dressed

This is the Hebrew word *shith* which means a garment, dress. Solomon wants us to know that this characteristic of the kind of clothes she is wearing is huge.

harlot

This is the Hebrew word *zanah* which means to commit fornication, to be a harlot. The idea here is that this woman is trying to dress so as to attract attention to her body so that a man other than her husband will notice her body and want physical intimacy with her. She is hoping, most likely, that through physical intimacy she will be able to hook him into staying and wanting emotional and mental intimacy.

Unfortunately it never works that way. A man does not go from physical intimacy to emotional and mental intimacy. He moves the other way around. He wants and needs physical intimacy so much that if he is given the end product first, there is no reason to work hard at what he finds difficult – emotional and mental intimacy. This is why marriage was set up the way it was by God. One makes a commitment to another person to pursue them, to take care of them, to meet their needs, to find out who they are, and then after the wedding comes the physical intimacy. Almost any woman can capture a man for a few moments with physical intimacy; it takes work on both his and her part for her to capture him emotionally and mentally for the kind of intimacy that she longs for and that a marriage needs to be a great thing.

Young ladies, if you dress in such a way that the first thing young men notice about you is your body, then do not be surprised when the only thing they are interested in is your body. It is unfortunate that our culture is constantly pushing young women to dress in more and more revealing ways. Do not follow this destructive tendency. You do not have to dress like a puritan, but do not dress so that your body is more noticed than your face.

This woman is right; she can capture a man's heart with the way she dresses but not for the long term. If you are going to dress to capture a man's heart, dress that way for your husband – not for other men.

she is cunning of heart

cunning

This is the Hebrew word *natsar* which means to watch, to guard, to keep, cunning. The idea is that this woman is watching intently and is strategic in her quest to drag this young man into her trap of illicit pleasure. It is unfortunate that she uses her smarts to capture the wrong man. She captures this other man instead of her husband.

Now sometimes a husband can be a very difficult thing to capture the attention of because he is on to career and other things, thinking that he has already captured you. But she needed to use all the smarts and strategy she is using in the wrong way to be used on the right man.

Solomon is saying here that this woman has planned out the whole affair. It is not spontaneous to her. She knows where she wants this to go and has known for a long time. If you are foolish to be involved in an affair or headed toward one, you can be sure that the woman is fifty steps ahead of you. As a man you are only thinking about the climax of physical intimacy, but she is thinking way beyond that. Sexual intercourse is only setting the hook and then the reeling you in really begins.

Solomon is screaming: Young men don't get caught in this trap of the attractively dressed woman who seems to want you when her husband is away! And, young lady, put your energy into your marriage and you will be so better off. You already have what you are trying to capture: a man. This new one is not any better than the one you have. In fact, you know that he is worse because he is willing to cheat and be unfaithful.

PROVERBS 7:11 - *She is boisterous and rebellious, her feet do not remain at home;*

This proverb gives us the character flaws of this adulteress and how she lures her victims. What is sad about our culture is that these qualities are now being touted as being praiseworthy instead of signs of a fool.

boisterous

This is the Hebrew word *hemya* which means sound, music, cry out, making noise. It is translated boisterous – meaning that this type of woman is loud and aggressive.

This woman – in the midst of betraying her vows to God and her husband and luring a man into unfaithfulness and destruction – is confident, loud, and aggressive. One would expect that there would be hesitancy or a level of guilt which would bring a sneakiness. But not this type of fool.

Solomon is trying to get men – and especially young men – to realize that the quality of sexual aggressiveness going outside of marriage is not a good thing. While it is tempting if a woman comes on to you like this, turn and run as fast as you can. This woman is trouble. She is offering candy-coated poison. She covers over the sin she is trying to commit by being loud, sure of herself, and aggressive. Some people take other people's surety as a sign of righteousness. In this case her aggressiveness and loudness toward sexual unfaithfulness is a sign of her depravity, not the rightness of what she wants to do.

The opposite situation is also true. Many young men act all sure of themselves to convince a young woman that sexual unfaithfulness is okay and even the normal or expected thing. Do not believe them; get away from this type of person.

rebellious

This is the Hebrew word *sar* which means to be stubborn or rebellious. In other words what they should be doing under an authority, they are not doing. They are powerful and aggressively doing what they want to do.

What is interesting here is that the rebellion that this woman is engaged in is not an open rebellion in that she opposes her husband outright. She may even be very engaging with him. She is rebellious to his wishes and to his basic expectations. She ignores the common rules of relationships and pursues instead her desires. When a person's desires trump what they should do, then a moral line will be crossed.

Solomon is trying to give us a heads-up that there are people out there who are like this; people who lurk waiting to ensnare the person who is going along having a sane life. The bait is sex, romance, and love. The real price is alienation, loneliness, guilt, and missed opportunities. There will most likely be someone ensnared by this person, but it does not have to be you.

PROVERBS 7:12 ~ *She is now in the streets, now in the squares, and lurks by every corner.*

Solomon wants to educate young people to the ways of the world in this section of the proverb. When a young man comes across an adulteress who is willing to break her marriage vows for the illicit pleasure of being with him, he feels that this is special, that he is special, and that she is special. Solomon is trying to strip that myth out of his and her mind.

He is not the long-lost love of this woman's mind; there will be others. She is not special; she is just responding to the age-old temptation. Everywhere people go there are people who are like this and who will get caught up in a moment of lust if given the opportunity.

When people are about to commit adultery, they begin to believe a myth that their relationship is special. This love is so different that it does not have to obey the standard rules of morality. This love is something that cannot be denied. That is a fabrication of lust. It is not special; this kind of cheap lust is everywhere. Breaking your marriage vows is never a good thing. God is not ever calling you to be unfaithful.

Notice that Solomon says she is in the streets, now in the squares, and lurks by every corner. He is not saying that this particular woman is in all of these places. But this kind of opportunity with this kind of woman is in all of these places. If you are dumb enough to advertise by the way you act, talk, dress, and flirt with members of the opposite sex, you can find people who will break their commitment to marriage for an adulteress affair with you. Solomon is saying these people are everywhere. It is not special. It is not a one-time love.

The movies and television have tried to play up the idea of love at first sight. This is the idea that you can look at a person and so totally fall in love with them and know they are the perfect person for you and that they love you in a deep and lasting way. That is not possible in one look. You can feel lust for their beauty in one look and want to believe that the other things are true. But this idea of love at first sight cannot tell you what type of virtue they have; how much they love the Lord; whether they will make a great wife and mother or a great husband and father. The steamy fantasy of "I have got to have you" is real but it is not usually love; it is almost always lust. Real love takes time to flower and develop.

Love is meeting needs, pursuing, and pleasing the other person whom God has selected for you. If you are married, God has already selected that person for you. This person is your mate. If you allow your head to be turned by the beauty or personality or sensuality of a different person, it is not love but lust and you should head in the opposite direction.

Let me say it again – it is not a special love that you cannot deny yourself. It is lust that you could find in any place you go. The New Testament says: Flee youthful lusts; flee immorality, every other sin which a man commits is outside the body but immorality is in the body.

Do not believe that you have just stumbled across the special one that you missed when you were getting married. There are people everywhere who shout that they are available by the places they visit; the way they dress; the provocative things that they say; the types of activities that they get involved with; the way they look at people; the way they touch people. Do not fall for this "specialness" myth.

Solomon is screaming: She is everywhere; it is not special!

PROVERBS 7:13 - *So she seizes him and kisses him and with a brazen face she says to him: (verse 18) Come, let us drink our fill of love until morning. Let us delight ourselves with caresses.*

The key to the actions of a harlot that entices a man is that the woman is sexually aggressive. Very few men can resist a sexually advancing, aggressive, seductive woman. This type of woman will usually get the man to give into the impulses she raises.

There are several lessons in this whole text:

The man cannot wait until he is in the presence of a sexually aggressive woman to start resisting and staying true to his wife (in the case of a single man – staying true to God's future choice for his wife).

It is sexual aggressiveness that moves a woman down the course of harlotry. When women come to understand and make use of the power that sexual aggressiveness has over men, it often becomes a destructive force in their lives. The television and movies of our day are like a training course in female sexual aggressiveness or how to be unfaithful. The tragedy is that there is no intimacy or true love waiting at the end of multiple sexual conquests for the woman any more than for the man. Intimacy and real love are not developed that way.

A man should mark sexually aggressive women to avoid contact with them for they represent a real threat to his happiness and prosperity.

What is interesting is that it is married women who are seeking to meet their husband's needs who really need to understand sexual aggressiveness within the confines of marriage. Most men find a sexually aggressive woman irresistible; it should be a man's wife who is trying to communicate through her sexual pursuit of her husband that she loves him and that she values him and wants depth with him. It is sexual aggressiveness of this sort within the marriage that has the power to transform the marriage. A woman can often communicate more of her needs and the marriage's needed changes through sexual pursuit with clear communication in the midst of it than through any other means. A man who has a wife like this is highly likely to bend in her direction and take her advice and in this case suddenly follow her into strengthening their marriage, which is a good thing.

While a sexually aggressive woman outside of marriage is a bad thing and a destructive thing, a sexually aggressive wife toward her husband is a good thing in that it meets a deep need in a husband for respect and intimacy. Many men develop a sense of their own self-worth by whether someone wants them. Many men conclude (erroneously): if she wants sex from me and she is initiating it, then she wants me and loves me. This has to do with erotic love's place in a man's life. It is one of his top five needs, and he measures how much he loves his wife by how much he wants her sexually. Therefore he assumes it is the same for his wife. If she initiates, then she wants sexual relations with me and therefore she wants me and therefore she loves me. On the flip side: If she never initiates, then he is forced to conclude that she does not want him or that he is undesirable or that her love for him is slipping. Little does the man understand that a woman's needs are different and that she does not think the same or have the same top five needs.

PROVERBS 7:14 - *I was due to offer peace offerings; today I have paid my vows.*

Solomon includes, in this picture of adultery, some of the very convincing arguments that the adulteress makes to try and convince this man that she truly loves him.

peace offerings

This is the Hebrew word *shelem* which means a specific offering made in the Old Testament called a peace offering. Leviticus 7:12-25 describes this offering. It was to be offered at the altar and partially consumed with the priests, but the rest of the offering was to be consumed at home with one's family as a joyful celebration of love for the Lord and one another. It had to be consumed in the day that the offering was made.

In this way the adulteress convinces her target that she truly loves him. She basically says that I cannot think of anyone that I would rather be with than you. You bring me joy. I must consume this offering with those who I truly love and I pick you. My husband is out of town but you are the one I truly love, and we can share this feast tonight together.

She creates a false time deadline which the young man thinking of committing adultery is up against. There is a sense that all this food will go to waste, and that she has created an artificial deadline to convince him to be with her. Men also do this in adulterous situations when they say things like "it's now or never" or "if you really love me then..." She has completely blown off the nature of the offering to God. The whole peace offering at the temple is just an empty ritual with a lot of meat left over for an intimate party at home.

There is a warped way that those involved in adultery also begin to think. They can begin to thank God for the person they are committing adultery with. They are so momentarily happy with this person and their illicit love that they can mistakenly attribute this person as a gift from God. So she may be making a peace offering to celebrate with God that in her mind He has given her a man who truly loves her. And the leftover food will allow her to continue her celebration with her new love. So for her this peace offering is perfect as a celebration of and indulgence in her sin.

I have heard this kind of twisted logic coming from those involved in sexual sin. They do not understand that God is not the author of sin. Some people have embraced the false notion that God wants them to be happy all the time. Therefore if something makes you happy, it must be from God. Realize He is not going to help you sin. He is not providing ways for you to sin. It is the Devil who is helping you do what is clearly immoral. It is your flesh that is racing to help you find ways to be selfish. It is the world system around you that wants you to find joy in immorality. It is not God. This will become painfully obvious when the consequences begin to show up in your life. Then the "god" who supplied you with the gifts of sin will fail you. You will be left facing the real God and His real opinion and judgment about what you did.

Just because it is easy to sin, do not take that as the will of God. It is not God's will that you sin.

PROVERBS 7:15 - *Therefore I have come out to meet you, to seek your presence earnestly, and I have found you.*

What is interesting about this proverb is that it details what the adulteress says that convinces the young man to give into temptation and cross the line.

Solomon is incredibly observant and gives critical insight into the ploys of the adulteress and the psyche of men.

She tells him what he is hoping to hear: "You are wanted!!!" Men are sexual creatures, but they are also wanting desperately to be wanted and to be desired. This is how they hope that their wives will be with them – that their wives will see them as an object of desire.

Notice that this woman does two things that are not the normal response of wives. She comes out to meet him; she is the aggressor; and she tells him that he is an object of desire. These are two almost irresistible aphrodisiacs. This is the classic case of a man wanting what he feels for a woman to be felt toward himself. Since a woman is a unique creation, she will not normally feel this. As a man, his number one need in a marriage relationship is physical intimacy. He needs physical intimacy. There are four aspects of this need that happen inside of a man in association with this need. He needs it; he wants her to want it; he wants her to want him; he wants her to enjoy it. The woman who speaks, as Solomon details here, communicates: I will meet your need; I want you; I want it; and I know how to enjoy this. That is why this type of temptation is so hard to resist.

Note to wives: This is what your husband needs from you on occasion – to be the initiator of physical intimacy and to communicate that he is desirable. The more that he receives these needs from you, the more drawn to you he will be and the more filled up he will be.

Note to married men: If any woman does these two things – seeks you out sexually and/or tells you that you are an object of sexual desire – run in the opposite direction. Cut off all connection to that woman quickly. This is temptation talking and you will not be able to resist.

Note to single men: If a woman does these two things – is the aggressor sexually and communicates that you are an object of sexual desire for her – have someone you trust help you evaluate whether she is really the right woman for you because you will lose objectivity. These two signals are such a strong temptation that this woman will often move to the head of the class for marriage when she may not be the right person at all. If she has done this with others, then she is not the right person. It is a ploy.

PROVERBS 7:16 ~ *I have spread my couch with coverings with colored linens of Egypt.*

The strongest sexual organ in the human body is the mind and the adulteress uses this organ to draw the hesitant person into her web. She can put you there before you actually decide to violate your marriage vows. If she can get you to accept her three-dimensional picture of extreme sexual pleasure with no consequences, she has already gotten you to give in before you have even decided to sin.

This is the way that the strongest forms of temptation work – whether it is pride, envy, anger, lust, sloth, gluttony, or greed. You are seduced into mentally enjoying the sin long before you ever commit the actual sinful act. It is in your mind that you must say no. Unfortunately, our culture says that you can say yes in your mind as long as you say no in reality. In order to really win against temptation, you must say no to enjoying the sin mentally. You must not allow yourself, someone else, the Devil, or the world to paint a mental picture of you enjoying a sinful moment in your mind.

We need to say no to these mental pictures and pursue righteousness. It is crucial that we do not linger over the sinful choice but move away from it mentally and physically. Pursuing righteousness means that we are seeking to benefit someone else in our life from within the boundaries of the Ten Commandments. Since sin at its core is selfishness, then righteousness is the opposite – the benefit of others.

The way to beat back temptation of any sort is to listen for the prompting of the Holy Spirit as to what positive act of love and benefit does He want you to do instead of the selfishness that is presenting itself to you.

Solomon shows us, in this section of Proverbs, the techniques of an adulteress to trap her hesitant subject into her web of foolishness. He is also saying – to those who will listen – that you must be ready to exercise mental discipline and positive righteousness. Are you ready to say no today to the sins that so easily entangle you and yes to the opportunities for good that will present themselves today?

PROVERBS 7:17 - *I have sprinkled my bed with myrrh, aloes and cinnamon.*

This is the continuation of the temptress' four-dimensional description of sin. One of the strongest nerve and memory connectors in the human body is the sense of smell. So if the adulteress can get you to imagine or remember these sweet-smelling fragrances, it anchors the sinful acts that she wants to entice you into directly to a sweet fragrance.

Those who are experts at luring people into sin know that you must have a person mentally participate in sin before this person will actually participate in sin. In this case the adulteress must, therefore, get you to picture yourself in her bedroom with her in the midst of the smells and sights and sounds. She must then make you take an active part in that mental picture that she is creating. If you enter into the mental picture, then it will be very difficult, if not impossible, for you to say no in the actual world.

This is why mental discipline is important. We are to fill our mind with godly, pure, wholesome, enjoyable, righteous thoughts and mental pictures. We are to say no to the mental constructs of sinful events. Embracing a sinful scenario mentally is a sin as Jesus says, "If you look on a woman to lust after her, then you have committed adultery with her in your heart."

Do not allow the agents of temptation to build a mental picture of sin in your mind. It always leaves out the consequences and the negative difficulties. Sin is never as good in actuality as it is mentally.

Do not allow anyone to build a fantasy world of sin in your mind – whether that fantasy world involves stealing, lying, blasphemy, rebellion, murder, or sex. Each of these types of scheming and plotting is not harmless but is the first step to giving in to temptation.

Right now you may not have a person painting a picture of the wonders of marital unfaithfulness, but you do have some aspect in your life presenting the glamour of sin and how moving in a sinful direction will fix your problem. This is a trap and a lie. It may fix your problem of boredom at the expense of significant negative consequences. Our whole culture is laughing at actual sin and encouraging thinking about it. Each and every person who plays with sin mentally or actually will pay a price for it. Don't be one of them. Listen to Solomon and his warning. Steer clear of thinking about the joys of sin.

PROVERBS 7:18 - *Come, let us drink our fill of love until morning; let us delight ourselves with caresses.*

This is the attitude of the adulteress that persuades the husband to stray from his marriage vows. Solomon accurately portrays the sexual aggressiveness of the adulteress. She causes the man to believe that he is wanted. She promises and delivers focused attention on him for an extended period of time.

What is sad is that it is this focused attention by a woman that causes the husband to stray because he craves it so much. In many cases if this man's wife would give him regular focused attention, he would be drawn to her instead of this adulteress who will wound and use him.

If a man feels that he is wanted, this becomes a very difficult temptation to resist. This is why a man must put an emotional and, at times, physical barrier between himself and women who are not his wife so that he cannot respond to any hints that they are interested in him and so that they are distant enough to not try.

Solomon is exposing three of the techniques of the temptress that allows her, over time, to weaken a man's resolve and lure him into an adulterous relationship: overt sexual aggressiveness or initiative, focused attention, and the feeling of being wanted. Watch out for anyone other than your wife who offers, hints, or behaves in these ways. They are trouble and this will be tempting.

These are three of the things that a man needs his wife to do to build a strong bond in marriage and a great relationship, but many wives slip into an emotional distance in marriage that puts a damper on their relationship. These three actions – overt sexual aggression or initiative, focused attention, and the feeling of being wanted – can become powerful tools in a wife's toolkit to build an intimate marriage. Wouldn't it be great if a wife worked with her husband to lure him back into his marriage, so the bond they share is strong and incredibly deep?

Do not be fooled, men, a woman who exhibits these three tendencies spells trouble. Get away from her emotionally and physically. Do not enjoy the attention, believing you can break away later.

PROVERBS 7:19 - *For my husband is not at home, he has gone on a long journey;*

What this verse points out is that when a husband travels, it can result in a wife not having her relational needs met and seeking to go outside of the marriage to have them met.

It is selfish and deeply damaging for either party in a marriage to go outside of their marriage to have their relational needs met.

Note that the adulteress in this verse has planned her husband's absence. One thing that many men do not realize is that if they are gone a lot to the point where they are tempted to go outside of their marriage vows, their wife might also be tempted to pursue a relationship with a sympathetic man.

The man who is lured by this sexually aggressive woman needs to realize that he is being lured into a trap. He may think he wants to be trapped, but the consequences will be devastating.

Men, don't travel so much that your wife is neglected.

PROVERBS 7:20 - *He has taken a bag of money with him, at the full moon he will come home.*

The temptress who is seeking to lure a hesitant sinner into her net – step by step – builds a mental picture of the pleasure that will be enjoyed by giving in to her suggestions and step-by-step answers his objections to going along with her sinful suggestions.

In this particular case it is that there is no chance of discovery. The husband has gone away for a long time. He has a lot of money to spend and is not expected back for a month.

Temptation works like this: getting you to visualize the sin, mentally giving into the temptation, and then answering the consequences question with "No one will ever find out." It is not true, of course; but this is always the way temptation works – whether it is stealing from a store, lying to your parents, intimidating someone into silence, sexual unfaithfulness, corruption, drugs, whatever.

Do not believe the assurances of those who want you to give into what you know is wrong. They would say anything to get you to join them in their selfish pursuit. If you are a young girl, do not believe the boy who tells you that no one will find out. If you are a young person, do not believe your "friends" when they tell you that no one will find out what you stole.

Solomon is trying to warn young people of the tactics of sexual predators, but the lesson is also for all temptation. You must believe the assurance that you will not get caught or you would not do the thing. You will get caught – either publicly and legally or internally – with true moral guilt and shame. Do not let go of the fact that you will be found out by at least God and you. Both of you will know that you did what was wrong.

The fear of the Lord is about consequences that God will bring into the life of those whom He cares about. He spanks or disciplines those He loves. The writer of the book of Hebrews says that the only ones who are without discipline are those whom He doesn't love. There will be consequences. He does love you.

When I am being tempted to do something that I know is wrong, I try and list the ways that I could be found out or caught if I were to give in. The more that you keep the consequences in front of you, the easier it will be to say no to the sin no matter how close to it you have been lured. Just walk away before anything more happens.

PROVERBS 7:21 ~ *With her many persuasions she entices him; with her flattering lips she seduces him.*

Notice that the adulteress woman is the aggressor. Without her actions the man would not be drawn into the destructive embrace of sexual sin. It is always this way: lust initiates, lust is the aggressor, lust seeks to persuade. It does not want to let you decide whether you should; it seeks to decide for you by more and more aggressive actions. This is true of men who are the lustful initiator and women who are the lustful initiator. This is why lust seeks more and more room to ply its trade. It wants to be protected under free speech rights so that it can be more aggressive with its images. It wants to break down laws so that predatory individuals can attack married partners and lure them away from their spouses without any danger of legal recourse. It wants to flood the mind with lustful ideas, images, and songs so that people are already primed for sexual suggestion.

persuasions

This is the Hebrew word *leqach* which means learning, teaching, instruction, persuasions. This predatory person has many teachings, many persuasions. This person is not just asking if you want to do this sin. Lust has many ways to instruct and compel you to move in its direction. Notice that the lustful person just keeps piling on temptations until you give in. There are multiple forms of touch, sound, sight, smell, words, listening, stories, etc., which seek to convince you that you are important and that you are the object of affection and desire – one after another after another until one begins to believe the hype and go with the fleshly urges that are boiling within. That is why Scripture says to flee. You cannot just stand there and resist.

I know of many young men and young ladies who have thought that they would be able to resist the suggestions of lust. But they weren't strong enough; they should have just run for their lives. The way to resist the temptation to lust is to get away from the source of it.

entices

This is the Hebrew word *natah* which means stretch out, spread out, incline, bend. All of the teaching and instruction that lust is doing is getting the student to bend into the lust and to want to know more. You don't want to know more; you don't want to bend in lust's direction. You want to learn about real intimacy, not the shortcut that lust offers.

flattering

This is the Hebrew word *cheleq* which means smoothness, seductiveness, flattery. The idea behind flattery is overemphasizing a person's strengths and/or inventing a strength that the person does not have. Everyone likes to have their victories and strengths celebrated. But one can become addicted to the attention and focus.

We are all drawn in the direction of those who will value us. Focus on our strengths and minimize our weakness. The formula for good people skills becomes the means of temptation when we celebrate what is not true, or when it is so overblown that even the praised individual knows that it is not true of him/her.

If a young lady begins to sing your praises in ways that you know is not true, then it is flattery. If a young man begins to sing your praises in a way that is not true, than it is flattery. Flattery is a tool of temptation. You are being led somewhere if someone is puffing you up with things that are not true. Figure out the endgame and disconnect the machine that is pumping hot air into your ego.

seduces

This is the Hebrew word *nadach* which means to impel, thrust, banish. Solomon uses a very interesting word here to talk about what the temptress is doing to the man. She is impelling him; she is thrusting him in a direction that he would not normally go. This is very interesting and provides a basis of evaluation of a temptation. Is this feeling that I am feeling at this moment something that I would normally do or something that I would pursue or is it instead something that I am being presented with that is not normal, or something that I am being sucked or pulled into? If it is the latter, then you are being tempted to do evil even though the activity may be pleasurable. There will be consequences. Watch out.

PROVERBS 7:22 - *Suddenly he follows her as an ox goes to the slaughter, or as one in fetter to the discipline of a fool,*

This verse begins a section of the consequences of adultery and unfaithfulness. A person needs to regularly be reminded, in the most graphic ways, what will happen if they commit adultery; and most importantly, what it will feel like eventually – like an ox to the slaughter; like a bird in a snare.

The key to this whole section on the harlot is that the young man is impulsive. Notice the word "suddenly." This verse is the climax impulsive action; an impulsive choice which is made in the moment. Okay, what can it hurt he says to himself. Or... Okay, let's get it on. He goes with the flesh.

If you stay in the zone of temptation long enough, sin will all of a sudden become the right or good or best action; and this feeling of let's do it or this feels good right now will come suddenly. It is destructive and the zone of temptation should be avoided. You will not be able to resist the impulses to sin within the zone effectively or if you stay there too long.

If you keep staring at the cheesecake you shouldn't have, it will become irresistible. If you keep in connection with the adulterer or adulteress, then it is inevitable that you will succumb to temptation. In a flash of fleshly insight, you will give in and suddenly you will do the wrong thing. Don't hang out near the place of temptation for you.

Take an honest look at your life and face the fact of what tempts you:

- It could be pride and false flattery

- It could be envy and the possessions of others

- It could be lust and sensuality

- It could be anger and the ability to get your own way through anger and even violence

- It could be sloth and the desire to procrastinate

- It could be greed and the insatiable need for more money, possessions, and stuff.

Whichever of these temptations connects to you the most, set up protections so that you do not hang around the particular source of temptation that draws you. Be willing to admit to yourself, God, and maybe trusted others that you are tempted by these things. If you think you are strong enough to resist all temptations on your own and especially in the presence of that temptation, you are fooling yourself.

There is a reason why the New Testament says to flee – to not become a "suddenly" statistic.

PROVERBS 7:23 - *Until an arrow pierces through his liver; as a bird hastens to the snare, so he does not know that it will cost him his life.*

liver

This is the Hebrew word *kabed* which means liver. This is also the word used from burdensome, heaviness, sorrow, weighed down. There is the idea that the Hebrews thought that the liver was the place where great pain was stored or kept – a physical location for guilt, pain, sorrow, disaster.

The idea here is that you think that you have found the way to really live, but you have added immeasurably to the pain in your life. When you are unfaithful to your spouse, you will have a level of heaviness, sorrow, and guilt shoot through you that will be very hard to deal with.

Betrayal of your spouse should not be entered into lightly because your body will keep score.

snare

This is the Hebrew word *pah* which means bird trap or net. The idea is that only an insane bird would fly toward a net or into a trap it could see. It just won't do it. Solomon is trying to paint a picture of what marital unfaithfulness is like. He says it's like a bird that knowingly flies into a trap so that it can be eaten.

No animal in its right mind goes willingly into a trap. Only the creature that God created in His image – who has freedom of choice – can use this wonderful power which was meant to produce noble choices and honest love to willingly move into a destructive trap.

In our culture we have minimized the meaning of marital unfaithfulness so that people don't believe it is a big deal. Even though it is not a big deal in our culture, it is a big deal. It is a big deal to the person you betray. It is a big deal to your children. It is a big deal in God's eyes. It is a big deal to the diseases and bacteria that you introduce to your body. It is a big deal to your soul. God is saying that you can't walk past this moral boundary without consequences. Do not do this.

Thankfully there is forgiveness in Jesus Christ. If you are willing to confess and repent of your actions, you can be forgiven by God. But that does not mean that all of the other consequences go away. The disease may continue. The loss of one's marriage may continue. The damage to one's other relationships may continue.

God is willing, through the propitionary death of His Son, to forgive your sin and open to you the path to heaven.

life

This is the Hebrew word *nephesh* which means life, soul, mind, etc. There are two different ideas that Solomon may be aiming at here. One is that in a pre-pharmacological culture committing adultery opened one up to all kinds of diseases, such as syphilis in which its final stage was insanity. The second idea or direction of this verse deals with the soul in that the person who betrays their spouse in adultery damages their soul and their life in significant ways. It is not possible to blast a hole through your soul and have your life continue on as though there is no damage or no impact to that kind of destruction. It is possible that both ideas are meant. The second idea probably carries more of the intent of the verse as Solomon has and will consistently suggest that one's life is lived through the soul, not the external body. If your soul is damaged through sin, selfishness, and stupidity, then one has significantly affected the size and functionality of your soul. Without a clear and open soul, life as it was meant to be lived cannot be fully enjoyed.

In fact, this is what we find when a person violates moral boundaries – they pervert their soul so that simple pleasures no longer satisfy them and they begin an endless selfish search for pleasures that will move them. They have left behind the simple pleasures of a good conversation, a child's love, a tender moment, a walk in the park. It must all be thrill, adrenaline, and risk. They have closed off the lower ranges of their soul's nerve endings.

PROVERBS 7:24 ~ *Now therefore, my sons, listen to me, and pay attention to the words of my mouth.*

sons

This is the plural form of the Hebrew word *ben* which is *benim*. Solomon is talking not to his literal sons of which he had many, but rather he is talking to those of us who submit ourselves to his spiritual fathership. He wrote the book of Proverbs at the Holy Spirit's urging to disciple young men especially but also all others who wanted to learn to live a wise life. Sons listen to their father – if they are really sons. Solomon is speaking as a spiritual father.

listen to me

The word *listen* is the word *shama* which means to hear. The Hebrew word and mentality was that you had not really heard if you did not do what the person talking had asked you to do – in this case especially of a spiritual father to his spiritual sons and daughters.

Solomon does not want to get done with all of this rich instruction – especially about the dangers of adultery – and have his spiritual children ignore his advice: You must do what I am telling you, he says. I do not want you to wreck your life. I do not want you to wander into the traps of foolishness and sin. Too often young folks think that things are so much different as they are growing up than when their elders grew up. And in some ways they are right, but the basic sins are still the same. The basic ways that you can mess up your life before it even gets started are the same.

pay attention to the words of my mouth

The Hebrew word that is translated *attention* is the word *qashab* which means to incline towards, to attend to. The idea again here is that Solomon is saying: Do not miss what I have been teaching for the last seven chapters; lean into this stuff. It will allow you to avoid the basic pitfalls of early life. There is the danger of gang or a violence-based life; there is the danger of adultery; there is the danger of debt, of laziness, of mocking, of pride; and so many others that Solomon has clearly laid out in this first seven chapters of Proverbs. At this point Solomon is saying it will take more than just a quick read through to grasp all the wisdom that has been packed in the first seven chapters. Go back, he directs, and lean into the learning of the warnings and dangers that I have included in the first seven chapters. Solomon says with this phrase: *pay attention.*

It is important to realize that Solomon has outlined in powerful ways the wonders of the life of wisdom and the difficulties of the life of foolishness. Foolishness confronts the young person on every side, and it seems so right. But it is not right, and it will destroy your potential. Avoid what seems right and choose what is right.

Yes, it pays to be wise. It seems like the teenager who is selfish, proud, immoral, a liar, and even a thief is having all the fun and really living life the way it should be lived. But this is all a sham. The foolish teenager is building up a life full of pain and hurt – both in themselves and in the people they are around. It is so much wiser to go past these landmines and take the straight and narrow road of righteousness. It grows brighter and brighter as you go along, and your wisdom will be shown to others.

You may feel like you are missing out. In some ways you are missing out on some things; but you always want to miss out on pain, sorrow, loss, hurt, stupid choices, bondage, guilt, and shame. See, these come with the things so many foolish teenagers go after.

PROVERBS 7:25 ~ *Do not let your heart turn aside to her ways, do not stray into her paths.*

This chapter of Proverbs contains 27 verses and they are all pointing to this verse. The command is in this verse. All the rest of the verses are designed to help you realize that you must do what is in this verse. This is the verse that will produce understanding if you do it. There are two separate commands which are crucial to turning back the destructive urges of lust:

do not let your heart turn aside to her ways

The heart is your mind, will, and emotions. Essentially what Solomon is warning about is that if your mind begins to think about all that this woman can do and what she is like – especially in intimate encounters – then you are finished.

You must think about other things. As the Apostle Paul said, you must think about positive, righteous, good, and lovely things. We all have control over our thoughts. Most of us do not exercise control over them, but we can stop thinking about one thing and start thinking about another thing anytime we want. It is when we let our mind graze on whatever it wants that we can get in trouble. The advertising culture that we live in today believes that most people will not exercise any mental discipline. They believe that people will let their mind go wherever the advertisers take it. The wise person does not do this. They realize that there are mental pathways that are destructive to a full and enjoyable life, even though they seem delicious at the moment.

Gather up a list of positive things that can be thought about when the wrong images are presented to your mind: great family trips; wonderful times with your spouse; enjoyable times with friends; great victories; hobbies; vacations; special times of learning and growth; accomplishments yet future, etc.

I believe that this same principle would apply to any temptation of a fleshly nature. This would include overspending, envy, slothfulness, anger, greed, and bitterness. One cannot allow one's mind to become occupied with the living out of sin. If you indulge in your mind, then you are moving toward engaging in the actions. Sin is crouching at your doorstep, ready to pounce.

It is not that God does not want you to have a good time or enjoy life. He just knows that the temptations to move outside of His moral boundaries are enticing but will not satisfy. Life in its fullness does not exist down that road. In fact, that road is a dead end.

do not stray into her paths

Here is the second admonition in regards to beating back the temptation posed by the strange or adulterous woman. Do not go where she goes. Don't arrange it so that you will bump into her.

The word *paths* could also be understood *ways*. In other words, don't allow yourself to become seduced by her way of acting and living.

Remember, temptation is only effective because you want to be tempted. There are many temptations that do not affect you because you have no interest in that temptation.

This is what the Apostle James says: "Each one is carried away by his own lust." It is your own strong desire that pulls you to the place of compromise. Recognize those temptations that have a strong pull on your life and don't put yourself in a position to bump into that sin.

Alcoholics should not sit in bars; thieves should not hang out in stores full of carelessly watched merchandise; young virile men should not hang out with loose women; angry people should not be around those who constantly disagree with them; lazy people should not do their planning in bed, etc. While each of us has to learn to win against the temptations that seek to pull our lives in the wrong direction, it is best to avoid the primary source of the seduction if possible – especially in the area of lust.

Remember that the way to beat the seduction to destruction is to be careful what your mind is allowed to freely think about. It is unwise to let your mind feast on the fulfillment of lust. That is why pornography is so destructive to the ability to resist temptation. It is designed as a mental feast on lust. It directly violates the admonitions in this verse.

Second, get away from where a willing, loose woman will be. You can't fall if you are not there. She will find another person who will fall victim to her charms; it does not have to be you. Our culture sends that repeated message that it is not a big deal to give into lust. It is a big deal and reaps a whole harvest of consequences: mentally, emotionally, spiritually, and physically. It is a big deal that you win this battle.

God devotes the better part of two chapters to the discussion on avoiding the problems of lust, adultery, and seduction. This is a life-killer that most young men face. They must beat this or they will destroy the potential for their own happiness. Solomon writes that at the end of this temptation are the ways of death. In other words, separation from all that is life. This happens mentally, emotionally, spiritually, and physically. Our culture has become a licentious culture bent on pushing young men into this form of living death by giving them every opportunity to be turned aside to this soul-killing way of life. Don't let it happen to you.

I am the father of three girls and am raising them to be righteous young ladies. I have warned them about the nature of lecherous young men, as well as the problem of pornography and lust in our culture. I have told them if a young man has a problem with pornography, that young man will need to constantly work a Scriptural program of memorization and meditation as well as confession to win over the temptation to lust. This is serious for it threatens the ability to enjoy life. If the problem of lust is not dealt with effectively, it will color a young man's whole life and twist his ability to interact with the opposite sex and change his ability to enjoy married love.

PROVERBS 7:26 - *For many are the victims she has cast down, and numerous are all her slain.*

Solomon is trying to give us a bigger perspective because when you are under the influence of adultery, it feels like it is love and it is different and your feelings are unique and it is an exception to the normal moral boundaries. But it is not different and this is how millions of people have destroyed their life.

Solomon talks about the sin of adultery as through it were a spirit inhabiting a new woman and luring a new man but aiming at the same destructive goal. You don't have to give into the pull of this temptation. Don't allow yourself to become a victim.

victims

This is the Hebrew word *halal* which means fatal wound. The idea is clearly that the sin of adultery or unlicensed sexual involvement results in a fatal wound. Giving in to lust in a physical action results in things changing. Our culture has tried to make sexual unfaithfulness an action of no consequence – something that happens all the time. But that is not how God treats it. It is giving into an impulse that needs to be contained in a lifetime commitment called marriage. Adultery changes a person; it kills things.

slain

This is the Hebrew word *harag* which means destroy, kill, murder, slay. Adultery begins stabbing those who engage in it and keeps stabbing them until much about their present life dies. It corrupts and destroys. Very few find their way out of the grip of this sin; most are slain by it.

Solomon is doing everything he can to bring the power and destruction of this sin into the open. It destroyed his life and he felt its power first-hand. Do not let this sin begin stabbing you. It will take everything you have and a deep connection to the grace of God, but you can resist. You do not have to give in to the temptation to lust, adultery, and sexual escapades.

PROVERBS 7:27 - *Her house is the way to Sheol, descending to the chambers of death.*

Sheol

This is the Hebrew word *sheol* which means the grave, the place of the dead. In the Old Testament it is the place where all the dead go – both the righteous and the unrighteous.

Solomon even defines Sheol with the second phrase of the proverb: *descending to the chambers of death*. Sheol is the place of the dead. It is the holding tank where people wait for judgment.

Solomon is saying that when a man is unfaithful to his wife, he violates God's law and is destined for the place of the unrighteous dead. Unless he repents and gains forgiveness, he will bear the penalty of his selfishness.

There is also the suggestion that a man who is unfaithful to his spouse will hasten his trip to Sheol. The idea is that this type of rebellion against God's law leads to other types of rebellion and selfishness. A bent towards doing what you want just because you want to leads to all kinds of sin, rebellion, and difficulties. It accelerates the moral decay process and moves you more quickly towards the place of the dead.

Solomon is saying: Do you want to make sure that you end up in the place of judgment for the unrighteous dead? Then by all means move forward with your infidelity and adultery. This was a real warning because the culture had the general understanding of the reality of judgment and hell. In our culture, people dismiss the idea of hell and judgment as myths of a bygone era. But just because we do not retain the memory or understanding of hell does not mean it does not exist. It is a real place and there will be judgment for everything we have done. For those who have admitted that they are sinners and embraced Jesus Christ as their Savior, there will be forgiveness and comfort. Amazingly there will even be rewards for our cooperation with Him in good works. For those who maintain that they are good enough to earn God's favor on their own and unaided by His gift of forgiveness in Christ, there will be exacting judgment.

The early church understood in parallel with Luke 16:19-31 that there were at least two general compartments in Sheol prior to the death and resurrection of Jesus Christ. There was the upper compartment called Abraham's bosom and/or paradise and the lower compartment called Sheol/hell/hades/death. The upper compartment was the place where the righteous dead waited. The lower compartment was the place where the unrighteous dead waited for judgment. The one was a place of comfort and rest the other was a place of regret, sorrow, and torment.

The early church understood based upon Ephesians 4:7-9 and 1 Peter 3:19 that Jesus Christ went to this place called Sheol (the upper compartment) and proclaimed that He had vanquished death and paid for the sins of the world. He then took those who had expressed faith in God (righteous through faith) to the Father. He emptied that upper compartment and took those captives who had been waiting for Him to finish His work of atonement to be with Him in heaven. The lower compartment is still filled with the unrighteous dead who are awaiting the final judgment day. Revelation 20:11-13; Daniel 12:2

Proverbs 8

Proverbs 8:1 - *Does not wisdom call, and understanding lift up her voice?*

What is amazing about this verse is that God tells us that wisdom is not unknown or mysterious. Wisdom is calling attention to itself; it is usually overlooked. According to this verse, wisdom is telling us what to do; we just don't hear its message.

The idea is that someone or something in your life is telling you the right thing to do. The question is - will you have the discernment to know which one that is and be willing to do it when lots of your own thinking says to do something different?

There are all kinds of reasons why we do not listen to the voice of wisdom; many of them are the reasons of a fool. It is not what we want to do. It doesn't feel right. It is a lot of work to do that. It means I have to work harder than other people. It means I have to be disciplined to pull it off. It means I don't get as much rest. It means that I would need to let others win and even promote their winning. It means that I will not get immediate credit for doing something. It means that I must let others win in order for me to win. It means that I can no longer just be the critic looking for the flaws in others plans. I must try to make a difference.

There are all these and many other reasons that any of us ignore the voice of wisdom that calls to us. The wise thing is never that far from any of us. It just doesn't sound easy or risk free or quick.

understanding lift up her voice

Remember that understanding is the connection between things. It is not a mystery why things happen as they do. We just often do not want to face the real reason - either politically, psychologically, or for some other reasons. We don't want to admit that a connection between one thing and another thing exists. In our culture people don't want to admit that there is a connection between pornography and child abuse.

People don't want to admit there is a connection between liberal enforcement of current laws and increasing violence. There are all kinds of connections that are real, but we do not want to admit that they are present. They scream to us, but we are often paddling on the river of denial.

Most importantly, there is a connection between the choices that you have made and the condition that you find yourself in. It is not a mystery why you have the career you have, the house you have, the marriage or children you have. These result from the choices that you make. If these areas are not what you want them to be, then make different choices starting now. Start listening to wisdom; start listening to understanding.

This is not to say that there is not injustice in the world where one person oppresses another person. This is present, but that also involves connections and choices. One should not submit to oppression, immorality, degrading conditions. New choices need to be made. It is true that the perpetrator of these things should be punished, but hoping they will be given justice will not make it happen. You may be the person who starts the wheels of justice turning. Potentially, just your act of no longer being under this immoral oppression may begin the change that will lead to justice, but at least it will change your situation.

PROVERBS 8:2 - On top of the heights beside the way, where the paths meet, she takes her stand;

Wisdom wants to get the word out to people to live a different way. She does not hide what she knows in some dark place reserved only for the special few who will spend years looking and recite some bizarre incantations. Wisdom is right out in the market place.

Wisdom is in a prominent place. When life is not working the way you have put it together, then look up for there is a wiser way of living. And right around you – in a prominent place – are the people who will give you the answer.

There are a few things that are interesting in this verse:

One is that wisdom is prominent – on the tops of the heights, right beside the way, where the paths meet.

Two, she calls for people to turn in and listen to a different way of life. She does not call out what to do. Wisdom does not spew her pearls to everyone. You must turn in and be willing to listen before you hear it. Some people are just not ready to listen that there is a better way than working harder and doing what seems best.

Three, the place where wisdom stations herself is the same place that the elders of a town station themselves or where the supervisors of a crew or company station themselves. There are people who have gone down the road you are on that would love to share the secrets of how to get ahead, but you must be willing to listen. You must turn in. In other words, you must be willing to listen and submit to those who have been down the road farther than you.

Now it is important to say at this point that wisdom – as delineated in the next few chapters – actually has succeeded at the area being considered. Unfortunately in our day we have a host of "experts" who offer their ideas on how to live, but they have not succeeded in that arena. They have degrees and the ability to lecture convincingly. This kind of academic learning is not necessarily connected with wisdom. It is important to recognize this distinction because we do have people tell us to learn from them, but they have not been wise themselves. We have pseudo wise people who have studied all the different things to do and then begun teaching the one they like – not because it worked but because they like how it sounds.

Do not be fooled. Those who have raised great kids should be listened to. Those who have succeeded in business without blowing out their marriages and kids should be listened to. Those who have amassed wealth without becoming greedy should be followed. Those who actually have a righteous walk with God should be listened to. Those who have a great marriage should be followed.

As you are reading this, it may be that some aspect of your life is not working. It could be your marriage; it could be your family; it could be your money or your career. God has stationed people around you who understand wisdom in the area you are lacking. If you ask, they will tell you. It requires humility and a willingness to change the way you live your life. If you are unwilling to do things differently, then any wisdom they would share with you would be worthless.

Four, wisdom is not internally discoverable. You can't just think about things yourself and come up with the better way to live. You need to read a book or talk to people who are wise. Many times we try and appear self-contained, not needing anyone to help us figure things out. This is the fool's plan. Wisdom is calling all around you about how to build a better life, but you do have to be humble enough to listen and change.

PROVERBS 8:3 ~ Beside the gates, at the opening to the city, at the entrance of the doors, she cries out:

The place described is the place that the elders of the city sat to conduct business and to govern the city. He is saying that wisdom resides in and near the place where the elders and successful businessmen are. They have done it. They have accomplished a level of success that has put them in a position to advise others who have not done it.

The key idea is that you should listen to what the leaders who have done it would say about your idea. You should be willing to listen to what these highly respected leaders say about success and prosperity and life. Wisdom is not hidden; it is out in the open in these men. They want to advise you. Listen to them.

These men have made many of the mistakes you are thinking about and have overcome those mistakes in order to have a level of prosperity that does not require them to be out in the field or store every day. They can dedicate a high level of their time to governing the city.

Now the type of thinking in this proverb is that those who have been successful and have lived life should give back to the community by governing. In this time the governors or leaders were highly revered people; not reviled as lying politicians. If you have a question, make sure you get the counsel of those who have already successfully navigated the waters you are about to sail in.

Wisdom is the triple-win: the win for God, the win for others, and the win for yourself. The kind of choices that result in this type of winning and understanding requires that you listen to the voice of experience. The choices that result in real winning over the long term are not always easily determined.

PROVERBS 8:4 ~ *To you, O men, I call, and my voice is the sons of men.*

This is an often-overlooked verse in the call of wisdom. It precedes a section where God, through Solomon, details what different people need to grasp to escape the folly of their lives. The naive need prudence; fools need wisdom; and everyone needs noble things, right things, truth, avoidance of wickedness, embrace of righteousness, understanding, knowledge, and instruction. All of these are different and powerful in helping everyone sort out the way in which they should go.

This verse, however, is about a more specific attention-grabbing group of people who often miss wisdom's call as they rush off to business. Specifically, men. It is often true that men miss the subtleties of wisdom, understanding, skill, and nobility in the hurry to make a name for themselves. But the glories of riches, honor, and life are won using the subtleties of these very things.

Solomon stops just before he launches into the meat of the subject and says: Men, are you paying attention? Don't miss this, men. Don't be in such a hurry that you miss the things that will be required to be successful. The desire that you have to make a mark on the world is good, but it will make a far greater mark on you if you do not listen but learn what I am about to tell you.

The phrase *to the sons of men* is the balance statement which would include all children.

Do not miss that wisdom has a special call to men to slow down on their rush to make money and a name for themselves; to learn the subtleties of wisdom. It is hard to get young men, who are so sure of their talents and energy and direction, to embrace subtle issues of discernment and interaction. But it is crucial.

In applying this verse, ask yourself the question: Do you know the definition of the things wisdom wants to teach? If you do and how they work in the real world, you are ready. If you do not, then stop a while and listen to wisdom teach us.

- Prudence

- Wisdom

- Truth

- Wickedness

- Righteousness

- Perversion

- Understanding

- Knowledge

- Instruction

These terms should live with meaning from our study of Proverbs. If not, re-read the previous sections of Proverb and learn what these words mean and how to live them out

PROVERBS 8:5 ~ *O naive ones, understand prudence; and, O fools, understand wisdom.*

The idea of prudence is very important. Many people do not have it or the desire to get it.

The English dictionary lists these ideas for the word:

1. the ability to govern and discipline oneself by the use of reason

2. sagacity or shrewdness in the management of affairs

3. skill and good judgment in the use of resources

The simple need to understand how to plan well and execute the various phases of a plan. It won't go as simple as we think it should; it will be complex.

If you are one of those simple people who does not understand that the shortest distance between two people is not always a straight line, then you need to grasp the words of the proverbs. Don't keep being so simple. If you keep saying, why can't people just or why can't this thing or that thing happen... Things are more complex than just one simple reaction triggering another simple reaction. There are multiple people and multiple reactions plus events outside of people's control.

These are the definitions for the word *provident* that prudent comes from:

1: making provision for the future: prudent

2: archaic: marked by foresight: prudent

To summarize these two ideas: To be prudent is to be ruled by reason rather than emotion and to see the present decisions and actions in light of their future consequences.

These sentences suggest prudence:

- I shouldn't do this because it will probably lead to this or that.

- I should do this because it will put me in a position to do this in the future

I want so much for my girls to be able to tie their present decisions and actions to the future that they will live in. It is absolutely true that we are creating the future that we live in.

God has given us great latitude within the boundaries of His will to create our own lives.

To be simplistic, naive, and impulsive and refuse to see how our actions affect the future is like taking our future in our hands and destroying it.

PROVERBS 8:6 - *Listen, for I will speak noble things; and the opening of my lips will reveal right things.*

Solomon is trying to get the reader to pay attention and not just read. "Listen!" he shouts, "I am about to give you pearls of truth that few have heard." The danger is that you won't know what to do with this information and will not treat it with the dignity and value it deserves.

I will speak of noble things

The word *noble* is the Hebrew word *nagad* which means to place a previously unknown matter or unknowable matter right in front of a person. It can mean telling the solution or proof to bring something to light; to make it visible. The idea here seems to be that wisdom is hidden from the naive and the fool and the average person. God, through Solomon, is going to begin sharing this hidden knowledge with us. We just need to be prepared for the information. Too often we miss the profundity of wisdom, mistaking it for a solution that is too hard or too remote or too simple for us.

One of the key ideas is that wisdom – when it is revealed – is that wisdom was hidden and not initially obvious or a contemplated solution. It is high, hidden. The translators of the NASB used the word *noble* to infer that it is different and higher and more sublime than the information and solutions that are regularly suggested in the marketplace of ideas.

When a problem or a difficulty is brought up, the typical solutions are bantered about and can be collected rather easily and often. But then there is wisdom: it is the solution that is stunningly helpful; it is unusual; it is right in a much higher way. It does not promote self as the justification for its actions. It promotes God and the common good as well as the individual's well being. It is high and noble and hidden from most people as they pursue the self-first solution.

When you are looking for the way out of your troubles, do you take the selfish solutions and its many variants or do you wait until wisdom speaks? Wisdom will speak if you listen. It will speak of a noble solution that honors God, promotes the value and worth of others – especially others directly affected by this problem – and it will over the long haul build your reputation and value.

the opening of my lips will reveal right things

Meyshar the Hebrew word at its root means to go straight and direct rather than the crooked or twisting way. In the moral and ethical realm it, therefore, means to go straight according to God's law and not to twist or pervert the rules of conduct that God has handed down; to not use myself or my actions in ways that God clearly did not intend. We do not talk about this "natural" or obvious rightness to what one should do, but it used to be called the natural law because morality obviously fit within that which nature allowed. Going against nature was a perversion of it.

One could rightly talk about the unnaturalness of premarital or extramarital sexual relations because it gave rise to sexually-transmitted diseases. Our physical bodies were not designed to handle more than one partner. The spread of disease was the result of the twisting or perverting of God's natural or right order. The same and even more could be said about the homosexual sins as these were a further twisting of obvious natural order. Murder was an obvious violation of the natural order because it produced death – an argument gone horribly too far. A discussion is supposed to produce cooperation, not death. Stealing is another twisting of the natural order – the goods of one person being abrogated to another without work and at great loss to the owner. To gain money or goods in the right way requires that all parties be pleased with the transaction. If one is displeased or feels defrauded, then the transaction has been perverted. Each of the Ten Commandments had a clear understanding in this natural law. It was natural to stay within its boundaries. Each violation was a form of selfishness and twisting what was clearly right in this natural order. We have abandoned this form of simple and profound wisdom because we as a culture want to do what we want to do. We see God's laws as too restrictive. Our culture has basically said: What Jesus says in the parable; we don't want this king to rule over us. We push the limits of what is acceptable and then wonder why we have the diseases and heartbreak and depression and crime that are throughout our culture. Until we get back to a basic understanding of what is right, it will be difficult – if not impossible – to dwell together in peace and safety.

I was on an airplane the other day talking with a 22-year old computer whiz kid who had never talked with someone who advocated abstaining from premarital sex until marriage. He was fascinated by my logic and morals and said repeatedly that he had never heard this line of reasoning before. "You mean to say that you think that I should abstain from going to bed with a woman until I get married to her?" he exclaimed! I had a fascinating discussion with him about the naturalness of godly morals and the selfishness that is in every heart. It was stunning to me that here was a college-educated and brilliant young man who had never encountered a cogent person make the case for premarital abstinence.

Until we are willing to listen to wisdom, our culture will continue on this twisted and broken path and our way of life will collapse. It cannot be sustained if it is not righteous. It is undoubtedly true that our culture will collapse if it does not repent of its immoral ways, but it is also true that each of us as individuals do not have to be a part of that collapse. We can choose to listen to wisdom and follow the right things that wisdom speaks, even if it is against the common wisdom of the office or the streets.

Follow God. It is worth it. Listen to His wisdom. I have read the last chapter... HE WINS.

PROVERBS 8:7 - *For my mouth will utter truth; and wickedness is an abomination to my lips.*

One of the forgotten things to consider is what wisdom is not capable of being. That is what this proverb tells us. In other words, if we think we are hearing wisdom but what we are hearing is one of these things that wisdom cannot be, then what we are hearing cannot be wisdom.

truth

This is the Hebrew word *emet* which means firmness, truth, and is a major part of the biblical word faith. It clearly has to do with that which conforms to reality; that which is truly true and not a perspective or only true in certain circumstances. When we embrace the Christian view of the universe and how to be right within it, we are saying that what the Bible says is true. We are putting our trust in the biblical record.

What Solomon is trying to get us to realize is that when a person tells us things that consistently don't happen, then they are not wise even though they purport to be very wise. Wisdom must actually conform to the truth of reality. There are a number of people who want to be our guides to life but who regularly tell us that this will happen or that will happen, but it does not happen.

I am amazed at the major universities and places of higher learning that make major pronouncements about what they say is true or what is the state of this or that thing, and then what they predict does not occur at all. It has been intellectual parlor games. It is all speculation, and it does not have any level of wisdom in it.

The other aspect that we must be aware of in this idea of wisdom always uttering truth is that one should be able to trace the wise action that is being recommended back to a bedrock truth. If one cannot trace it back to a truth, then it is not wisdom. Let me give you an example: I have heard of women who advise their girlfriends to have an affair – it won't hurt anyone – in fact, it will probably help your marriage. There is no bedrock truth to this statement. I have heard of teens who tell one another to go ahead and try this pill; it won't hurt. But there is no truth to the statement and, in fact, the truth is something completely different.

The classic case of this type of trickery was performed by the advocates of evolution in the 1960's and 70's. They taught countless children that babies move through their evolutionary stages in the womb based upon drawings from a respected scientist that were not true. They suggested that experiments done by a scientist proved that electricity passing through the atmosphere of the early earth produced the building blocks of life. When they knew that their "atmosphere" was not the early earths and the building blocks of life is far from life. These bogus sets of truths – along with trumped up fossil evidence – convinced many that there was no God because life's existence had been completely explained by science.

When you are moving in a direction wisely, there is some truth that is a fixed compass point from which you can navigate.

It is also clear from this proverb that if you do not know the truth about what you are thinking about doing, then you do not know whether it is wise. I am amazed at the number of people who rush into investments without knowing the truth but just because someone said it was a good investment. If you are willing to do the research to find out the facts, then you can make a wise decision. In fact, it often presents itself as the obvious choice when the facts are clear.

wickedness

This is the Hebrew word *resa* which means wrong, wickedness, guilt. Remember that in the Proverbs, a quick definition of that which is wicked is that which is outside of the Ten Commandments.

This is an area that our modern world has completely lost track of. We think that we can gain some new insights into life if we will investigate the realms of sin and moral degeneracy. No, you will not find wisdom there. You will find wrecked lives and twisted logic but not wisdom. In certain circles it is fashionable to suggest that you must go beyond traditional moral boundaries to really live a full life. This is not true. It is not wise.

Solomon is here to tell us, in shorthand form, that if someone is advocating an action or a position that requires that we have another God; bow down to an idol; use a spell or charm; swear or curse God; fail to worship God regularly or work hard each week; not honor our authorities instead rejecting authority; commit physical violence; steal another person's goods; deceive another person, scheme, or plan; lust after the possessions of another, then we are not hearing a wise suggestion. It can't be wise if it requires that we go outside of God's moral boundaries.

So think about what you are going to be doing this next week or the decisions that you will be making. Are they based on truth within the moral boundaries? If so, then you are being wise. If not, then you are being foolish no matter how high-sounding what you want to do is.

PROVERBS 8:8 - *All the utterances of my mouth are in righteousness; There is nothing crooked or perverted in them.*

utterances

This is the Hebrew word *emer* which means speech, words, arguments, declaration, etc. In this proverb Solomon is giving voice to wisdom. He says that you will hear wisdom speak in various people, in various situations, in various ways; but there is a consistency to what wisdom says. It will never say that which is unrighteous. It will not be involved in what is crooked. It will never suggest that the answer to your dilemma is to do something morally twisted.

righteous

This is the Hebrew word *sedeq* which means justice or righteousness. The actual Hebrew words read, *righteousness is what I utter.*

Now it is important to remind ourselves about what righteousness looks like in the Proverbs. It is actions that are within the boundaries of the Ten Commandments and are reflective of the intent of the Ten Commandments. The Ten Commandments are both a boundary and a positive direction. Just as wickedness is defined as that which is outside of these moral lines, so righteousness is defined as living within these lines and living in accordance with the spirit of the commandments.

Solomon is trying to alert us to the fact that there will be many voices claiming to be wisdom. They will all be telling us what to do. Just as the adulterous women of chapters 5 and 7 say similar phrases to wisdom, so there will be lots of other fake wisdom counselors. They will tell you that embezzling is the wise thing to do. They will tell you that getting drunk is wise or hitting the party scene will advance your career or that letting go of your Sunday School morality is required to make it in the real world or that you need to experience other religions to know which one is true. These and all kinds of other advice will be offered to you as wisdom. ANY WISDOM THAT SUGGESTS THAT THE RIGHT COURSE OF ACTION IS OUTSIDE THE TEN COMMANDMENTS IS NOT WISDOM. This is what Solomon is saying. It may sound impressive, clever, and cunning; but it is not wisdom and it will not result in a long-term win.

crooked

This is the Hebrew word *patal* which means to twist, crooked, clever, cunning. This would be the opposite of straightforward.

perverted

This is the Hebrew word *iqqesh* which means twisted, perverted, crooked.

These two words are somewhat similar but when used together, it seems best to understand the difference between the words in this way.

The word *patal* translated crooked should be taken to mean cunning, clever, or deceptive. This is something that wisdom will not be saying. So if someone is talking to you and what they are saying to you sounds deceptive, cunning, and wickedly deceitful, then it can't be wisdom.

The word *iqqesh,* which is translated perverted, should be taken to mean actions or behavior that is beyond just normal sin moving into abhorrent sins. Sin begins with a violation of God's law. But it doesn't stop there. As selfishness progresses, people are able to invent all kinds of ways of sinning: bizarre false religions, blasphemous words, unusual forms of rebellion, sadistic forms of violence, unthinkable forms of sexual debauchery, etc. Some people will suggest that the only way out of some dilemma that you will face is to think outside the box of your old morality; that the way to truly learn wisdom is to let go of your Sunday School morality and embrace a "higher" truth. What they are about to say cannot be wisdom and following their advice is being sent on a fool's errand. But this is how "normal" people get sucked into incredibly abnormal things.

Another way that people get sucked into this kind of behavior is they begin a relationship with a person who does these things and that friendship, romance, or partnership at first doesn't require that they participate in what is clearly crooked or perverted. But it will down the road. It is better to end the partnership, friendship, or romance before it begins because it is headed in the wrong direction from the start.

PROVERBS 8:9 - *They are all straightforward to him who understands, and right to those who find knowledge.*

Here we hear about the nature of wisdom. It is straightforward to those who have understanding. In other words, what sounds wise to a person who has understanding will not sound wise or straightforward to those who don't have understanding. If a person does not see relational connections between people, activities, and things, then they will think that the wise choice is a convoluted mess and will not make it.

The person who understands how people live their lives and how things really work will understand that in order to get to point A, sometimes you need to move in the direction of point Q. This type of thinking makes no sense to the person who does not realize that there are connections between people.

What is fascinating here is that the people who hear about wisdom, but do not have understanding, will not get it. Even if they are given the wise answer, they will not see it as the answer. How many times have I seen this... The person who cannot see that taking any job in order to have a track record will lead to a better job. No, they want the high-paying job right now or they will not work at all. The person who must apologize for their actions when they were only five percent wrong in order to begin to thaw the relationship and allow the other person to apologize for their five percent. The employee who refuses to do things the boss' way because they don't like that way and cannot understand why they are not promoted. The person who is always talking about themselves and what they think without asking about other people, wonders why they have no friends. "I want them to be my friend so they have to know about me."

I have told people what the wise choice is in all types of situations: teen to parent; student to teacher; employee to employer; employer to employee; pastor to church. And yet if they do not understand that life is an incredibly complex arrangement of relationships, they will not do the wise thing they have been told, because they just don't get it. Some people cannot understand that the best way to catch a fish is to go to where the fish is going, not to where the fish is. Some people cannot understand that the shortest distance between two points relationally is not necessarily a straight line.

PROVERBS 8:10 - *Take my instruction and not silver, and knowledge rather than choice gold.*

Solomon sets before us key choices that will come our way and advises us not to get sucked into the wrong choice that looks momentarily better but is really a dead end. All of us will be faced in our life with choices of learning key information or making money.

- It may be presented as a job that pays okay or going to college where you have to pay them. Choose college almost every time; it is the better deal in the long run.

- It may come as the promotion or raise to do something you would hate, learning a new skill, having time to balance life, and/or quality time with loved ones. Choose the new skill or balanced life over a promotion or pay raise almost every time.

- This type of choice may come to you in terms of a get-rich-quick scheme that a friend is peddling which you don't really understand or as a diligence, limits, savings, get-rich-slowly plan that you do understand.

instruction

This is the Hebrew word *mosawr* which means chastisement or correction or change. We must be open to constructive criticism even if it comes from a source that does not want our best. It is always hard to hear where we have messed up, but you must be open to it. Solomon says that constructive criticism is more valuable than a stack of gold.

One of the things that we continue to watch and try and stress to the kids is that they need to be able to take correction well. Even if you think the other person is all wrong, hear them out with kindness and gravity. But do not get into the habit of dismissing people who come at a situation differently than you or those who suggest that you might be the problem.

93

Another way to look at this is that the companies, churches, and organizations that move forward, ask people to rebuke them. They ask the question, "What could we improve on?" "How could we have served you better?" Many people do not give accurate helpful criticism because they do not believe anybody will listen or take their concern as an action item. Organizations that want to get better, get bigger, or serve more people, force themselves to listen to ways they could improve.

knowledge

This is the Hebrew word *daath* which means information, skill, perception. This completes the couplet that is often found in Solomon's thinking. One must be able to take correction and hear new information without defensiveness or withdrawal. This Proverb is about not being willfully ignorant – I would just rather choose to get along than to really know how to handle this situation. This is how corruption in a company starts; how a government begins to take bribes and is no longer just for every person – when someone would rather take money, silver, or gold rather than truth; whether it fits their political direction or not.

Money, if you have it, will be spent but instruction and knowledge once it is used is more yours than before you used it. You grow more wisdom and knowledge the more you use the wisdom that you have. Use it, give it away, and you get more. It is not that way with money.

PROVERBS 8:11 - *For wisdom is better than jewels; and all desirable things cannot compare with her.*

This is quite a claim. But it is dependent upon the existence of an afterlife and a God who rewards. Moses says in Psalm 90 that we should ask God to help us number our days so that we will present to God a heart of wisdom at the end of our life. This means that wisdom is one of the most valuable commodities in the new life that follows death.

This is one of those comparison proverbs scattered throughout the book. These help us reevaluate our values and make sure that we haven't allowed the Devil or the world to change the price tags on things in our life. The world and the Devil are constantly trying to convince us that worthless things are the most important and the important things are worthless. They try and get us to throw away our marriages, to disregard our children, to avoid honesty, to pursue the adrenalin rush of gambling or illicit intimacy. It is the wise Christian who allows this ancient God-breathed wisdom to keep us from falling prey to this re-pricing scheme.

There is too little discussion about the impact that heaven should have upon how we live here and now. Christians are firmly committed to the fact of a life after death and how you live today affects that life. Now is the warm-up for that life. But many Christians live with the values of the world's culture which is "live for today."

Wisdom is the best policy for this life also. Wisdom is the everybody-wins policy – looking for the action that produces a win for God's glory, a win for the others in your life, and a win for yourself.

This comparison proverb slaps us in the face and says that we must value the wise choice enough to sacrifice some things in the short-term to gain it. There will be many choices that present themselves to us during our life, and many of them will require giving up some desirable things. If we forego a desirable thing to gain more wisdom, then we have done well. God will reward that choice.

Solomon is saying that knowing how to live life and what is important and what is not is far more valuable than having a lot of wealth, fame, power, or any sinful pleasure. For wisdom means that life is lived well and others have received blessings from it, God has been glorified, and you have benefited. A life well lived and filled with loving relationships is far more full than a life filled with possessions and other trinkets of this world.

Many times we have to be reminded of this truth because we get sucked in by all the advertising and babble from this world that tries to convince us that the stuff of this world is more important than wisdom and peace and righteousness from God. One day it will be revealed that the baubles of this world were silly vending machine jewelry. Only the qualities of Christ are really valuable.

On a personal note, it was this verse a long time ago that God used to help me see how right Dana was for me. She has been such a wise counselor, friend, confidant, and wife. I have benefitted a thousand-fold because of her willingness to marry me. It was because of her wisdom that God got my attention. One day when this life is over and I present her to the Lord as a major aspect of my ministry on earth, I pray that I have added in some small way to the wisdom that she possessed. What a blessing for God to give me a woman like her.

PROVERBS 8:12 - *I, wisdom, dwell with prudence, and I find knowledge and discretion.*

This is one of the most amazing groups of verses in the Scripture. It stretches from verse 12-14. It could be titled: How to Make Great Decisions or The Eleven Friends of Wisdom or How to Find Wisdom in the Toughest Situations.

This group of verses tells us how to find wisdom; how to find that elusive thing called the wise choice or action. When you don't know what to do, then this is the way. You will recognize wisdom by the company it keeps. If you find these other things, then you will find wisdom on any subject and in any situation.

Remember that we are looking for wisdom or the wise choice among several alternatives or the wise path among many possibilities. The short definition of wisdom is the triple-win: the choice that God wins, others win, and I win. This could also be called God's will. The other choices that are not wise are various levels of foolishness. Foolishness is the selfish, impulsive, rebellious choice or path. It looks good but only for the short term.

The passage in front of us is a template to objectively evaluate each possible decision or life path and make sure that you are not duped into a foolish short-term path.

These are the Eleven Friends of Wisdom that must be used to evaluate what to do so that you are doing the wise thing. These, in effect, form a grid for evaluating potential choices and decisions. If you run your options through this gauntlet, it will be clear what you should do.

You are looking for these friends of wisdom:

- Prudence

- Knowledge

- Discretion

- Fear of the Lord

- No Pride or Arrogance

- No Evil Way

- No Perverted Mouth

- Counsel

- Sound Wisdom

- Understanding

- Power

I wisdom dwell with prudence

The Hebrew word *prudence* is the word *ormah* which is guile, prudence, subtlety, planning, strategy. This verse is very interesting because it says that when a person is acting wisely, they will have prudence also. They will have a plan for what they are doing. They will have objectives, reasons, and plans that make sense to accomplish the desired results. Wisdom is not usually spontaneous. It thinks through what is wanting to be accomplished and how to bring about the desired result.

Solomon is saying that those who would be wise must have the ability to be focused on a goal and to be able to be emotionally objective in the midst of the decision.

Solomon would ask, "Do you have a goal?" "Do you have a strategy?" "Are you using your reason or your emotions to make this choice?"

As a very good friend of mine always says when his children ask if they can do something, "If this is wisdom where is the prudence?" Show me that your idea or thought or desire is wisdom by showing me the prudence. What is the goal? How are you going to get there? Is this just emotional or temptation?

The reason people who abstain from sexual relations before marriage have been called prudes is because they kept in mind that they wanted to have a great marriage in the future and not just a good time in the present. It is their planning, their strategy, their goals, and their objectivity that allows them to say no to the present impulse.

A few questions that parents have to continually get children to answer: Where will this activity lead? What do you want to accomplish with this activity or friendship? What do you want your life to be like in ten years? What is your plan to get there?

Wisdom dwells with prudence. Wisdom has a plan. Wisdom looks at the opportunities and objectifies which ones will accomplish the desired results and which ones will not. Foolishness is very spontaneous and impulsive. It just waits for the next interesting thing to come along. It cannot non-emotionally evaluate the options.

This clearly means that we must ask ourselves what is our plan to accomplish the goals and dreams that God has put in our heart. Without those plans and goals, we will not have wisdom. Wisdom lives with prudence. Many times the only way to avoid temptations, destructive opportunities, and interesting non-productive rabbit trails is because you don't have time, energy, or money because of your pursuit of the goals you have set. Avoiding sin is often about not having time for it: "I have more important things to do." Keeping away from subtle, unknown destructive pathways is often about being too busy fully pursuing what you know is God's will.

If you believe that a relationship is wise, where is the prudence? What is the objective? What is the plan? How are you going to pull this off? What would be a violation of a godly plan? Go find knowledge and discretion. If you believe that a business opportunity is God's will, then what is the objective? What is the plan? How are you going to pull this off? What would be a violation of a godly plan? Where will this end up?

Sometimes a choice or opportunity is God's will and it does represent wisdom, and prudence clearly emerges the more you think about it. You know what should be done. How to get there also emerges, but as you are moving forward you can begin to dwell not on the goal or the plan but the benefits of the plan or the results of the wisdom, the money, relationships, prestige, and power of accomplishing the goal. Stay objective and live with prudence rather than coveting the attending blessings of wisdom. Keep working the plan. Keep your head down.

The English dictionary for *prudence*: the ability to govern and discipline oneself by the use of reason

Prudence is the ability to evaluate potential choices and actions using reason with a detachment and lack of emotion and see where that choice/action leads. It clearly carries with it a goal orientation; a future orientation. If you are going to truly find the wise choice, have you evaluated each choice with this level of precise detachment? What will happen if I go down this road? Where will it end up? This is close to the T aspect of the Myers Briggs Temperament Type scale: Just the facts ma'am, just the facts.

This means that you must get past what you personally feel about different orientations and detach from it enough to really evaluate it with as little interference from your emotions as possible. Whether it is a win choice for you will come later.

I find knowledge and discretion

This tells us that if we are going to find the wise choice, then we must get as much information as possible and maximize our skills. This is what knowledge is – information and skill. Sometimes you can only get information at certain times or in certain places, so you have to go there and get it to find the wise decision. Notice that wisdom doesn't always have knowledge, but it goes and finds it. What are the real facts about the options that are facing me – not my guesses or suppositions?

knowledge

This is the Hebrew word *daat* which means information and skill. In the ancient biblical view of knowledge there were two forms of it. That information form of it is where new bits of data are added and new facts and new ideas. The second form of knowledge is skills you can learn, ways of behaving, and tactical strategies and actions that allow you to accomplish a particular goal or desire.

Solomon is saying that you must have knowledge if you are to be truly wise. It is not the same as wisdom, but it is the raw material that wisdom requires. Realize that since this is true, it means that coming to the wise decision or wise life may take time as you gain the information or skill that are required to accomplish the wise action.

discretion

This is the Hebrew word *mezimma* which means purpose or a plan or a plot. It is consistently translated as discretion when it is used in a positive context and scheming or plotting when used in a negative context. Discretion means the ability to make discrete and responsible choices. Or it is focused on the key decisions that are a part of a plan or accomplishing something. You cannot have found wisdom unless you have or find a plan on what to do. Wisdom is not impulsive; it is very thoroughly thought through. What is the plan for each option and how do they unfold? You do not have wisdom if you are always making it up as you go. Clearly there will be some improvisation and some spur-of-the-moment thinking and course corrections; but by and large, wisdom does not fly by the seat of its pants. It plans

When decisions, choices, and potential actions are evaluated against and with these perimeters, then the wise choice will be clear.

These are the eleven friends of wisdom:

- Prudence

- Knowledge

- Discretion

- Fear of the Lord

- No Pride or Arrogance

- No Evil Way

- No Perverted Mouth

- Counsel

- Sound Wisdom

- Understanding

- Power

When you can't find wisdom clearly among the choices available to you, then find his eleven friends and he will be very near by...

PROVERBS 8:13 - *The fear of the Lord is to hate evil; pride and arrogance and the evil way and the perverted mouth I hate.*

This is a very interesting section in the midst of how to make a good decision. It brings in a whole different set of parameters than the positive qualities of prudence, knowledge, and discretion. It means that you must live in the boundaries of the fear of the Lord. Where has God said "no"? The Ten Commandments quickly come to mind. I would understand this reference to be that if a choice or action or decision will take you outside of the boundaries of the Ten Commandments, then it cannot be the wise choice because it would mean that you are no longer living in the fear of the Lord and no longer hating evil.

Also, Solomon adds that one must not even – within the boundaries of the Ten Commandments – develop a proud I-don't-need-anyone or I-can-make-it-on-my-own mentality. We must realize that we are interdependent.

God adds that wisdom will not take an evil way to accomplish a good purpose. The means to the end is as important as the end. It is not okay to resort to tactics of evil as a way of life – especially as a positive strategy to accomplish or find the right or wise decision. Sometimes it is the thought that I can accomplish a great good through the short-term pathway of bending the rules or the short-cut of going outside the boundaries of the Ten Commandments. If it is clear that a certain decision or pathway requires this, then it fails on two counts: the fear of the Lord and the evil way.

The next bit of negative way to find wisdom is that if you have to begin to speak in a twisted or perverted way in order to move down a certain road, then it can't be the wise thing to do. There will be paths and choices that look far better than others but demand a certain type of language or a lie to begin the journey. That path or choice cannot be wisdom.

PROVERBS 8:14 ~ *Counsel is mine and sound wisdom; (judgment) I am understanding, power is mine.*

counsel is mine

There is an aspect to the word *counsel* that is more than just advice or influential wisdom. Good counsel involves the purpose or the ultimate aim of a thing or plan. Why do you want to know how to do this thing? What are you going to do with it? What are you trying to accomplish? If the person giving the counsel knows the purpose, then their counsel will be much better; but if the purpose is unsound or unknown, then the counsel or advice or recommendations will be suspect.

Give counsel that is really reflective of the purpose of God and you will meet with good success. Do not give counsel that would work at counter-purposes with the purpose of God or you will not succeed long term.

Counsel is the idea that you have bounced the various ideas and potential paths off of several people and received their point of view about it. You must let other people help you evaluate potential choices or you are not interested in finding wisdom. It is sometimes helpful to make a list of people you want to run a certain idea by. Then get their counsel.

sound wisdom

Sound wisdom could be the input you get from the counsel and/or it could be talking to people who have gone down the roads that you are thinking about going down – people who have actually done the various things that you are contemplating. What are they saying? It is sound wisdom in that it is not potential; it is real or solid – a been-there-and-done-that kind of wisdom. Would you think this would be the best way to go? Would you do it again? What would you do differently?

I am understanding, power is mine

Understanding is looking at decisions and seeing their effect in every direction. How will this decision effect this or that or my relationship with so and so or such and such a person? It has the feeling side of the Myers-Briggs scale in mind; seeing a decision for its effects. This is the opposite of prudence which is detachment.

Solomon adds the unexpected dimension of power. The wise decision will come with the power and the authority to accomplish it. If you think you have found the wise choice but it involves no authority or no way to make it happen, then you need to keep looking. Wisdom brings power, authority, and might. The word is the Hebrew word for might and even lady or queen.

Let's look at this idea very practically. Let's describe this phrase *power is mine* in real world terms. If I have found the right decision, then the people in authority will give me the okay to do it. If I have found the right choice, then the energy, power source, and labor will be available to do this right choice. The right choice is not pie-in-the-sky which cannot be done because no one will approve it or I don't know how I will find the people or equipment to pull it off. A lot of people excuse themselves from what they should do because they have convinced themselves that the right choice is beyond them. The right choice is never beyond them. It is not the right choice if you can't do it. That is someone else's right choice.

In Solomon's day to have the physical power to do a project meant people, horses, mules, and oxen. In our day it means equipment, electricity, and people; but the concept is still the same in this sense. You must have access to the actual power to do your right choice or it cannot be the right choice.

Another aspect of what Solomon is saying by including the phrase *power is mine* is that the wise decision increases authority and power rather than diminishes it.

Will the decision that I am making today or the path I am contemplating move me along a path that will increase my might or authority or will it really diminish or leave my authority at the same level? Which choice or path will move me towards more might, authority, and power?

Are you making decisions or taking actions that if people found out it would cause them to diminish your authority and power? If you are, then those cannot be the right decisions. Wise decisions add power and increase authority, not diminish it.

The only exception to that rule is when the authority above you is committing acts of evil and your actions are righteous; then they will demote you for being righteous. And even in those cases your moral authority goes up even if you are being diminished in other areas.

Remember that this verse is a part of a whole section in Proverbs 8:12-14 that could be called the eleven friends of wisdom.

When decisions, choices, and potential actions are evaluated against and with these perimeters, then the wise choice will be clear. These are the eleven friends of wisdom: Prudence; Knowledge; Discretion; Fear of the Lord; No Pride or Arrogance; No Evil Way; No Perverted Mouth; Counsel; Sound Wisdom; Understanding; Power.

When you can't find wisdom clearly among the choices available to you, then find his eleven friends and he will be very near by.

PROVERBS 8:16 - *By me princes rule, and nobles, all who judge rightly.*

The reference here is to leadership under the influence of wisdom and that those who are good leaders are looking for the triple-win solution. They are not willing to settle for the easy, selfish-win solution or the corrupt I-win-you-lose solution. Good leaders evaluate their decisions on the basis of who wins if I do this. Does anybody lose, and if so, who is that? If it is anybody other than the wicked, then I cannot make this decision.

The key idea here is that Solomon wants leaders to think before they make decisions and not just act out of their own universe or their own little world. Too often what seems right from their limited perspective is clearly wrong when seen in a larger context. When you are in positions of power and authority, you must ponder how to bring about the triple-win solution and what the triple-win solution is.

princes

This is the Hebrew word *sar* which is translated prince, chief, captain, governor, steward. This is a leader who is not the ultimate leader but still has real power. These are also young leaders who have been given authority to test their abilities, giving them real experience in leading, managing, and directing.

It is these people who must be taught to look for the wise choice. It is often this level of leader who can become corrupt quickly, looking only for how they can win and even being willing to cause others to lose so they can win.

nobles

This is the Hebrew word *nadib* which means generous man, noble, even prince. The idea seems to be that there are those who have, through their efforts, become wealthy or successful and are known as generous people. They do not have positions of power in government, but they have respected places in the community because of their generosity and service. They live out the idea of wisdom: others winning through their choices and actions.

judge

This is the Hebrew word *saphat* which means to judge or govern. We think of this word as a person who must decide whether a person is innocent or guilty, and if guilty, how much punishment. This was not the case in those days. The judge was a ruler and a person who actually handled all the branches of governance. If they were to lead their people in a righteous way, then they were looking for the triple-win decisions.

PROVERBS 8:17 - *I love those who love me; and those who diligently seek me will find me.*

The discussion is about wisdom and this verse clearly states that God will make sure that the wise choice, action, and direction will be found by those who consistently seek it out.

It is not hidden from us – if you diligently examine the choices before you. Get counsel from wise people; examine the relationship between each choice and the people and situations around you; and you will find wisdom and know what to do.

There is an interesting play on words in the Septuagint in this verse. It says that God or wisdom *phileo* (loves) those who *agape* (love) Him. Wisdom comes as a friend and the companion when we have surrendered to it first; when we realize how desperately we need it and we have chosen God and wisdom to meet our needs. This is similar to Jesus and Peter and His asking him if he loved Him three times.

PROVERBS 8:18 - *Riches and honor are with me, enduring wealth and righteousness.*

Solomon is selling the advantages of going after wisdom. Everything that temptation promises, wisdom actually delivers with none of the bitter aftertaste of foolishness. Too often we, as believers, have taken the route of saying that God will make up for our sacrifices in this world with rewards in the next one. This is true but this is not the inducement that Solomon or Jesus give. Both say that the path of wisdom and faith will be highly rewarded in this life as well as the next.

It is important to say that the Christian way of life – the life of faith and righteousness; the life of wisdom – is the best life here and now. If one has to sacrifice wisdom, righteousness, or faith in God to have this world's goods or this world's adulation, then it means submitting to a fool's world that will fall apart. Do not run after the world's fools gold; instead run hard after wisdom and God will reward you. If you seek first the kingdom of heaven, He will add all these other things to you. The life of faith and wisdom is worth it. It pays off in this life and in the one to come.

Let's take a look at the four payoffs that Solomon knows we are all looking at:

riches

This is the Hebrew word *oser* which means abundance or riches or plenty. Solomon's perspective is to try and get the young person to understand what is very difficult to understand from an American cultural perspective. He is saying that when you embrace the life of wisdom, you will have more than just one of something; more than just what is needed at the moment. Instead you will have multiples and abundance of food, clothing, shelter, and resources. American culture, being built upon a whole culture of people who embraced wisdom, is experiencing this plenty – even those who are themselves fools. This was also true of Israel during Solomon's day. There was so much plenty that even silver was common. The economy was good in Solomon's day. Our culture is, however, fast forgetting the wisdom of our past and embracing the fool's way of believing that our position of abundance is ours by right. American young people can often not imagine a world where one does not have multiples of everything. This is why a mission's trip is often so enlightening to American youth.

Solomon's selling feature of plenty is important to mention. It suggests that it is not against God's will for a person who follows His will to have plenty. It is not more spiritual to be poor. It matters whether the plenty is handled with righteousness and justice.

honor

This is the Hebrew word *kabod* which means glory or honor or weightiness or even heaviness. The idea of this word is heaviness or weightiness and is applied to both good and bad ideas. In this context – as in many – it means that a person is a valuable or weighty and respected person. This is what people want as they progress through life. They want to be respected and valued. They want their opinion to count and their presence to be noted.

Solomon is saying that those who embrace wisdom and look for the win/win/win scenario will become a person who is respected and valued. The opposite is also true: The people who only look out for themselves will be devalued and diminished in their respect and place of prominence.

American culture has begun to substitute a fool's honor for real honor and is beginning to convince teens and others to pursue it. The fake honor is fame: I want to be known or noticed. What is amazing is that people don't care what they are known for as long as they are noticed or known above others. This is not the honor that Solomon is talking about; it is vainglory of the pilgrim's progress. It is pride and vanity. What is interesting is that if people actually become famous, then they enter a prison of their own making. They cannot go out like they used to because everyone notices them. They are not respected for who they are. They are followed around by paparazzi and hounded. This is portrayed as a shortcut to honor and adulation; it does not end up where you think it does.

We do want honor where people value us; where they want to know what we think and we have something of substance to say; where people give us room to live because they value us. We want honor and the path to attain it is wisdom.

wealth

This is the Hebrew word *hon* which means enough, riches, abundance, and/or wealth. There is not a huge difference between the word riches used in the first phrase and wealth used in this second phrase. What is different is the describing adjective: enduring.

righteousness

This is the Hebrew word *sedeq* which means justice; righteousness. It comes from the idea of conformity to a standard; staying within God's proscribed boundaries.

One of the grave concerns of those who are raised in a religious context or supernatural worldview is: What if I am good my whole life and then near the end I make a major error and blow away – through giving into temptation and sin – my righteous life. We may have a hard time understanding this great concern, but Solomon is addressing this concern with this word. The person who embraces wisdom will have enduring righteousness. They will not destroy all they have been through evil choices later in life.

This does raise issues about Solomon's own life as he made very poor and unrighteous decisions near the end of his life.

enduring

This is the Hebrew word *ateq* which means durable or in this case translated enduring. It is this word which changes the meaning and gives the significance to what Solomon is promising. If you embrace the path of wisdom, you will not only have abundance and value but it will not be fleeting. The danger of those who gain abundance and honor is that it could go away, especially those who gain it the fool's way. They do not know how they really got it and it is not necessarily repeatable.

We don't just want abundance and value. We want to make sure that we won't lose it and that we won't make major mistakes so that whatever value we have built up will be snatched away.

PROVERBS 8:19 - *My fruit is better than gold, even pure gold, and my yield better than choicest silver.*

fruit

This is the Hebrew word *peri* which means fruit. Fruit is the product of trees that are planted and cared for. It is a way of turning sunlight, water, and land into useable and saleable commodities. It is also a way of collecting sugar and making a dessert in a non-industrialized society.

All of these ideas are wrapped up in the word *fruit* as Solomon uses it. He is saying that when a person goes after and then gains wisdom, they will have turned breathing, working, choosing, and relating to others into a useable and even saleable product. The process of collecting wisdom will also sweeten life.

better

This is the Hebrew word *tob* which means good but in this instance is translated as a measure of contrast between the yield of wisdom and the yield of gold. Gold just sits there and can purchase things, but wisdom has a much better yield. It grows and grows.

What is the better yield of wisdom over gold? Well, wisdom can accumulate material possessions, but it can also accumulate relationships which make life worth living.

It is important to realize that without relationships, all the money or power in the world is not worth it.

If you are chasing power or prestige or fame or popularity – but you have no real relationships – then you are chasing a dream, a shadow, even a nightmare. I was recently talking with a young woman who was trying to adapt herself to those around her so that she could be powerful and popular. Every time she thought she was about to arrive, it still did not satisfy and it did not yield two-way relationships.

gold

This is the Hebrew word *charuts* which means gold.

yield

This is the Hebrew word *tebua* which means produce, yield, increase, gain. The idea is that there is significant increase or gain. Solomon is saying that the gain or increase from having stockpiles of wisdom is greater than from having stockpiles of gold. Don't go after the wrong one. If you go after wisdom, you will most likely get all the wealth you need; but if you go after gold, you will usually not end up with wisdom and, in many cases, even riches.

Again let me remind you that relationships are the real key to a satisfying life. Relationships are what give meaning and depth and joy and satisfaction. Whatever is needed to produce these is what you are after. What you need is wisdom.

Solomon is approaching this as though he were talking to an investment banker. Do you want to invest in the better yield or the less secure yield? He knows that everyone will choose the higher and more secure yield.

Even if you are a loner you will want to have at least a few people who love you and know you. Relationships are the real keys to life. Everyone has nine relationship possibilities in their life:

- The relational possibilities with God
- The relational possibilities with their spouse
- The relational possibilities with their family
- The relational possibilities with their work
- Their relational possibilities with their community of faith
- Their relational possibilities with their finances

- Their relational possibilities with their community and society

- Their relational possibilities with their friends

Take each one of these relationships and rate them from 1-10 in terms of how much wisdom you have on how to make that relationship really blossom.

PROVERBS 8:20 - I walk in the way of righteousness, in the midst of the paths of justice.

It is important to realize that this is wisdom talking, not God. The wise course is the one in the midst of the righteous way. If you have to be shady to accomplish something, then it cannot be the wise course.

A caveat is that wisdom is not flowing with your feelings or making others feel good; it is objective and shrewd. It makes sure that justice is done. Someone stabbed in the back will come back to bite you. So many people believe that the only way to get ahead is to cheat people and to play at the edges of what is right. This is not the biblical way of wisdom.

It is, however, unconventional wisdom to walk down the middle of the morally right path and stick with it.

PROVERBS 8:21 - *To endow those who love me with wealth, that I may fill their treasuries.*

One of the side benefits of wisdom is that one gains filled treasuries. Seeking wealth is not the goal of wisdom but one gains understanding and, therefore, gains an ability or gifts that will fill the treasuries of their house. I think this is material possessions but also relational prosperity. One is not really rich unless one has a depth of relationships with which to share it.

If one makes the decisions that consistently have God, others, and yourself win, then you will be in a very good place.

PROVERBS 8:22 - *The Lord possessed me at the beginning of His way, before His works of old.*

at the beginning of His way

This is a very interesting statement, and it reminds us that one of God's attributes is wisdom. He has infinite knowledge and infinite wisdom. He can and does search through all of the possibilities and implements the best scenario given the goals that He has in mind.

This verse reminds us that before God ever began the creation, He was prepared with wisdom. We would call it doing advanced planning. Now God did not need to sit down with a piece of paper and lay out all the different possibilities of worlds and materials and choices but, in essence, on a much larger scale this is what God did. He did it in an instant of our time. He planned and explored all the various possibilities before He ever created anything.

Solomon is wanting us to understand that this trait of wisdom that he wants us to develop is a part of the way that God is. We have to learn to develop wisdom, but God is wise. He contains and has a natural part of His nature, this thing we call wisdom. Everything He thinks and evaluates must come through this ability to see where the win is for everyone. We must gain this way of mental action, but God automatically has it.

Solomon is using God as an example that we should emulate. In order to bring this world in which we live into being, God had to use applied knowledge in precise ways, and so do you need to apply knowledge in the maximum win-win-win ways to navigate the various choices that you will face.

PROVERBS 8:23 - *From everlasting I was established, from the beginning, from the earliest times of the earth.*

This is a section that is establishing the antiquity of wisdom. It is quite an impressive section. God, through Solomon, is declaring that the quality or attribute of wisdom is an aspect of God and, therefore, did not begin with the creation of the world. Wisdom existed in eternity before there was a universe and space and time. In fact, wisdom is that which allowed God to "choose" among the various options that were available to Him about this coming universe. This passage suggests that of all the possibilities that presented themselves to His limitless mind, He chose to use, employ, and direct those which would be for His glory and our benefit. This is exactly what the scientists are finding – that the universe has been fine-tuned for our existence and benefit. They call this the anthropic principle.

Within the last thirty years the scientists have been astounded at various fixed values that have been hardwired into the universe because they all are specifically designed to sustain and provide for our form of life. Some astrophysicists have suggested that it looks as though someone has been monkeying with the physics. I would suggest that you could read *Mere Creation* by Dembsinki or *The Creation Hypothesis* by Moreland.

What this passage tells us is that God – from outside our dimensionality – planned the universe for our arrival and specifically chose to provide for us in what He created. It is an amazing thing and deserving of great worship to God. As the various avenues of scientific research pour their information on us, we are continually reduced to shock and awe and stunned worshipful silence. God did design the universe with us in mind. He exists and brought the universe into being after having planned every detail of it for our arrival and existence.

Solomon's argument in this whole section is that wisdom predates the universe, our world, the mountains, the sea, and resides in the presence – if not essence – of God. It is the way that God acts and it should be the way that we act. If you want to be like God and live as you were intended to live, then live out a life of wisdom. Wisdom is not just a technique that God invented for living in this world; it predates the world and is the way that He acts. Get in step with wisdom or you will be out of step with God.

The other side of this argument that is not mentioned here in this section is that foolishness is not at all like God. If you are selfish and possessive, you will destroy yourself and move against God's nature and His will. The world was His perfect creation, and it has been infected through the Devil and Adam and Eve with a virus called selfishness (sin). This contagion has spread throughout our world and is why we no longer live in a good and beneficent world. The world has gone wrong because of the foolishness of the Devil and the foolishness of mankind.

God allowed – in His wisdom – angelic beings and mankind to have the power of choice. They have used that choice to rebel against wisdom, generosity, and love and instead have embraced selfishness, impulsiveness, and rebellion. He gave us the power of choice to give us the power of true love. We would do well to fight back against those who choose the path of selfishness with wisdom and generosity and love. At some point God will end this experiment and collect those who have embraced His love and wisdom. He will eliminate the foolishness and set up a world without the contagion for those whom He loves and who loved Him. Every day you embrace wisdom you make yourself more fit for heaven.

PROVERBS 8:24 - *When there were no depths I was brought forth, when there were no springs abounding with water.*

This is a fascinating reference to the eternal planning process. God planned and arranged everything that was going to happen in this universe that we live in before the first atom or particle appeared. God not only planned what could and would take place, he also invented the laws – physical, spiritual, relational – that would be needed to govern this universe. This proverb deals with the fact that wisdom had to be brought out and used in the process of deciding which of all the possible worlds that could be invented would be invented. A limitless number of worlds and possibilities in those worlds presented themselves to God's infinite mind. It was wisdom that allowed Him to choose to bring this one into actuality.

Paul refers to this planning time before the beginning of the world when he states that Christ was slain before the foundation of the world. Before there was ever anything, God was planning how to work through the various problems that a universe with stars, creatures, and choices would cause. The greatest problem was the problem of how to redeem mankind when it chose to disobey and turn away from its creator. God planned before the foundation of the world that His Son would become a man, live a perfect life, and sacrifice that perfect life so that certain members of mankind could be bought back from the slave market of sin.

It is interesting that this proverb uses the words *brought forth;* this is the Hebrew word *chil* which means to whirl, dance, writhe. The idea seems to be writhing like in childbirth. Solomon describes God's application of wisdom to the infinite number of possibilities as though He is birthing this world through the appearance of wisdom. It is important to realize that wisdom does not exist as speculation. It is the actual application of knowledge, strategy, goals, and counsel which brings about the win, win, win scenario. Of all the worlds that God could have created, He chose to create this one with you having the choices that you have. He has put you in a position to glorify Him today, to benefit others, and to succeed personally. Choose the choice that does all three of those things. It is what the universe was founded upon, and it is one of the bedrock principles of how to navigate through this life to get to the next one in the best possible situation.

Realize that God also planned you and all the choices that you would ever have in this life. He knew you before the world began. Through His wisdom He gave you the choices that He gave you. Use wisdom to make your choices and you will glorify Him, benefit others, and succeed for yourself. He used wisdom to create the universe and He wants you to use wisdom to live in it.

PROVERBS 8:25 ~ *Before the mountains were settled, before the hills I was brought forth;*

Solomon is reaching for ways to explode the ancient nature of wisdom in the minds of his hearers. Wisdom has been around much longer than the most stable constant thing in your world, the mountains, and the hills.

We embrace the idea that we have access to the same wisdom that planned the universe, the stars, the earth, and the hills. We can do better than just exist or muddle through; we can actually express wisdom even in a fallen, broken world.

God calls us back through Solomon's imagery to the time when there was nothing fixed or settled about the earth – when it was still covered in water and undetermined. It was God's wisdom that planned out the various ways it would be formed and the various shapes that it would take.

Before the hills or mountains ever came to be, your life was plotted and God knew you. He knew that if you choose a particular thing, then certain choices and a certain result will come from it. He knew that if you choose something different, then a whole host of different choices and results would become available to you. We can choose wisely and change our destiny, or we can choose foolishness and destroy our potential. Use the wisdom that God has made available.

PROVERBS 8:26 - While He had not yet made the earth and the fields, nor the first dust of the world.

Solomon wants to emphasize the point that God, during the planning process for the universe, evaluated all the possible worlds and options using wisdom to decide how He would have the world unfold. He decided that those choices and options that would give Him glory and allow people to win would be the ones that obtained reality. He could have made any kind of world. But He made this one.

Everyone must have a theory about how the universe and our world got here. That theory controls the way you live. If you believe that the universe just randomly happened and is the result of accidental mutations with no guiding purpose, then you will live your life like a random accident or like you are the god of this life you have. If, however, you realize that the universe we live in is too complex, too planned, too designed, then you will seek to live your life with wisdom and planning like the One who designed the universe.

If everything is random and chance, then wisdom is folly. But if wisdom comes out of the very essence of the being who planned and created this universe, then we should do as He did and use wisdom and planning for our lives.

Stop and think through your day today. What will you do this morning? How can you be wiser in your choices and actions this morning? What things shouldn't you do that you will probably have the opportunity to do? What things could you do that will significantly bless others, God, and even yourself?

What are you planning to do this afternoon? How can you be wiser in your choices and actions this afternoon? What should be done to get ready for a great afternoon? Is there anything that you are planning that you should cancel? If you were really to be wise, is there anything that you should add to this afternoon to get ready for the weekend or some upcoming event?

This verse says that God spent considerable time in the process of planning, using wisdom. Embrace this idea: everything goes better with wise planning.

PROVERBS 8:27 - *When He established the heavens, I was there, when He inscribed a circle on the face of the deep,*

The ancient origins of wisdom are being celebrated in this proverb. Solomon speaks of the eternality of wisdom in this section. God puts on display the wisdom that He alone possesses: the application of knowledge, its interconnections, the fine detail, the understanding of the consequences of billions of different actions, the construction of a world in which everybody wins.

when He inscribed a circle on the face of the deep

This passage and others like Job 26:10 and Isaiah 40:22 are what caused many to understand that the ancient Hebrews understood that the earth was a globe. The idea is that God, in His use of wisdom, has brought forth the circle as a way to boundarize the planet.

This passage should cause you to celebrate the wisdom of God and the amazing interconnections of creation. As we find out more and more of creation we find detail, design, and wonder at every level we penetrate.

The point is that if God used wisdom to create the universe, then we should use wisdom to live in the universe. Look for the everybody-wins choice.

PROVERBS 8:28 - *When He made firm the skies above, when the springs of the deep became fixed.*

We don't often contemplate that there was a time when the atmosphere was unstable and not fixed. Scientists tell us that it is possible that other planets in our solar system may have had an atmosphere like ours, but it was swept away by meteor showers and other cataclysmic events. God, however, firmed up the atmosphere around this planet and protected it from those types of events that could have stripped this planet of its atmosphere. We are told that by placing our earth in a solar system with numerous planets and especially with Jupiter and Saturn – much bigger planets near to us – whatever meteors and asteroids that enter our system are usually drawn to their gravitational field rather than earth's rather small one.

We are learning all the time about the fine-tuning that God did to establish our planet and protect it. It is these displays of wisdom that is convincing many scientists of God's existence and of His love for this special planet and its inhabitants.

when the springs of the deep became fixed

This is another reference to the early earth when it was not settled; its landmasses, oceans, and inner core were not fully established. God was at work in this creation, and Solomon says to look at the wisdom in all of this. He used wisdom in the creation of this unique and wonderful planet, and we need to use wisdom to live on it.

Other creatures cannot choose wisdom or foolishness, but we have been given that incredible privilege. Don't waste it by "just doing what comes naturally." Be wise and live out the highest forms of humanity. Glorify God, benefit others, and win for yourself.

What is interesting about this verse is that it wasn't until fairly recently in modern history (the last 100 years) that we could really understand the truth of the second statement. The springs of the deep has reference to deep underwater and underground springs. Recently they have discovered at the bottom of the ocean floor springs that have whole colonies of life that live around the super-heated water that is emitted from these deep springs.

PROVERBS 8:29 ~ *When He set for the sea its boundary so that the water would not transgress His command, when He marked out the foundations of the earth;*

Solomon continues to call out a time before any of the world was settled back in its formation stage. He is trying to reinforce the ancientness of wisdom. It comes out of the time before there was time. Wisdom is what invented the various laws, physical conditions, and natural phenomena we know of as the physical universe. Solomon is saying to examine how things in God's creation fit together and you will realize the power of wisdom. Without this underlying wisdom, we would have chaos instead of order and design.

In the same way, your life will descend into chaos if you do not follow wisdom. If you give into the selfish impulses within you and the temptations pushing on you, then your life will become disordered and chaotic, looking for some way up and out of the wreckage of your relationships. Wisdom is the only way.

The two main features of this verse of Proverbs is the boundary for the sea and the pillars of the earth. Solomon is calling specifically upon the Jews who lived in a coastal country to give thanks for the boundary of the sea. The sea was to the Jew a dark, foreboding, and evil place. So to put a boundary on the sea was not just a physical boundary on the water in the sea but also to boundarize evil and declare where it must stop.

One can stand in Israel and see the wonder of the sea lapping against the shore and marvel at the beauty. God, in wisdom, understood that raised land would be the best barrier to the sea and then arranged the conditions so that would happen at the appropriate times and in the appropriate places.

One also understands that God has placed a boundary on evil. It cannot advance beyond the place where He says. It also can be pushed back by our actions.

The second aspect of wisdom that Solomon would have us celebrate is the pillars or foundation of the earth. This would refer to the solid structures of the land – that which allows for human life and community. It is the land that shows wisdom in its diversity: coastal zones, forests, mountains, deserts, wetlands, hills, and valleys.

Out of the timeless reaches of eternity, God used wisdom to design and then create the world in which we now live. Even though sin has marred its true radiance and wonder, we can still see the wisdom and glory of God in its design. Solomon is speaking to us from 3,000 years ago. Don't go against the wisdom that built the universe. Don't embrace the stupidity of selfishness and begin the descent to chaos. Make the little choices today that will allow others to win as well as you. Your life will become more ordered and rich.

PROVERBS 8:30-31 - *Then I was beside Him, as a master workman; and I was daily His delight, rejoicing always before Him, Rejoicing in the world His earth, and having my delight in the sons of men.*

These are interesting verses because they talk clearly and specifically about what the world was like in its interaction with God before sin and the curse.

We have a tendency to believe that the way we experience the world is the way that it has always been. But that is not the case. Our world is a broken world – a world that shows the evidence of what it once was like when God created it. But it is not what it once was.

This proverb tells us more about that phrase that appears in Genesis where God says that He saw what He had created and it was very good. This proverb expands our understanding of those times. It says that the wisdom of the universe that God was building was so astounding that it was like wisdom and God were playing. Wisdom was every day a delight to God. What He was doing in actual space-time dimensions was so powerfully superb and intricate that it can only be described as rejoicing or playing.

master workman

This is the Hebrew word *amon* which means master, artisan, master worker. It has the idea of a fully-trained, gifted worker who creates beautiful work that displays a level of skill and artistry that are not easy to come by. The image here that Solomon is trying to paint is that wisdom was at God's side as He was creating the universe. This wonderful thing called wisdom that looks for the choice that brings God glory, the group a win, and the individual a win was "informing" the Lord about which of all the possible options which presented themselves to His infinite mind He should choose to actualize.

Realize that God could have chosen to create a different world than the one that He created but because of the guidance of His infinite knowledge and wisdom, He chose to actualize this one. All of the underlying structures, interactions, mechanisms, and life were designed by God. Think through the wonder of the world that God created even in our damaged broken version of it and marvel at the wonder of it: DNA, planetary orbits and distances, seasons, cellular structures, properties of water, unique forms of life from plants, to bacterial, to animal, to aquatic, instincts, communication, climate, various metals and many more. All of these testify to the brilliance of the wisdom of God.

rejoicing

This is the Hebrew word *sachaq* which means to laugh, to amuse, to play, to celebrate, to rejoice. Wisdom and God were rejoicing at the actual application of wisdom to the creation of the world. There is a wonderful difference between planning something and having that plan come together in actuality. It is this kind of joy to which Solomon is referring. God had that kind of joy in the creation process.

We are only now coming to understand, through science, the incredible fine-tuning of the universe that allows for life on this planet – some 180+ perimeters and values that needed to be set within very small ranges in order to have life be able to survive. It is quite thrilling to realize the degree to which God fine-tuned the universe for us.

When you and I embrace wisdom and apply knowledge to bring about an actual result that causes God to rejoice, others to win, and us to win, there is a release of joy. This is why we search for wisdom. This is why we dig past the easy, selfish answer and push past the martyrdom answer and keep seeking until we find the wise answer. Wisdom brings about rejoicing.

daily

This is the Hebrew word *yom* which means day. The idea here is a clear reference to the six days of creation. On each day God brought out more evidence of His incredible wisdom. Each day was a masterstroke in the progressive development of our world. Each day was a testament to the wisdom of God. Solomon pictures wisdom being amazed and delighted with how God solved the myriad problems, challenges, and possibilities that creating our space-time dimensional existence created. It is almost like wisdom is standing back saying, "Oh, that is the way you choose to solve that... wonderful. And you used that to get around this issue... brilliant." Every place I look I find more of the astounding use of wisdom by God.

sons of men

Ben is the typical Hebrew word for son and men. The interesting thing here is that we would have expected sons of God or angels here, not sons of men. Often when creation is referred to it is the angels that are seen rejoicing with God over the unfolding panorama. But in this case it is the sons of men that draw the delight by wisdom.

The idea here is that wisdom found a focus to its involvement in the sons of men. The focus of creation is clearly humanity. We are the crowning achievement of creation and the preeminent focus of God and, therefore, where wisdom is seeking to focus.

The proverb could be saying that wisdom found such delight in the creation of humanity – in terms of its spirit, soul, and body interaction – or it could be that the choices of mankind during the initial stages of the creation were absolutely delightful.

We, of all the creatures, were made to be able to embrace wisdom and live it out so that we would be a glory to God. Today live wisely and reflect the glory of God in your decisions.

PROVERBS 8:32 - *Now therefore, O sons, listen to me, for blessed are they who keep my ways.*

Solomon draws down the conclusion from all the above verses dealing with wisdom and its role in creation. The conclusion is that if all the planning and executing of creation involved wisdom, then you get in step with the universe when you embrace wisdom.

therefore

This word does not appear in the Hebrew text but has been added to point out the concluding nature of this section of Proverbs 8:32. The Hebrew reads with the word now *attah* as the critical connective between what went before and what is coming after. Solomon is summing up or drawing to a conclusion. This is why the translators felt justified in putting the word *therefore* in the passage.

listen

This is the Hebrew word *sama* which means to hear, listen, and to obey. This word is in the imperative or command mode. Solomon is saying: LISTEN TO WHAT I AM SAYING.

blessed

This is the Hebrew word *eser* which means happiness or blessedness. Solomon is saying that what you are really looking for out of life is in living out of a wisdom orientation. The kind of life you are really wanting does not come out of a selfish, prideful life. You can't get what you want by going at it straight away. You get it by going round about through wisdom. As one person put it: "You can get everything you want, if you help enough people get what they want!" A blessed life is through looking for the triple-win, not the selfish win.

keep

This is the Hebrew word *samar* which means keep, guard, observe. The idea is that one would live a life of wisdom and not just occasionally do something non-selfish. Live this way is what God is telling us through Solomon.

We must ask and answer the question: How does everybody win in this situation?" How do I allow the company to win as well as me? How do I cause my spouse and family to win as well as me? How do I bring a win to the community as well as to me in this situation? Many times the wise choice is a more long-term win or stretched-out win for us on the short end. But it will lead to a greater relationship and build a climate of winning.

Remember that celebrating a win in life is only really sweet when it is celebrated with loving, deep relationships and friendships. How often have we seen people who went after the money, the fame, the prestige, the pleasure to the exclusion of the relationships in their life? And when they attain what they seek, it is hollow and devoid of the joy they wanted because there are no people to enjoy it with. I want to enjoy life and embrace all the blessings that God wants to give me; but I will not sacrifice the love of my wife, children, colleagues, community, or country to have them.

ways

This is the Hebrew word *derek* which means way, path, or road. Wisdom has a way it approaches situations and difficulties. Wisdom does not say, "How do I win here?" It says, "How do we win here?"

All of us are tempted to be selfish from time to time. We feel the impulse to win at the expense of others; this is not the way of wisdom and pushes us down the fool's road.

PROVERBS 8:33 - *Heed instruction and be wise, and do not neglect it.*

The great danger in life is that you would be wise in one area of your life or with one decision and then lay wisdom down and not use it in other areas of life. Some people are the best versions of themselves at work but a horrible version of themselves at home. In one world they are selfless and think about the greater good. In the other world they are all about themselves and incredibly impulsive. Don't let this be you. Solomon is telling us that we need to become wise in all the areas of our life: Dig for the Triple-Win in each arena of life, not just one or two. Some people employ wisdom for a period of time and then think they don't need it. Some wander away from wisdom as they become fascinated with the new. Solomon wants to remind young and old alike that we need to keep digging for the wise action, the wise choice, and the wise direction.

All of us have a default setting that is foolishness. In theological terms it is called Original Sin and our sin nature. What this means is that we are oriented toward selfishness. Adam and Eve as originally created were oriented toward God. Their first impulse was to please God and expand His glory. This was their natural impulse and allowed them to enjoy the wonders of the Garden for as long as they were there. They also were oriented toward others and ministering, serving, and giving. Their own personal interests were in the background. What the Devil did was to tempt Adam and Eve to put themselves first and think about what they wanted and believe that somehow God was holding out on them by restricting this one tree and its fruit. When they sinned, something changed in them. They spiritually died as God said would happen. They became oriented to self first which resulted in alienation from God and others.

All of this to say that we are now naturally oriented toward neglecting wisdom. We feel the most drawn to the fool's solution. We will drift to neglecting wisdom. Solomon screams at us: Don't do it!

The word *heed* is the word *sama* which means to hear, listen to, obey. Life is giving us instruction; we just have to be willing to pay attention to it. Solomon is letting us know that too many people go to sleep about further learning – after their early years. "I am an adult, I don't need to learn." Develop a constant delight in learning and your life will unfold in many delightful ways. Close your heart to learning as an adult and life will close down and become routine and unsatisfying.

The word *instruction* is the word *musar* in the Hebrew, and it connotes that you have received information, knowledge, and step-by-step instructions about how to do something. There is another idea that is also a part of this word that is often overlooked. This is the idea of feedback. Solomon is also saying to the adult: Don't neglect the feedback that you are receiving. As we go about our lives, we receive feedback (instruction) from a lot of sources. Don't neglect that information: if you didn't make the sale; if your spouse is becoming cold toward to you; if your bank account is getting smaller; if your career options are increasing in one direction but shrinking in another direction; if you are not as close to God as you were. These are all feedback

Too often we establish a way that we want to live life and then blame others for how they are reacting to us. We need to be open to feedback (instruction) about how we are coming across; about what we are doing; about who we are associating with; about our manner, dress, and tone. Life is giving us feedback but we must be willing to listen. This is why Solomon is saying: Heed instruction (feedback) and be wise.

I am interested in how this works in so many areas and how the feedback changes. The clothing that I wore ten years ago now blocks some people from hearing my teaching because they have a different reaction to those colors and patterns than I do. I must receive that feedback and discern a wise course of action.

The very same patterns of behavior and routine become boring, predictable, and potentially suffocating to a relationship at a certain point; and I must discern that feedback and interact with my spouse, my friends, and my colleagues in order to receive that instruction and see if there are new patterns of behavior that would breathe life into those relationships.

The word translated *neglect* in this passage is the Hebrew word *para*. It means to set free, to avoid, to let be naked, to allow something to go without restraint. Solomon is telling us that we are receiving instruction about life all the time. Don't let this valuable commodity wander through your life without your capturing it. Do not neglect feedback.

I interact with people all the time who have the chance to learn how to have a better marriage or grow in their knowledge of God or learn a new skill at work or learn a new hobby; but they are more interested in movies, TV programs, or the latest inane thing their friends are saying. If you have the chance to grow and to become better, take it. And then once you have gained this information, do not neglect it.

Don't become that person who says to me at church one day: "I used to be really into God but I have gotten away from it." Or "We used to have a great marriage but we just kind of drifted into other things and have grown apart." "We used to be the fun family but somehow that just faded away."

The instruction that God sends and you receive from friends will not always be kind, but it will be helpful if you are ready to receive it and pay attention to it.

Heed instruction and be wise. Do not neglect it.

PROVERBS 8:34 - *Blessed is the man who listens to me, Watching daily at my gates, Waiting at my doorposts. For He who finds me finds life And obtains favor from the Lord.*

Solomon shares a simple process for making sure that we don't make as many foolish decisions. Find a way to listen to wisdom every day instead of just barreling forward with your first reaction. Have a wisdom place. Have wisdom resources. Have wisdom people. Solomon reminds us that life exists where there is wisdom. If wisdom is not allowed then really enjoyable life will not be there either.

Blessed is the man who listens to me, watching daily at my gates

We tend to think in our culture that being blessed is a state of existence instead of a series of process that consistently deliver a blessed life. But Scripturally it is more accurate to see being blessed as having build a series of process into your life that consistently deliver a wonderful life. In this particular case the process that Solomon is asking us to build into our life is listening to counsel on the issues, problems and dilemmas that face us. The danger is that when we graduate from some level of schooling we will stop listening and believe we have all the answers. This is never the orientation of a blessed man or woman.

The blessed man or woman is always learning. The blessed man or woman is willing to hear a contrary point of view. The blessed man or woman has people, resources and conduits of information that bring practical knowledge. The blessed man or woman has built into their life every day to think, evaluate, listen and mentally explore alternative decisions than the ones they are drawn to initially.

What is interesting about this phrase is that it tells us that wisdom speaks everyday it is just that we are not listening. The triple win choice speaks every day. Here is how God can win, you can win and others can win. The blessed man or woman listens as wisdom speak. Solomon goes back to the statements that he makes at the beginning of this chapter, wisdom calls out at the gate of the city. The dilemmas and problems of your day have a wisdom solution, you just have to be willing to listen and not launch into the self-focused solution that immediately presents itself to your mind.

Watching daily at my gates

Each of the choices that you make requires wisdom and could jeopardize the decisions you have already made. We cannot rest on our laurels. Each attainment on the path of wisdom is to be cherished and protected by the next choice. This phrase suggests that we should take time every day to make sure that we are being wise before send out a bunch of decisions. I like to have a time with the Lord the night before and work through the decisions of the next day. Some people get up early and spend time with God praying and searching the Scripture for the wisdom they need for the decisions of that day. However you do it, it is important that you establish a routine that has you wait at wisdom's gates before you make decisions.

In the ancient cities of Israel the wisest people of the city would sit in the gate of the city making decisions for the city and helping people with the decisions that they faced. They would also listen to the complaints that people had against one another and render decisions about how those situations should be solved. So when the original readers of these proverbs saw Solomon refer to the gates of the city to receive wisdom they saw the physical gates of the city and the line of people who were waiting to receive the wisdom from the elders and wise people of the city.

This process of looking for wisdom every day to handle the issues of your day, week, month and year is a sound one. Keep bringing your issues to God every day and allow Him to show you wisdom and to build wisdom over a number of days and weeks as He guides you. I have found that sometimes in God's guidance of me, I am only able to receive a part of the wisdom I need for a particular issue and I need to come back day after day, and week after week letting His wisdom for that decision unfold over time, fact upon fact, insight laid upon insight.

One of the things that Solomon is trying to help us see is that we have never arrived. You never are at a place where you don't have to have wisdom for the situations and issues of your life. The next day will bring new pressures and new problems. Build a habit of getting alone with God every day. Make it a regular part of your life to call wise people to get counsel. Take walks to think before you make decisions.

It is somewhat disconcerting to realize that every day I face decisions that could put in jeopardy everything that previous wise choices have accumulated. This calls for a level of vigilance and alertness beyond what I was expecting. Let me say again what I think Solomon is saying, build a process that will give you time to pursue wisdom every day.

It also though means that every day I have the opportunity to begin to climb out of the foolishness that I may be in by my actions and choices of the day before. Wisdom is a continual opportunity. One cannot rest on one's laurels and coast after a certain attainment. Today is the day, and I must praise the Lord and listen for the spirit of wisdom to speak.

He who finds me finds life

Wisdom is the goal. It is there for everyone but few find it. It takes diligent searching. It is worth the searching. It is life, but it takes daily maintenance and alertness. It is interesting that you could have wisdom and then lose it because you are not watching constantly, vigilantly for the next choice that requires wisdom. When you make the wise choice life springs up around that choice. People feel validated. Relationships are strengthened. Righteous businesses flourish. Good works are performed. Wisdom is like water, where wisdom flows life springs forth.

I just talked to a man who has been selfishly directing his family to do what he wanted and they resent his dictatorial style. I challenged him to become wise. What is the way to have your wife and children have a win in accomplishing your righteous goal? He admitted that it was just easier to bark out orders and demand obedience than sit down with his children and walk them through the why and the how of what he was saying. He had alienated his whole family by selfishly pursuing his goals. I asked him to think through how to accomplish the same thing in a wise manner. A manner in which God won, his family won and he won. It will take more time, it will require more listening, but it will allow everyone to feel listened to and have time together as the same chores are done, the same goals are accomplished.

And obtains favor from the Lord

This phrase is often seen as a throwaway line which one expects in the Bible, but Solomon did not put it here for that reason. Solomon is saying that if you build a process that allows you to pursue wisdom every day and you pay attention to the wisdom that you receive then two things will follow. First, life will follow. This means that your relationships will improve and your life's joy will increase significantly. The second result of building this process for the pursuit of wisdom and then doing what you discover is that God's favor will come to you.

Solomon is saying what he has observed and that is that the people who regularly pursue and listen to wisdom seem to be the luckiest people around. They have things "happen" to them that are beyond just the wisdom they learn. They have the favor of God on their life. God makes sure that things go well for them. God works out some of the details that would derail some of the joy, love and peace they are enjoying.

Just to be clear, we don't get the favor of God unless we are pursuing wisdom daily and doing what we discover is the wise thing. But if we do those things an extra measure of God's favor accompanies those kinds of people.

PROVERBS 8:35 - *For he who finds me finds life and obtains favor from the Lord.*

When a person finds the wise choice, it almost always requires a level of faith to embrace this wise choice. Therefore it is a fulfillment of the verse in Habakkuk 2:4: *The righteous man shall live by faith.* When you find the wise action, it usually means that you as an individual have to look at a longer-term win. The wise person has to, by faith, commit to playing for the longer-term win. The wise person tells themselves that they will win far more through this wise decision than if they made the selfish choice. The wise decision is the one that takes the colleagues at work into account. The wise decision is the one that takes the children into account. The wise decision is the one that factors in your health. The wise decision factors in the needs, strengths, and weaknesses of the spouse.

The selfish decision just thinks about what you want and what would make you happy. This impulsive, foolish, and destructive choice almost immediately pops to mind when faced with a choice. It is the wise person who knows that the truly wise choice must be pursued and that rarely is the best decision the first one a person thinks of.

The wise choice makes God a winner, allows others to win, and causes the individual to win. It is this quality of the triple-win that makes it more difficult to find.

But here Solomon states that when you find the wise choice, it is relationship sustaining and a powerful increaser of energy into a great life. We have to spend some time talking about success from God's point of view. When Solomon says that the person who finds wisdom finds life, he means that the person is successful. God sees success differently than we do in modern western culture. We can tend to see success as material prosperity, as power and prestige. When God talks about success, He turns the discussion to the relational side. When Jesus says that there are only two commandments that need to be followed in Matthew 22:37-39, He is saying that these are the key

146

ingredients in success. What does Jesus say are the crucial elements in a successful life in God's definition of life? Loving God and loving others with the assumption that we are loving ourselves appropriately (I have to say that in these days because people can be so abused by the evil in our world, they do not know how to love themselves righteously). In other words, God declares that success is relational and not material. This is the idea that Solomon is promoting here in this verse. Wisdom promotes relationships which leads to a successful life. If you have all the possessions and status in the world but do not have loving relationships with God and others, you have nothing. A lack of wisdom will destroy relationships because it values things over people.

I heard a true story the other night about how three families lived this out. It started with a birthday gift being stolen from the front porch of one family. They accused their neighbor's daughter. They called the cops on the daughter. This set the feud going. The neighbors now looked for things they could call the cops about against the people who had called the cops on them. And of course they found a few things. This then escalated to shouting, honking, and screaming as the neighbors went by each other at all hours of the day and night. This led to the first neighbor going into full combat mode – hunting and killing his neighbors. Three families were shattered over a missing birthday present. If one of the neighbors had found the wise choice and thought beyond the impulsive desire to win, the whole tragedy could have been avoided. What is interesting is that they admit this now.

I see this with couples who start fighting and clawing over where the couches are placed or whether too much money was spent on some outing. Realize that the relationship is more important than these petty things. I see companies destroy the morale of their employees through policies designed to stop something that has already happened with no regard as to how this makes people do their job. I watch as friends walk away from deep, helpful relationships because of some little disagreement and then when the friendship is really needed, it is not there anymore.

The New Testament says the same thing that Solomon is saying here in this way: *the wages of sin is death.* Death means separation from life. Sin is self-centered foolishness that hurts or damages others. Wherever you have self-centered actions with no regard for God or others, then you will have foolishness and you will have death. Some relationship will die when sin is present. When relationships die, life is lost. Solomon is trying to get us to see this fact. The Apostle Paul is also trying to get us to see this fact. But we so often want what we want and push on with our selfish choices because they seem right to us, and we kill something good in our life or we harden our hearts even further towards God.

When you begin to consistently choose the wise course of action rather than the foolish or selfish ones, then your life will grow in connection to others and become more deeply satisfying. This person also gains a measure of grace from God.

The next verse is ominous: *Those who hate me love death.* Those people who are thinking only selfishly will end up alone and separated from others in depth of soul. Even if others are around, they will suffer separation. How tragic...

PROVERB 8:36 - *But he who sins against me injures himself; all those who hate me love death.*

sins

This is the Hebrew word *hata* which means miss, miss the way, sin. This is the idea of the sin of omission – something that you should have done but you didn't. The search to find wisdom can be a sin of omission. Solomon states that you should have kept looking for more options or another alternative so that you could find the one in which God received glory, the right people win, and you win. If you don't look hard enough or seek enough counsel or look at all the possible things that could be done, you could miss wisdom and that would be a sin against wisdom.

We all do this from time to time. We just take the two or three options that present themselves to us. We assume that these are the only choices, and we choose one of these. It is convenient and quick. The problem is that we are short-circuiting some of the good that could happen to us. Keep searching until you understand wisdom.

injures

This is the Hebrew word *hamas* which means wrong, do violence to. The idea here is that the person who does not complete the process of searching for wisdom and just takes the short-term solution is doing violence to their life. When the easy, selfish, impulsive choice works its way through your life, it represents a significant shortfall over what could have been your lot had you kept searching and found the wise action or choice.

I remember young people who knew that their present girlfriends or boyfriends were not God's best for them but rather than break up and be lonely trusting God to bring the right person later, they just hung onto this okay person. Eventually they marry and live out their life with its problems and adjustments that they were never supposed to make. They injured themselves.

I have seen men who don't want to send out all the resumes and do all the interviews that they should and then settle for the job that is easy, convenient, and quick. They then have to deal with the parameters of that job and its demands and lack of satisfaction because they refused earlier to push through to the wise action.

I have watched people injure themselves in terms of their friends, in terms of their church, in terms of their marriage, in terms of their family, and in terms of their finances by settling for an easy solution by not doing the extra work to do something right or by not asking for counsel. They miss God's best because it is easier to settle for what is already available.

hate

This is the Hebrew word *sane* which means to hate, hold in derision. This means to hold a negative emotional response to a particular person, action, or activity.

Solomon says that those who don't search for wisdom are those who have a negative emotional response to the work, the discipline, and the restrictions that are required to be wise. They are involved in loving separation and alienation. The idea of death is separation and alienation. They want it their way to the extent that they would rather have separation, loneliness, and even alienation from others than give up this thing they want.

This is true in that as a person comes to embrace foolishness or a particular brand of selfishness, they cut off themselves from some group or relationship that they could have and in that way experience death in a certain part of their life. Many times people don't even realize that they are killing off a section of their life. The man who commits adultery and runs off with another women doesn't realize that he is cutting off and killing the relationship that he has with his children through his betrayal of their mother. The person who embezzles money from his company does not realize that he is cutting off a future employment opportunity that would have brought satisfaction and financial reward to him. The woman who openly disrespects her husband does not realize how it will cut her off from developing a lasting relationship with him. She is killing a part of her life. The young person who selfishly skips class and/or flunks a core class does not realize that they are killing a college admission or key piece of information that will be needed for a job.

Solomon is trying to say that we should not give up on wisdom because doing so has disastrous consequences.

Proverbs 9

PROVERBS 9:1 - *Wisdom has built her house, she has hewn out her seven pillars;*

The book of Proverbs -- and especially chapters 8, 9, and 10 -- are about the acquisition of wisdom. And this opening of chapter 9 notes a crucial aspect of wisdom. Wisdom is not in the speculation or talk or dreams of people. True biblical wisdom has actually produced something that has lasted. Notice the verb tenses of this section. Wisdom has built her house. She has hewn out. She has prepared her food. She has mixed her wine.

In other words, when you want to find wisdom, you look for those who have actually accomplished something and not the salesmen who can talk about what they will do and not the professor who spins logical fantasies. When you want to really lock onto wisdom, you ask yourself who has actually accomplished what I want to do. There is always someone. Wisdom is practical and real. Too often we listen to the dream weavers and wordsmiths who make it sound like their ideas will work, but they bring devastation.

Our culture has followed the visions of fools with open marriages, domestic partners, the children will be better if we divorce, junk bonds, stock speculations, all religions are the same or lead to the same place, completely free speech, pornography is not harmful and is protected speech, we evolved from monkeys and slime.

It doesn't matter which relationship in your life needs a dose of wisdom -- God, Self, Marriage, Family, Work, Church, Money, Society, Friends. There is always someone who actually has a very together relationship; someone who has actually put that part of their life together. Listen to them. Ask them.

We all desperately need wisdom, and we are often deceived as from whom to receive it. Get it from those who have actually accomplished the wisdom you are looking for. If you wanted to build a building, would you talk with someone who has never successfully built a building or someone who has built a number of buildings and they are beautiful and functional. If you want to fix your marriage, would you talk with someone who has a broken marriage or someone who is living in a happy and contented marriage? If you wanted to become financially free and solvent, would you talk with the person who is deep in debt and working many schemes and plans or someone who is contented, solvent, and debt free? If you wanted to build a church that was healthy, growing, strong, and vital, you should talk with those who have grown a church that was healthy, growing, strong, and vital and not those who theorize about how a church ought to be. If you wanted to enjoy a great family life, you should talk to those who enjoy a great family life and not those who can make great speeches about family life but don't want to spend time with their families.

The Bible is clear: Wisdom is in the heart of those who over a significant period of time have demonstrated the type of wisdom that you are looking for. Do not be fooled by those who are merely rhetoricians - those who can make things sound nice but have not done anything in their own life.

I am greatly concerned that our culture is about to collapse because we do the opposite of this principle of wisdom. Most of our marriage counselors have failing or dreadful marriages. We are more interested in listening to actors and actresses who have played farmers or bankers than we are listening to successful farmers and bankers. We want to explore the boundaries of licentiousness so we let those who are mired in depression, guilt, and brokenness advise us about what is normal, acceptable, and desirable. We are unwilling to really look at the consequences of our actions but want to just keep telling ourselves that these problems we are seeing are normal. We do not want to admit that we are living with the consequences of our foolishness.

PROVERBS 9:2 - She has prepared her food; she has mixed her wine; she has also set her table;

Solomon mentions three aspects of the preparation of wisdom to receive guests. These give us a metaphorical picture of what wisdom does when you become its student.

It has food prepared

It has drink prepared

It has a table prepared

she has prepared her food

The word translated *prepared* is actually the Hebrew word for slaughter. In fact, the actual Hebrew phrase is *she has slaughtered her slaughter*. The idea is that real meat has been prepared for this wisdom banquet. The question is raised as to what the food is when pulled out of this analogy. It is clearly wisdom. Wisdom offers to its students meaty chunks of wisdom to nourish the soul and to give strength. In many ways the book of Proverbs is the meat for it is deep wisdom that must be meditated upon and contemplated and used for energy and action.

she has mixed her wine

This is interesting in that it can mean that the wine was diluted which was the typical Jewish custom as straight wine would be too strong for the average Jewish taste and sensibilities. Or it can mean that wisdom has mixed wine with other juices or alcohol to make it stronger as in Isaiah 5:22. It would seem that in this analogy that wisdom prepares wine in the common way just as the slaughter of meat is in the common way. Therefore, this is most likely a diluted wine which was the custom of that day. What is the wine? It is also wisdom and/or understanding or counsel or prudence or one of the other aspects or partners of wisdom.

she has set her table

Wisdom is not impulsive and unprepared. There is a table set. This speaks of preparation and desire to entertain. This is contrasted with the impulsiveness with the woman of folly. She counts on the impulsiveness of desire to draw her guests. Wisdom has been planning to have students and she has a table prepared. Also note that in Proverbs 7 the woman of folly prepares her bed and not a table. Wisdom does not do illicit things, and the preparation is for discussion and at a table where relationships and information are gained.

The point of this section is that wisdom wants people to learn how to live better. There are results to show that have stood the test of time. Wisdom is projecting potential but has real wisdom to share that comes from the rough and tumble of real life. There are real discussions about how it applies in business, at home, in friendships, etc.

Too often what is passing as wisdom in our colleges and places of higher learning today are new theories that have not been proven. When you are listening to teachers and the supposed wise, keep asking yourself whether what they are saying has really been tried in the real world. Has it accomplished something? I grow weary of theories and ideas about leadership, marriage, families, business, friendship, normal life that has never been tried or comes from a person who has only failed at the very thing they are trying to help us with.

Don't get your marriage wisdom from someone who has been divorced three times.

Don't get your parenting wisdom from someone with rebellious kids who hate their parents.

Don't get your business wisdom from someone who keeps failing in business even if they do it spectacularly.

Don't get your view of meaning in life from someone whose life is a train wreck of marriages, failed business, abandoned friends, and addictions

Don't get your spiritual advice and wisdom from someone who has no prayer life or who is more greedy than godly.

Get your wisdom from those whose lives have stability and look like what you want yours to look like. They will have something to say that is meaty and worthwhile.

PROVERBS 9:3 - She has sent out her maidens, she calls from the tops of the heights of the city:

The characteristics of wisdom are personified as a king with servants. It is to allow us to see when we are listening to wisdom and how to find it when we need it.

Verse 1 is clear that wisdom has accomplished the thing we seek. It is successful, over time, with a balance of Glory to God, help and honor for others, and personal development and enrichment. Too many charlatans can talk a good game but cannot show any real evidence of their success. Wisdom has results to show.

Verse 2 is clearly another characteristic of wisdom: it has figured out how to present its wisdom in a way that others can grasp. It wants to share its information, but it has thought through that presentation in some detail. Notice prepared food, mixed wine, set table. It is true that many are successful, even wise, who cannot communicate the essence of what they know to others in such a way that others can grow from their knowledge. It is either too deep within or its presentation is too muddled and thus indigestible.

Verse 3 is clearly another dominant characteristic of wisdom. It wants to have others gain from the wisdom it has learned. It sends out maidens. It seeks to enlighten others. True biblical wisdom does not have to be pried out of the hands of those who truly have it. They want desperately to communicate it. It is just few who really want it. Notice that there are others beside wisdom itself that are enlisted. It is developing a communication strategy.

she has sent out her maidens

Wisdom wants to help. The message from these verses is that you cannot do this alone. One person totally alone, even with a book of wisdom, cannot discover and maintain a life of wisdom all by themselves. They need to be shown the way to do things: "mix their wine."

There is a complexity about life that demands that you need others helping you, advising you. Do not be so selfish and proud that you are independent and will not accept help.

she calls from the tops of the heights of the city

Wisdom does speak from a place of superiority and accomplishment, and it means that you must put aside your own pride to listen to the message. She is saying that there is a level of complexity and sophistication between where you are and where I am, and I would be more than happy to show you if you would listen. Are you willing to be humble enough to listen?

Too many times we see the rewards of wisdom – the prestige, the prosperity, the power – and we believe that we can get to that place on our own without help. Or we think we see the way that you get there: a straight line. But that is not true. That is a simple person's approach to life.

PROVERBS 9:4 ~ *Whoever is naive, let him turn in here!*
To him who lacks understanding she says, Come, eat of
my food and drink of the wine I have mixed.

The naive see everything as much more simple than it really is, and they need to come to someone who has achieved what they want to achieve and ask them for the real truths that bring about that level of success.

This is truth whether it is the corporate executive of a large company or the successful housewife in a loving and enjoyable home or the successful pastor in a large church or the teenager enjoying good grades and popularity at school. Each of these successful enterprises involve far more than meets the eye. We are tempted to think that people are just lucky or it comes easy to them. No, it doesn't come easy to them; but they have learned to make it look easy.

The food they eat is varied and complex. They combine things that would not naturally be combined. The wine they have mixed. It is possible that the food they eat and the wine they mix are the different sources of information they receive and the skills they have acquired.

The key to understanding is perceiving how a choice or decision will affect everything before it happens. This takes lots of information, skill in choosing a path, and avoiding or steering around those consequences. Understanding is seeing relationships and reactions and implications – even two or three steps beyond where you are presently.

The person who is simple believes that championships are won by individuals with lots of talent but does not see the hours of practice, weight training, film work, and such that go into each championship team.

Naive or simple people seize on one characteristic of a winning program, organization, or team and think that is the full explanation of a group's success. They must be willing to be shaken out of their naiveté. They need to start chewing on some real food and drinking some strong, mixed drinks of the real information and skills required to build a winning program. Remember it is never as simple as it seems.

Just doing more of your simple formula for success will not get it done. There are hundreds of pastors who believe that if they just preach better, then hordes of people will come. There are hundreds of restaurant owners that believe that if they just had better cooking, they would have lots more customers. There are hundreds of companies that believe if they just made a better product, they would be successful. Each of these approaches is naïve; it is too simplistic. The development of a successful church is more than the sermon; the development of a successful restaurant is more than good cooking; the development of a good business is more than a good product. We have all seen successful churches that have lousy preachers, successful restaurants with lousy food (McDonald's), successful companies with lousy products.

The Proverb screams "stop your folly" – selfish, simplistic ways that will not accomplish what you want. Start living in the real world with real complexity and lots of variables – especially people variables.

What follows in verse 7 and following is pure, distilled understanding. When you do this, you get this – watch for it. If you do that, you will get this – be aware of this.

This is one of the purest courses in real humanity that exists anywhere in the world.

- Correct a scoffer – results: dishonor for self

- Reprove a wicked person – results: insults thrown back

- Reprove a wise man – results love

- Instruct a wise man – results greater wisdom

- Teach a righteous man – results: increase his knowledge

- Give in to the strange woman – results death to relationships and eventually to self

PROVERBS 9:5 - *Come, eat of my food and drink of the wine I have mixed.*

Wisdom does have an agenda. It wants more people to enjoy the fruits of wise choices. It does not try and hoard what it knows. In fact, wisdom is trying to get the message out. It is just that many are not interested in long-term gain. Many are only interested in short-term pleasure and fulfilling their selfish desires at the moment.

This proverb continues the banquet analogy with food being the substitute for wisdom. The food of wisdom looks different than the food of fools. One is filled with selfish delights; the other is filled with deep and abiding joy. They look different. One is pastry and immediate sugar highs; the other is vegetables and fruits and whole grains for stable health.

come eat of my food

Wisdom is doing a recruiting job for people to mentor. If you are not passing on your leadership secrets, then you are not being wise.

The picture of wisdom being food is that wisdom brings nourishment. Wisdom is what the soul feeds on – a long-term plan to build a successful family, a good marriage, a satisfying career, and a deep relationship with God. It is the nourishment of wisdom that feeds the pursuit of real life. This is not the quick-fix of sin and selfishness.

The obvious questions arise: Have you been feasting on wisdom's nourishment or the folly of selfishness? Do you have a reasonable plan to have a better marriage in five years than you have today? Do you have a workable plan to have a great family that you are working and that has worked elsewhere? Are you planning your career in such a way that you have a constantly renewing sense of purpose and satisfaction? Is there a growing amount of resources so that you can smooth out more of the difficulties and storms of life?

drink of the wine I have mixed

Notice that the wine is mixed. This means that the alcoholic content was cut, not strengthened. This analogy continues with the drink being healthful. In that day and age, diluted wine was much better for the stomach than straight cistern water. This was the way to decrease your exposure to disease and quiet your stomach. This wine was not designed to get a person drunk but instead to satisfy thirst in a healthful manner. Wisdom and understanding are like that. They may not be flashy, but they get the job done. And over time there is a significant difference between the results that flow from wisdom and what flows from folly.

Let the slower satisfaction of the nourishment of wisdom and understanding minister to you rather than seeking the thrill ride and consequences of selfishness.

PROVERBS 9:6 - *Forsake your folly and live, and proceed in the way of understanding.*

Those who are simple and do not know how to handle a particular problem or accomplish a particular goal often hold onto the wrong things or act impulsively because they are unable to understand how things really work.

The words *forsake your folly and live* is really let go of your selfishness, impulsiveness, and rebelliousness in certain areas and you will find the solution; the goals that you are looking for coming to you. Realize that there is a relationship between what you want and what you must do that right now in your selfishness you are blocking yourself from accomplishing.

Another clear point can be made from these verses. One can never really live when one is operating out of a selfish mindset. It is cooperation, compromise, interaction, togetherness, etc., that will produce the life we really want. People so often want other people to like them and do things for them, but they try and get them to do this by force or seduction rather than voluntarily through wisdom and good will.

One could make an interesting case that biblically it is selfishness (folly) that keeps us from the abundant life God created us to enjoy. What is it that you want? If you are not enjoying the bounty of the Lord, it is selfishness that is keeping you from embracing it – either yours or others.

Forsake your folly and live is a command. Live away from selfishness. It may seem like it is in the direction of what I want to the exclusion of others, but that is really the way of death and separation. What is the type of selfishness that you are most prone to embrace? Pride, Impulsiveness, Anger, Rebellion, Mocking, Lasciviousness, Lying, Gluttony, etc. Forsake that type of folly and learn to live. It is this type of selfishness that clings to you like a wet T-shirt that must be abandoned.

Realize that if you can't find the way of wisdom when facing a decision, it is because you are still clinging to folly and your own brand of selfishness. All of us have ways in which we win and the others around us lose. These are our folly. We must be willing to strike out in new directions and find those actions that produce wins for all. What is the choice or action that the most people in my life win along with my win? What is the pathway which will allow God to be exalted and me to prosper and others to benefit? That is the pathway of wisdom.

PROVERBS 9:7 - *He who corrects a scoffer gets dishonor for himself, and he who reproves a wicked man gets insults for himself.*

This is the first lesson for those who enter into the house of wisdom. Cynicism and criticalness are not welcomed by anyone and especially those who need it most. Keep your negative comments about others to yourself or those who will listen.

scoffer

This is the Hebrew word *lis* which means scorning, mocking, derision, put-downs, etc. This is the person who uses the tool of critique to make himself look intelligent and superior. It is very easy to see what we don't like or what is wrong with a person or their work or their style. The ability to pick at people is a selfish pursuit. That is why it is labeled a fool's pursuit. It is selfishness expressed through condemnation, critique, and mocking. Sometimes this is just the tone of voice one uses to describe one's achievements. Sometimes it is the words that are chosen. But what Solomon is trying to get us to understand is that this type of behavior will not build a great life. It seems like this is an easy way to build one's reputation – by critiquing others. But even if you are insightful and get paid to do it, it does not build life; it builds alienation and death.

Nobody likes to be corrected or have their flaws pointed out. Everyone wants people to focus on the good points, the helpful or positive aspects of what was being done.

There are some who become scoffers in every area of their life. At home they can point out the one flaw when their children attempt to clean their room. They can point out the one thing at the restaurant that is not right about this meal. They can detail all the mistakes of their boss at work. They are ready at a moment's notice to tell people what is wrong with their church. If you are this kind of person, stop.

You don't have to be this way. It will accomplish a shallowing of relationships and distance from others.

I grieve as I watch people adopt this critical attitude about every area of life and then reap a life of bitterness and loneliness with no one to understand. It seems unnatural for this person not to be critical. But this was a learned behavior and can be changed. Start forcing yourself to list five positives about any person, place, or thing you come in contact with. You will find that as you would change from noticing the negative to digging for the positive that people will open up to you and a new kind of life will develop.

I know from personal experience a person can change from a scoffer who always sees and points out the negative to a person who enjoys the positives realizing that in a sinful, fallen world there will always be negatives. I was a scoffer during most of my teen years. Thankfully God brought me to Himself and began to deliver me from this selfish negativism.

Correct = dishonor, reproof = insults

Notice that all the results are negative when critique, correction, and reproof are involved with those who are not wise. Do not assume that people are wise and want to be corrected. By far, most people don't want it. This is the great temptation for those who think that they are intelligent – that they can make a critique of other people's life and work or that they are superior because they can see what is wrong with other people. It is not a sign of advanced intelligence that you can see what is wrong with other people. Any idiot can do that. That is called pride. It is the truly intelligent person who can see the strengths in a person when their negatives are so glaring.

Suppress the impulse to critique. It is not wisdom.

PROVERBS 9:8 - *Do not reprove a scoffer, or he will hate you, reprove a wise man and he will love you.*

We are always trying to influence people to see things our way. This proverb is a lesson in who you can do that to, who you can't, and who will listen. It also will allow you to understand the kinds of people that you are dealing with.

The word *reprove* is the word *tokeha* in the Hebrew which means to correct, to rebuke, to bring about a new perception to the listener. This proverb is saying that the scoffer will not receive any perception except their own.

The scorner is the person who puts themselves in the superior position of critic of everything. They accept nothing or are rarely pro anything but instead see themselves as the analyzer of everything. This kind of person does not want to be the subject of someone else's critique, no matter how deserved. Their pride will not allow them to receive it. This proverb says that they will hate you for even suggesting that they need correcting.

The word *hate* is the word *sani* which means hated or held in aversion.

This lesson of the proverb tells us that the scoffer will not receive a direct correction without an emotional reaction against the person who gives it. So, therefore, do not give them direct evidence that they are wrong. Do not confront them with their error directly.

The scoffer must be taught or developed in a different way than directly. It is a shame because it means that they will not make as much progress as if they could receive correction directly. This means that you have to ask the scoffer to explain to you how the previous situation could have been handled differently. It means that the scoffer must be presented with new evidence and allowed to change their mind themselves. They must make the application, not have it done to them. Their pride is just too great to receive direct correction without a severe emotional reaction.

The process of Nathan and Joab confronting David was a way to get around the emotional reaction of being hated in case David had become too proud to hear correction. They gave him scenarios that he could emotionally connect with and that would largely not allow him to hate them for bringing this corrective. It was not a direct confrontation in the beginning.

Another way that the scoffer can be approached with correction is through the other person's perception. This is their perception of the events. Since they are in this situation, how could you change your behavior to adjust for their perception? In this way the scoffer never has to believe that they were wrong, just that they need to make allowance for other people's faulty perceptions.

The point of this proverb is that the scoffer has a severe emotional reaction to direct correction. This identifies the scoffer and also should cause you to change your way of bringing about change in the scoffer's life. They need correction just like everybody, but they cannot handle it directly. It is too much of an affront to their pride.

By the way, one of the important tasks of parenting is to make sure that our children can receive direct correction and to talk with them about allowing others to point out error and inappropriate action without overwhelming negative actions. A truly wise person is willing to listen through a direct confrontation about things that they did wrong. They examine the information for truth, not the giver for reaction. If your children cannot receive correction from another, then they are not ready for the world at large.

reprove a wise man and he will love you

Notice the totally different reaction of the wise person. The wise person loves the person who has the courage to directly correct them. After all, it is a timesaver and gains them the ability to make even better decisions next time. The wise person is excited when someone has the courage to directly correct them. They want it and see it as a sign of love.

One of the things that wise people do is that they do not worry about how it was said or when it was said as to whether it is received. The only thing that matters is the truth of the statements and the fact that the wise person can grow and become better.

Is this your attitude? Or do people have to tip-toe around some big flaw in your life, not wanting to get you upset?

Everyone in Western civilization considers themselves competent to criticize everything in their world, so we must be very careful about becoming scoffers and not receiving correction.

What is also amazing is that these are still the reactions of people who have embraced the character traits of scoffing or wisdom. God's Word nails the truth about us even when it was recorded over 3,000 years ago.

PROVERBS 9:9 - *Give instruction to a wise man and he will be still wiser, teach a righteous man and he will increase his learning.*

This is one of the litmus tests of whether you have really arrived at a point of being wise. Are you capable of being corrected and incorporating the correction into your thinking, life, and design?

The word *instruction* is not in the original Hebrew and so the sentence is really given to a wise man, and he will be still wiser. The verse is in the context of rebuke and reproof so that the translators put the italicized word in to help bring about understanding. The Hebrew word *natan* is here translated *give*. What is the wise person given in this proverb? It is what would be despised by those who are not wise: a set back; a criticism; an obstacle; a difficulty. God gives these and only the wise realize that they are gifts.

The New Testament echoes this sentiment in James 1:2,3: *Count it all joy my brothers when you encounter trails as they come to test your faith.*

The second phrase – *teach a righteous person and he will increase in his learning* – two ideas are here. Teach means to share new information or new methods. If a person is really righteous, then they can be shown new information or methods; and they will add it to their collective knowledge.

If you try and teach a person who is not righteous, they will often reject the information. Too many men are too proud to really grow from information that was given in a rebuke.

This is evidence that wisdom involves a level of humility; be ready to learn even if the information comes from an enemy.

When was the last time you paid attention to what a critic was saying? Wise men do.

To be wiser means that one can make better choices and application of the information they have; to increase in learning is to have more information.

PROVERBS 9:10 - *The fear of the Lord is the beginning of wisdom, and the knowledge of the Holy One is understanding.*

The truth contained in this one proverb is so profound. Do not miss this.

The word *fear* is the word *yare* which means the emotion of fear, being afraid, reverence and awe, and formal religious worship. Too often we assume that what is being talked about in these types of passages is only reverence and awe or formal worship. There is a need to realize that the word fear is used for a reason. Reverence grew out of the word fear for a reason. The beginning of wisdom is when a person understands how awesome and terrifying the Lord God, the Supreme Being of the Universe, is.

Our society has lost its understanding of how big God is and, in many cases, His existence at all. We believe that we are the biggest and baddest creatures on the planet and in the universe.

What Solomon is saying in this proverb is that you are beginning to go down the road to wisdom when you embrace the idea that there are consequences to all actions that come from an absolutely Almighty God. There is reason to be fearful. There is reason to tremble. There is reason to be giddily grateful when you have done what He wants and He rewards you.

Living within the fear of the Lord is like living in the spotlight of God. As long as you are in the spotlight, then the blessing and grace of God is upon you. If, however, you abandon the place where the spotlight shines and run into the darkness, there are consequences and results that occur to those in the dark. To live in the fear of the Lord is to live voluntarily in the spotlight. It is to embrace wisdom and righteousness and prudence and counsel. It is loving and enjoying and pursuing the triple-win solutions of wisdom. It is also being afraid and worried to disappoint God or to wander outside of the arena of His blessing and grace.

In our day and age and cultural proclivities, we do not like to talk about actually fearing God or that He will bring people into judgment or that He allows the consequences of people's choices to rain down upon them; but that is the testimony of the Scriptures and it is the way that life really works. If you move away from wisdom, there are consequences for folly.

and the knowledge of the Holy One is understanding

This truth is so central to analyzing what happens to us. God is the major connection point for all that happens. So to understand or grasp the connections between things, one needs to understand or know God.

This truth also brings up what is sorely lacking in the Christian realm in our present day. Average Christian people do not know Christian doctrine. They do not know basic facts about God and Salvation, about Jesus Christ, about the Holy Spirit, about Judgment Day, about Heaven and Hell and Mankind. It is the knowledge of these truths that allows a wise person to grasp what is happening and why it is happening in the world. Take for instance the nature of man from a Christian point of view. According to the Bible, mankind is created in the image of God and endowed with certain traits, characteristics, and abilities that echo God's traits, characteristics, and abilities. Mankind is supposed to act like God would as a steward of this planet. He has within him or her a nobility born of his/her creation in the image of God; but because of the fall of mankind into sin, through our first parents Adam and Eve, mankind also has a sin nature which is dominant in their being – a selfishness that pushes to the forefront of who they are and damages their reasoning ability.

Therefore mankind is noble but also base. He is capable of wonderful things that echo God and also capable of abominable things that scream selfishness. It is both of these truths that are needed to understand the world in which we live. Some have tried to say man is deep down only good; others have tried to maintain that deep down mankind is only evil continually. But knowledge of the Holy One through the Scriptures gives us a complete picture of the world in which we live and God who created it all.

This is why it is tragic that almost everyone has a completely inadequate understanding of a Christian worldview. It is a thorough-going Christian worldview that will explain and allow understanding of what is taking place around us.

PROVERBS 9:11 - *For by me your days will be multiplied, and years of life will be added to you.*

This is an amazing proverb when you stop and examine it. He is saying that it is possible to change your destiny by your embrace or lack of utilization of wisdom.

If you are wise you will have a different destiny path than if you were not wise. How this is possible we do not know. God knows all the possibilities but is able to offer you real choices with real consequences.

If you look consistently for the everybody-wins solution, then you will have longer life than if you look for the selfish choice.

Notice that he says that your days will be multiplied and years of life will be added. This can be thought of as both the elimination of many of the consequences of living wickedly – disease, fights, stress, bitterness, etc. There is also the positive blessing of God that he adds – jobs, relationships, extra gifts, etc.

PROVERBS 9:12 ~ *If you are wise, you are wise for yourself, and if you scoff, you alone will bear it.*

This verse deals with the underlying reasons why a person is trying to be wise or foolish. Some choose these pathways as ways for fame and fortune.

This verse brings a number of behaviors into focus.

Some people try and act wisely to impress others. The wisdom they speak and do is not really theirs; it is a means to a goal. This approach will not work. Wisdom is not a tool to be used by the fool to accomplish selfish means. Embrace wisdom completely – not just as a technique for handling life but as a way of life.

Some believe that they owe it to the world to discover new levels of wisdom because they are so smart and intelligent. No, you are wise for yourself. There will be many times when you are called upon to be wise and no one will ever know what you did. Only God and you will know. It is those encounters that will determine whether you are truly wise and will reap the rewards of wisdom.

Some try and be wise for others while they are not wise themselves. This charade will always come crashing down. Children, employees, and citizens will eventually see the hypocrisy and reject your phony wisdom.

In the same way, some people try and use aspects of foolishness in order to further their life. In this case Solomon speaks of scoffing.

Some people become critical of everything and everyone, believing that people want to know when they are wrong and everything that isn't right. Often very observant people are tempted in this way.

Some try and develop a whole life out of being critical or cynical. They become critics of everything – negative commentators on others. With very few exceptions this is a lonely, difficult, scorned, and hated road. Unfortunately because of television, this superior critical position has been elevated and rewarded and so many fall victim to its temptation.

Some believe that it is funny to be critical. They cannot pass up a joke that points out the failings of another. They cannot overlook a comeback line that puts people down. They seem to believe that there is a laugh track playing, and they will be rewarded for how savagely they criticize the people closest to them. It is extremely tempting to put people down – especially parents, siblings, co-workers – and point out their faults and foibles, but there is a price to pay for this guilty pleasure.

Embrace wisdom because you want to live a great life. Embrace wisdom realizing that there will be many things you will do, sacrifices that you make, things you discover that others will never know about except God and He will reward you for your life of wisdom. You will bask in the glow of many wonderful relationships. These people will not care about nor want to hear about the sacrifices that you have had to make to help bring about these relationships. They will just want to enjoy the relationship and so will you. Your wisdom is to produce something – great relationships – not fame or fortune or prestige or power. It is true that a wise person many times gains these perks, but it is not why one pursues wisdom.

If God brings to your mind this verse – *if you are wise you are wise for yourself...* – it often is to help you realize that you need to do something that is hidden and to keep on the pathway of wisdom.

If God brings the other side of this verse to your mind – *if you scoff you alone will bear it* – it will often be to keep quiet about the critical comment that you are about to make; it will destroy or damage a relationship.

Proverbs: A Devotional Commentary

PROVERBS 9:13 - *The woman of folly is boisterous, she is naive and knows nothing.*

This section is a thorough description of the adulterous woman – who lures men into adultery.

the woman of folly

Proverbs is trying to get you to recognize certain characteristics about people who will suck you into sin. Solomon calls this person a woman of foolishness. In other words, foolishness has been fully embraced as a way of life for this person. This person is selfish, impulsive, and rebellious; but the characteristic of this woman who commits multiple adulteries are the three that are listed below.

boisterous

The Hebrew word translated *boisterous* is the word *hamah* which means loud, roar, clamor, noise, tumult, disquieted.

The idea seems to be when you notice this attention-gaining woman, take a step back instead of a step forward. This woman is loud and noisy in her manner and actions. She presents herself as a notice-me type of person. It is her notice me, all eyes on me, that brings her the attention she needs to begin the seduction.

The Septuagint translates this *tharsos* or bold and spirited. This aggressive trait is what is brought out in this early Greek translation.

Men can be easily attracted to an aggressive woman. It makes it seem as though they are wanted and desired. But this woman does not want you; she only wants what you represent.

naive

The Hebrew word is the word *peti* and comes from the verbal root *pathah* which means open, wide, or spacious but also is used in the Old Testament to mean entice, seduce, flatter, persuade. Exodus 22:16; Judges 12:14-16.

The Septuagint says that she becomes or presents herself as a favorable morsel.

Older translations use the word wantonness; disregard for moral boundaries.

This description of the foolish woman is very helpful. She is naive in that she does not really think through what will be the end results of her actions – either for herself or the men she seduces – but she also is a person schooled in the work of enticing, in flattery, and sexual persuasion. She knows how to use a man's natural sexual desire against him. She has a notice-me aggressive style with an enticing, flattering manner.

Men are warned to put some serious distance between themselves and this type of woman. No matter how attracted you are, make a space for her charms will destroy her and you.

knows nothing

This is a combination of words: knowledge, nothing, and at all. So she knows nothing at all. There seems to be the idea that she, in contrast to wisdom, does not add anything to the men she seduces. She has nothing to add. It appears that she will add some carnal knowledge and secret information to their lives, but she has nothing to add for she knows nothing at all. She actually takes much away.

This is important because one must contrast the offerings of wisdom at the beginning of this proverb with this woman who is offering sexual aggressiveness. It seems like a person will gain by being with her, but she knows nothing at all and has nothing to give except feeding a sexual appetite. The man comes away empty like feeding on cotton candy; it looks filling but will make you sick and leave you empty.

Another view of this verse is that these negative qualities are what young girls are being taught through the television and magazines to aspire to in our culture. The role models in our culture – for millions of young women – are loud, sexually aggressive, seductive, simple-minded, and consumed with useless pieces of information. We have almost become a factory for turning out prostitutes and porn stars instead of intelligent, virtuous, stable, godly, and beautiful women of God.

It is important to constantly work with your daughters to not give in to the pressure of this culture and become these things that do not end up in a good place. They will be alone, used, often battered, and lacking in basic financial resources with many emotional, mental, and spiritual scars.

I believe that it is important to limit the amount of this type of modeling that comes to your daughters and increase the amount of positive role models that your girls are exposed to.

Another interesting study to do is look at the opposite of these qualities and how they often signal a godly woman:

- Not boisterous but instead meek and humble.

- Not demanding the limelight with their manner, voice, clothes, and style.

- Not seductive and sexually aggressive but virtuous and patient.

- Sexually pure and responsive.

- Not trying to trap a man through sexual desire but instead living a life of industry and virtue, allowing a godly man to pursue her.

- Not knowing nothing at all but engaged in the real issues of the day, developing skills and taking action to fix real issues and real problems.

Realize that our society is working against us and is trying to turn out broken women who will feed an increasingly sexual culture.

PROVERBS 9:14 ~ *She sits at the doorway of her house, on a seat by the high places of the city,*

This verse is controlled by what the woman of folly is doing and where she is doing it.

sits

The woman of folly is in contrast to the call of Lady Wisdom. Lady Wisdom is seen active and diligent about the business of education and preparation for training. The idea here seems to be that the foolish woman is relaxing or resting. She is not industrious but instead sitting, or more likely lying on her bed, working. Clearly this is a woman of ill-repute waiting for customers to come visit her. She calls to them but she does not want to give them training, education, and wisdom. Instead she gives them lust, disease, unfaithfulness, impurity, etc.

doorway

The woman of folly sits at her doorway while Lady Wisdom is busy preparing for training and has sent out her maidens. Clearly this is a reference to the activity of the woman who is a prostitute and her waiting for customers and her orientation to leisure rather than industry. People in the city begin to know that this is where one can be unfaithful. Don't turn in that direction. These types of places will spring up near the power centers of a city.

high places of the city

What is interesting here is that this house of prostitution is set up in the places of power and authority in a city. This would be the downtown power corridor. This ancient insight is still active in the modern world. There are still houses of ill repute near the places of power and decision so that the naive and foolish can be serviced.

Solomon is saying that if you make it to the place where you are powerful and have authority, there will be this kind of temptation calling to you. Do not turn aside from the path that you were on to get to this place. Do not listen to lady foolishness. She will destroy you. You can count on her appearance to tempt you. Get ready. The more powerful, wealthy, and honorable you become, the more these types of temptations will be available. But you must not give in. Do not be a fool. Do not throw away what you are building for a few seconds of pleasure. Do not get training at the hands of the foolish woman. It is a dead-end street.

Lady Wisdom is a personification of wisdom in and through those who embrace her. The woman of folly is an actual woman who sells her body to destroy the lives of the men she services. You may see the actions of Lady Wisdom in a business in men who have embraced wisdom as their way of life. The woman of folly is a prostitute, whether male or female, who seeks to tempt men in positions of power to give in to lust.

PROVERBS 9:15 - *Calling to those who pass by, who are making their paths straight*

We do not often realize who the greatest temptation is leveled at. It is the person who is trying to stay righteous. The person who is not cheating and unfaithful will feel a higher level of attention from temptation and folly than those who are enmeshed in living outside of God's boundaries.

Notice that the woman of folly – and really foolishness itself – targets those who are trying to live righteous lives. One would expect that foolishness would target people who have already given in, in some way. But Solomon here points out that the goal of foolishness is to tell half-truths to those who are trying to live good moral lives in order to get them off the straight and narrow path.

Foolishness – or the woman of folly – specifically sets up her place where there will be a lot of people passing by: ordinary people, businessmen, and regular people. These are the people who are her special target. Can she get them to give into radical selfishness? Can she tempt them to stray from what they know is right for a little "naughty" pleasure?

We could debate why God would allow this kind of person to be so near the people who are trying to do good, but really it seems that God is testing us to see what is in our hearts and which things will we choose (it is not as if God does not know). This means that in every office, church, school, business, and home there will be temptation to be selfish. The temptation will come through those we know. The temptation to be selfish will come in various forms and in various ways, but it will come. Get ready for it.

making their paths straight

This is the Hebrew way of saying that this person is trying to live within God's moral boundaries. They are trying to be righteous. They are trying to be a good person. What is interesting is that so far they are succeeding. They have not given in, through an overt act, to the lure of foolishness.

Making your paths straight is a good thing, and it will result in a great life if it is accompanied by wisdom. There will be some things that you do not experience because to get everybody you love to win, you will have to give up some things. You will still win yourself, but there will definitely be something that you do not get to do. It is these sacrifices that foolishness and selfishness wants you to dwell on so that you can't bear to give these things up; but the small sacrifices of illicit pleasure are nothing compared to the great life that is waiting for those who persevere in doing what is right and being wise.

PROVERBS 9:16 - *Whoever is naive, let him turn in here, and to him who lacks understanding she says,*

The main phrase in this proverb is, "Whoever is naive, let him turn in here..." This is the same kind of phrase that wisdom shouts to us. If you really do not understand the level of complexity and skill that you need to, then you will seek to be grown by someone. The danger is that you may choose the wrong teacher.

In this case the one who is offering to grow you up is a person of wicked credentials. This is crucial in our quest for wisdom. Who are you turning to help you become more strategic, more experienced. Just as the first Psalm of David says that the person is blessed who does not follow the counsel of the wicked, so his son Solomon is telling us that you must not turn to the wrong teacher for your lessons on how to live life.

naive

This is the Hebrew word *pethi* which means simple, naive, open-minded. This is the person who does not have an agenda or mental framework for understanding the world or a way of filtering all the information that is going to begin coming at them. What Solomon is saying is that you should make sure that the person building your mental framework is a person who lives inside of God's moral boundaries.

If the person, who is going to show you how to understand and live life lives outside of God's boundaries, then that person will give you a twisted mental framework. You will accept certain things as normal that will not work and will lead to destruction. Your philosophy of life will be faulty. Most people believe that their mental framework is the right one and works. They do not know why certain things in their life don't work - they just ignore those aspects of life.

All of us are naive in certain areas - especially when we are teens and young adults. We may like to think that we have life wired, but we really need to build a much bigger mental framework in order to comprehend and live life well.

It is a shame that in most colleges and universities in America the professors live their life outside of God's moral boundaries and then try and instruct students on how to live in the "real' world. It is very damaging for a young person to be instructed by those who do not have a personal morality that is righteous.

In this particular example a young man is being offered an "education" by an older woman. Her education will produce a twisting on this young man's soul. Even though men are strongly tempted by this type of education, they need to resist. There are some kinds of knowledge that you do not want to know for it will twist the learner in the process of knowing it.

Our culture is just now barely returning to the idea that there are bits of knowledge that are best left unknown - moral deviancies and oppressive techniques that are best to not learn about. God declares that one does not need to study wickedness for in its study one is twisted.

Remember that there are types of education that a young person really wants to study, but it is best not to study: adultery, stealing, debt, coveting, cursing, intimidation, witchcraft, etc. We are seeing this kind of argument advanced for education for children. They really want to read and learn about these things. Yes, they do but they should not do it for it will change them in ways that is not healthy for them. Educators are all excited that boys and girls are reading books about witchcraft and adultery and bullying and murder. One gets an education by studying those areas, but one is forever changed by the experience. We will find once a whole generation has studied these wicked pursuits that the results in our children are undesirable for it will activate in some percentage of those children - 10-25% perhaps - a living out of those images and ideas. Instead, study righteousness. This is the advice that Paul gave to Timothy (1 Timothy 6:11): Pursue righteousness, godliness, faith, love, perseverance, and gentleness.

PROVERBS 9:17 - *Stolen water is sweet; and bread eaten in secret is pleasant.*

Solomon brilliantly puts the actual words of the con artist and adulterer in the Scriptures. It is amazing how the sentiment and words have not changed in 3,000 years.

There is truth to what the adulterer, con artist, and embezzler say: There is a sweetness that comes as a result of going outside moral boundaries; of getting or receiving what you should not have. But the problem is that it is only sweet for a brief period. It is like a diet drink; it has a bitter aftertaste. The sweetness changes after a short period of time and becomes cloudy and bitter in its taste. In Proverbs 20:17, Solomon adds what is not here in this section since he is mouthing the sayings of the woman of folly. After the sweetness, the stolen bread tastes like gravel. This is the part that is never fully spelled out when you are being seduced to be immoral.

Wouldn't it be great if there was truth in temptation's advertising: *Come and enjoy the fruits of lust; free sex. Realize, of course, that there will be great guilt afterward; there will be diseases which could result in your inability to conceive later; there may be significant relational entanglements; participating in these activities may result in the loss of your marriage and the loss of over half of your assets in a divorce settlement; this will also result in the loss of a number of friends (if not all of them); there will be a loss of prestige and respect within the community and in your family when this comes out; your children will be deeply damaged and have an inability to trust you in certain situations.*

Wouldn't it be great if there was truth in advertising temptation and that there was a contract with all the fine print spelled out? This is what will happen to you if you give in to this temptation. It will be sweet for a period and then there will a number of difficulties and results that are not as pleasant.

Unfortunately, there is no fine print when temptation speaks. But God, through Solomon, is giving us in the book of Proverbs the fine print. He is trying to get us to wake up to the fact that temptation will lie to us. It will only give us a small portion of the facts about what will happen when we move into sin and selfishness. There is a significant amount of side effects from taking this bait.

Don't fall for temptation's pitches; it isn't the whole truth. If you have been duped by temptation and gone after money or possessions that were not yours; gotten involved in an affair; lied to protect yourself – then confess to God that you have done these things and move away from them. Repent and ask for God to give you the power to walk in the opposite direction the next time you hear the voice of folly offer you a deal to good to be true.

This phrase "stolen water is sweet and bread eaten in a secret place is pleasant" seems to be a saying or proverb itself. It is referred to a few times in the book of Proverbs. This proverbial half-truth has survived to this day by its inclusion in the Scriptures. It most likely refers not just to stolen items but also to immoral sexual activity as water is used of sexual intimacy in Proverbs 5 and bread is also thus used.

Remember that the words of a person who is trying to get you to move outside of God's Ten Commandments are not totally true. They seem true and will prove true for a period of time, but there are a lot of things that they are not telling you. You should realize that you will receive much more than the momentary pleasure that you are after if you follow folly down its road to destruction.

PROVERBS 9:18 - *But he does not know that the dead are there, that her guests are in the depths of Sheol.*

This whole section of Proverbs, beginning in verse 13 of this chapter, is about the woman of folly. She is using her beauty, her sexuality, her personality, and men's insatiable need to make her popular and in charge. She is offering the same things that wisdom offers, but that is not what the men who are foolish enough to follow her actually receive. She is selling life but what she is really doing is destroying herself, her own marriage, the men that she seduces, the families of the men she seduces, and the society at large. What she is doing is clearly evil, but because it is so pleasurable many turn a blind eye. Because it is so common, it is not seen as evil.

Let's be clear, evil is when you do something (usually to gain in some way) and it results in damage, abuse, or destruction of another person. Doing harm is the definition of evil. It is usually considered more evil if it is done repeatedly. It is considered a greater evil when it is done to the innocent. It is considered an even greater evil if there is no gain; the perpetrator just likes to see people be damaged, abused, or destroyed. It does not matter that your intentions were honorable. It does not matter that you didn't know (you should have checked it out). Evil can be done in many different arenas: marriage, finances, employment, personal development, words, authority, property, religion, and others. In this particular case that Solomon is dealing with, the evil that is being done is to marriage and sexuality.

I am amazed that Solomon could so accurately describe the seduction of a naïve young man in this whole section. Solomon perfectly describes the activity, the thinking, and the results of adultery. It has not changed in 3,000 years. It is not "educational" for a young man (or young woman) to be seduced. It is not an innocent thing where everybody wins when an older, more experienced person seduces a younger person away from the path of righteousness and away from their family. Unfortunately we are seeing more and more of this type of seduction in our day and age. Today sexual license and sexual boundaries have been cast aside, and this increases the death spoken of here in Proverbs. It is called love, coming of age, educational, needed, and common; but it is really evil and changes the psyche of the young person permanently. It is not education or loving to become prey for the rapacious appetites of an evil person.

There is a new form of harmful sexuality in our day that was not around when Solomon was writing. It deserves some special attention because it is seen as harmless in our time. It is not harmless. I call it wholesale adultery. It is pornography. This new form of adultery promises to give all the thrills of adultery without the diseases and without the entangling relationships. It still produces death. It still destroys those who are engaged in making it and producing it. It still damages those who consume it. It still harms the families and friends of those who engage with it. It still is a seduction of naïve people. Please do not think that because you are not actually having sexual contact that pornography is not harmful. It is very harmful for the viewer, for the producer, and for the people being photographed. It still produces death. It is not innocent.

Sexuality was meant by God to be a beautiful unfolding of the whole person with their lifetime opposite sex mate. It was designed to produce responsibility, not irresponsibility. Its primary function is not pleasure or even procreation. Its primary function is a form of knowing and being known. Do not be led astray by your desires. Sexuality is a form of transparency but if you are not being authentic in your transparency, then how dark is your understanding of yourself and the other person.

It is worth it to be chaste and reserve yourself sexually for your mate – both before marriage and when you are married. There is something delightful and deeply satisfying to following God's way of meeting our needs. Yes, it seems like there are other ways to meet our sexual needs, but they do not last and they leave the person damaged. God's design for sexuality is one woman with one man for life and this is a good plan. A person is not a fool to turn away from all the other ways of meeting one's sexual needs and landing on God's revealed plan. There is something powerful that happens when serving someone else is how one expects to have their needs met. If the marriage relationship is not served faithfully and lovingly, then something is missing from both of the people. Yes, we live in a sinful world where the selfishness of one or both spouses causes or even requires the dissolution of the marriage, but that is to be the exception not the norm.

the dead are there

The thing that escapes the thinking of the lustful person is that the consequences for their folly are exactly what they are trying to avoid. They want to connect with another person soul-to-soul, and yet they increasingly become dead to soul-to-soul contact as they give the body more and more control over their actions. Solomon could be referring to a number of things when he says that the dead are there. He doesn't mean that dead bodies are hidden around the room where you are committing adultery. He could be referring to the fact that the people who commit adultery and have frequent, varied sexual contact develop diseases and maladies that kill them sooner than those who do not. He could be referring to the fact the more one clamors after sex, the less it satisfies; and eventually they become dead to the thing that gave them so much pleasure. Then they are forced to push further and further into perversion to feel alive. Solomon could be speaking spiritually when he says that the dead are there. Death is a separation of the soul from the body usually at death. This could refer to the separation that takes place between one's soul and body. When one gives themselves to sin, they experience a kind of spiritual death. In a sense they are walking dead people. They are alive, but they cannot connect with the noblest things in their soul and spirit. The other people who are in this world of sin and compromise have become hollow. People who give into lust give themselves to bodies and carve out the substance of their souls. Addictions to sex are like all other addictions – people end up alone. They lead increasingly isolated lives. Aloneness moves in on this person at a new level even while they are trying to combat it. Solomon is right, the dead are the guests of the woman of folly..

her guests are in the depths of Sheol

There are consequences to perpetrating evil. As a society we have tried to forget about hell. But it is still there and still waiting for those whose selfishness needs to be contained over the eons of eternity. Sheol is a Hebrew word for the place that the spirit and soul of the dead go after they die. In the Old Testament before the death and resurrection of Jesus Christ, Sheol was understood as the place of both the righteous and unrighteous dead. Jesus tells us (Luke 16) that Sheol has two compartments: a lower compartment where the unrighteous dead are being held and an upper compartment where the righteous dead are being held (if you wanted to learn more about this whole arena of theology, read my book, *Why There Has to be a Hell.*

In the depths of Sheol means that the people who die after they have given into the seductive song of the woman of folly will be in the lower compartment of Sheol – the place of the unrighteous dead. Solomon is unequivocal here. Breaking the trust of your spouse and your God by looking for love and/or pleasure outside of God's design is sin that will condemn you to hell. It is wonderful to be able to offer at this point the forgiveness that is in Jesus Christ. Jesus the Christ lived the perfect life and offers His perfect love for those who will admit that they are sinners and accept Him as their Savior. One does not have to live with the weight of their sins. They can be transferred to Christ. There must be repentance which means a changing of the mind. You no longer think that adulterous relationships are okay. You no longer excuse your behavior and you own the fact that you sinned against a holy God and against your mate. God powerfully offers His mercy and His grace so that we can live up to the design of God.

The woman of folly says that she is inviting you into the best life, into real success, and real joy; but she is wrong. She is introducing you into damnation, death, addictions, and loneliness. Turn away from this path no matter how alluring it is. Do not believe that you will make it out the other side unscathed; you won't. You will become a shell of your former self and something inside of you will die while you are enjoying the pleasures of sin for a season.

Proverbs 10

PROVERBS 10:1 - *The proverbs of Solomon. A wise son makes a father glad, but a foolish son is a grief to his mother.*

This chapter marks the beginning of a new section in the book of Proverbs. These are still inspired by God and written through the pen of Solomon, but these are more individual in their attention than the last section.

This section of the proverbs are insights into life and comparisons that point out unique and little-seen ways of finding and living out life wisely. Notice that Solomon will point out a truth by comparing it with another thing in order to highlight a particular truth. He will say that this is more valuable than that. In this way he is helping us establish priorities for our decision making. He will show cause and effect that is often overlooked in the ordinary course of life.

Remember, also, that he will connect these proverbs through thought rhymes. This Jewish device provides the context to the proverbs. In the west we are impressed with word rhymes, but in the ancient culture they used thought rhymes where each verse is linked to the verse directly before it or two verses previous by a similar thought. This insight hooks to another insight about the same or similar idea even though the application is in a completely different aspect of life. This is a very powerful form of learning called hooked learning. It is almost like a person is saying, "I found that insight fascinating; do you have any more insights about that truth?" The teacher then tells you about another place that truth applies.

a wise son makes a father glad

There is a question whether this is written for parents or for children. One of the things that all boys want to do is have their dads be proud of them. Solomon is saying that the surest way to have your dad be proud of you and burst with pride about you and your accomplishments is if you become wise. If a father can show how his son has beat the odds and is a wise man with others respecting his advice and demonstrating a real level of success through that wisdom, this will make a father proud. Solomon clues children in with this so that they do not have to guess as to how to make their parents proud. Become wise and your dad especially will be proud.

This proverb is also aimed at parents in that it is the parents who largely determine whether the child becomes wise. It is their shepherding and care that determines whether a child has any interest in becoming a giving, patient, team player. If a parent is never around and does not demonstrate the essential qualities of wisdom, then where will the child pick them up?

On a personal note, I have to say that a large percentage of the desire for wisdom that I have comes from being raised by my father who is one of the wisest men I have ever known. As I was growing up he constantly pointed out the difference between two choices and where the results would go. He was there to love, support, direct, and correct me. He also was an incredibly consistent role model of what a wise man looked like. My hope is that I make him proud in my attainment of wisdom.

Parents, there is nothing but grief waiting for you if you neglect to raise your children with love and wisdom. There are few things more painful than watching one or more of your children turn their lives into a train wreck. Put the time in to make sure they know that you love them. Point out the good and bad choices that are available to them. Correct them and nurture them. Listen to them and don't always feel like you have to have the last word.

Wise children are a wonderful gift that you have a big part in creating.

PROVERBS 10:2 - *Ill-gotten gains do not profit, but righteousness delivers from death.*

The three-word phrase translated *ill-gotten gains* here in the New American Standard Bible is actually in the Hebrew two words: *wicked trea*sures. The idea is that there is a treasury of wickedness or material gains that can be had from the storehouse of wickedness, but it does not profit a person.

This is such a valuable lesson to learn. The younger that a person learns it, the better it will be. All of us will be tempted to gain money, wealth, possessions, power, prestige, popularity, etc., in ways that are just not right and we know it. But we can see how what we want can be had by just a little cheating, by just a little lie, by just a small theft, by just a little sexual license, by just a little greed or anger or intimidation. Riches and prosperity look like they are there for the taking, and in many ways they are there and they can be had. But they do not really profit. They will, at some point, destroy you. They will at some point – if not immediately – suck out your soul so that the very things you wanted are no longer enjoyable.

I think of politicians who plagiarized others' speeches and were never prominent on the national stage again. I think of football coaches who lied on their resume and had to give up dream jobs they had just won. I think of executives who are behind bars today because they played fast and loose with the books and lied to investors. I think of pastors who had huge churches and incredible ministries and then were selling used cars because they committed adultery. I think of stockbrokers who made billions of dollars using illegal schemes and were drummed out of their profession. I think of accountants who went along with schemes to fool investors who destroyed their whole company. I think of bankers who cheated in investment schemes to line their own pockets and who, in the process, brought down companies that had been in business for hundreds of years. I think of sports heroes who took steroids and other drugs to win and when exposed, lost everything.

Remember in the game of life you will be given opportunities to cheat. It does not matter what field of endeavor you find yourself working in. There will be chances to cheat and shade and take shortcuts. Don't do it. For even if you do gain, it will not profit. It is better to be poorer and have your integrity. For the life of a person who makes withdrawals out of the treasury of wickedness is not the life you think it will be.

but righteousness delivers from death

Doing the right thing instead of the cheaty, wicked thing causes you to escape the death that is stalking the one who has profited by the treasury of wickedness.

Notice that Solomon uses the word *death*. He is saying that some form of death is following those who play on the wicked side of the street. There may be profit there, but there is also death. What is death? It is separation from: Physical death is separation from our bodies. Spiritual death is separation from God. Emotional death is separation from our emotions or from our feeling; going dead in the sense of enjoying our feelings or having real joy. Mental death is separation from coherent thoughts and logic. Each of these forms of death stalks the person who uses the treasury of wickedness as their personal bank account. When anyone crosses the lines of righteousness and makes a profit by doing what is against God's Ten Commandments, they ask death to follow them and cling to them. They may not die physically for a few years or a few decades; but emotional, mental, or spiritual death is also following them and attaching itself ever deeper to their lives.

Notice that one of the benefits of righteousness is that it delivers from death. When we act righteously and refuse to go along with wickedness, then life wins and death loses. I think of the businessman whom I heard was involved with a business that unbeknown to him was cheating people. When he discovered what this business was doing, he told the person what he had discovered and said you will either quit or I will completely pull out. The wicked person refused to stop, so the righteous businessman withdrew from the arrangement at considerable cost to himself. In a few short months the government came and arrested the wicked man and was amazed that the righteous person had removed himself from that business. The wicked person went to jail and the righteous person received a commendation and escaped jail and fines because of his refusal to participate in wickedness.

This proverb is a way of saying to us: Don't be tempted to gain in the wrong way. It is not worth it. Gain in the right way. Make progress on building up a pile of goods for yourself the right way.

You may be tempted to cheat at school or lie about your age to get into a place or be tempted to lie on a job resume or be tempted to be wicked in a thousand other ways that this world, your own selfishness, and the Devil will come up with. DON'T. It is not worth it to have the milky film of death begin to coat your life, your emotions, your mind, and your spirit.

I must say at this point that the only thing or form of righteousness that will deliver from the spiritual death – that is the condition of all of us – is the righteousness of Jesus Christ, the Son of God. The New Testament tells us that Jesus Christ lived a perfect life and was perfectly righteous, completely satisfying God's demands for entrance into heaven. He willingly gave up that perfect life and submitted to death on a cross to be able to substitute His perfection for the sins of all who would embrace Him as Savior. Each one of us is being stalked by spiritual death and, in fact, are already separated from God because of our sins. But Jesus Christ and His righteous life and sacrificial death makes a way back to a living relationship with God.

If you are willing to pray and tell God that you know that you are a sinner but that you would like to be forgiven and have a vital and active relationship with Him, tell God that you accept Jesus Christ's death as the full substitute for your sins, mistakes, misdeeds, and wrongs. Invite Him to come into your life and make you the kind of person He wants you to be.

PROVERBS 10:3 - *The Lord will not allow the righteous to hunger, but He will reject the craving of the wicked.*

This proverb contains a very important clarification on some myths that exists in Christian circles. Many people will read this proverb and then draw direct applications to the lives of people they know or people they read about. If the person was truly righteous, they would not be hungry. If this person is going hungry, then they must not be righteous. If they are going hungry, then it is their fault and we do not need to be concerned with what God is justly doing to them. The problem is that this is not what this proverb actually says. The actual Hebrew sentence reads: *The Lord will not allow the soul of the righteous to hunger, but He will thrust aside the cravings of the wicked.* This proverb deals with how God responds to the internal needs and impulses of people.

the Lord

This is the Hebrew word *YHWH,* the unspeakable name of God. It was the name that God gave to Moses at the burning bush. The Jews, in order to protect themselves from violating the Third Commandment and speaking the name of God in vain, outlawed speaking the name completely. Every time they see this term in the Hebrew text, they say *Adonai* which is the word for Lord in Hebrew. What is interesting is that this is the personal name of God. When God is acting in the most intimate caring ways, He gives Himself this name. The actual definition of this word is that it is a derivative of the verb *to be* or we understand it as God saying that He is the great I AM. He is the ever-present one. There is no past, present, and future to Him. He is outside our time domain and exists in the eternal now. It is this One who has no time constraints and who wants a personal relationship with His righteous worshippers.

will not allow

God does allow a lot to happen to people that is not His perfect will for them. He allows the individual to make choices that result in devastating consequences. He allows unjust governments to build evil, oppressive systems to treat people unjustly. He allows other people in your life to treat you poorly or even do evil to you. One of the problems that we, in the modern world, have with God is how much He allows to happen. How come He is not the overprotective grandparent keeping all the bad stuff from happening to us? This type of question would not have come from the Ancient World. They understood that their choices mattered; that the choices of their leaders mattered. They understood that God was looking for people who would choose wisdom and who would choose to honor Him. It was in the next life that God would remove the evil influences and sludge of sin.

There are some things that God will not allow, but they are not what we assume they would be. This verse contains one of those things. He will not allow the soul of the righteous to hunger.

the righteous

As we have already stated, the actual Hebrew phrase is *the soul of the righteous*. God is promising, through the lips of Solomon the king, that He will not allow the person who is righteous to hunger or to be without what they basically need. The righteous in the book of Proverbs is contrasted with the wicked so that the definition of what it means to be righteous could be understood to be the person who stays within the boundaries of the Ten Commandments. However, we know that it is not possible for anyone to stay within this boundary perfectly (the only exception was Jesus). The Jewish sacrificial system was put in place to deal with the righteous who sinned. So righteousness is something deeper. The Old and New Testaments state that the righteous man shall live by faith or trusting in what God has said to do.

In Abraham's case it was trusting that a child would be born to his wife Sarah who was too old. In Rebekah's case it was trusting and favoring that God wanted to bless and honor the younger son Jacob and not the older more manly son Esau. In the life of the Jewish believer it was bringing their offerings to atone for their sins because God said this would fix the problem. Therefore the righteous one is the one who trusts God and thereby acts in accordance with God's commands and in the New Testament the guidance of the Holy Spirit.

The proverb says that God will not allow the soul of the righteous to hunger—hunger being defined as actually going without the needed thing to the point that death occurs. The soul of the righteous needs different things than the body. The soul needs relationships and it requires connection to God, to others, and to emotional support. God says He watches and will make sure that those who trust Him will not suffer soul-hunger to the point of the death of their faith. Notice this proverb does not say that God will keep a righteous person from ever going hungry physically. I would suggest that I have heard and seen God do this in a number of different ways. I have read reports of those who were locked in concentration camps or prisons where God sends an angel to minister to them or even gives them a new level of vision of His presence. I have seen God send new friends to those who were cut off by those who should have been their support and encouragement. I have watched God draw a person deep into His presence in the midst of disastrous, emotional trauma happening to them or around them. I have read reports of God actually calling a person home to heaven because there was not an adequate way to meet the needs of that person's soul here on earth.

We as a society have become fixated on the health of someone's body and their physical well-being – in many cases as though that were the issue of supreme importance. The body is important, but it is only the tent that houses the soul. And the soul will enjoy at least one other house. I have begun to think about the soul as an operating system and the personal files on my computer that I can download and transfer to another computer when the computer that I am on begins to fail. I collect programs and files and information and the software gets bigger and bigger and defines MY computer. But my stuff is not the computer; that is just what runs my stuff. I have changed computers a number of times and all my stuff is still there running on a new computer. One of these days we are all headed for an upgrade in terms of our hardware. God is going to take our soul and cleanse it of the parts of our operating system that orients it to selfishness and sin and put it into a new body to enjoy a new life and in a new place with a new level of relationship with Him.

Just remember, it is more important what we put in our soul than what we put in our body. It is the soul that lasts for eternity. It is the soul that God will make sure does not hunger to destruction.

PROVERBS 10:4 - *Poor is he who works with a negligent hand, but the hand of the diligent makes rich.*

poor is he who works with a negligent hand

The word *poor* is the word that refers to those who are destitute or have little or nothing. They have less than they really need. The principle here is that those who have less than they need have in some way been negligent. They had an opportunity to obtain what they needed, but at some point in the past they did not take advantage of that opportunity.

This clearly suggests that God has placed opportunity around us, and we are responsible for what we do with that opportunity. If we just expect others to provide for us, then we will be poor in some area that opportunity could have provided.

The word *negligent* is the word *remiya* which is the word used for slackening, sloth, looseness. When something is needed to be tight, this is loose. When something is needed to be diligently pursued, this is just followed with a half heart. Go after the opportunity that God puts in your pathway. If we do not work hard on the opportunities that God has given us, then we will find that we are destitute and not having what we really need to enjoy and live a fulfilled life. Some people do not have what they need to live a fulfilled life because when opportunity came their way, they were too busy doing something else to be bothered by it or they pursued it with only a half heart.

Personal responsibility is essential if one is to build a wise life. There are opportunities around you every day. Take advantage of those opportunities. Now these opportunities for a blessed life come disguised as problems, hard work, or service; it is not gathering baskets of money. There is a process of turning your opportunity into something usable in your life.

While this proverb is clear, a balancing principle is also needed to understand the poor or destitute in any major city. The balance to this principle is this one: abundant food is in the fallow ground of the poor but injustice sweeps it away. There are opportunities that are given to everyone but the wickedness of some takes away that opportunity from those people. They never see that opportunity or are restricted from pursuing it.

but the hand of the diligent makes rich

The word *diligent* is *charuts* in the Hebrew and it is the word for sharp, decisive, diligent, and decision. This word is the key idea in this verse on the positive side. Diligent is contrasted with negligent. This word means one who is decisive and/or diligent. The translators chose to put the emphasis on the constant application of action and power, but the word also carries with it the idea of decisive, sharp, and clear actions that are unambiguous. Poor people are lazy procrastinators who do not take action; they do not continue to apply power to a situation over a long time. Their *modus operandi* is laid-back and tomorrow-oriented. The person who wants to have abundance must act constantly, consistently, and, at times, quickly. Solomon is telling us that we must be ready to take diligent and decisive action when opportunities come our way or they will be missed.

It will be interesting if we can play the tape of our lives and look back at the opportunities that we could have taken and how our lives would be different. The poor person misses most of these opportunities because they require work or decisive action. Don't let this be you. Develop the life which is diligent and decisive rather than the one that is always looking for the quick, easy score.

You may recognize your hand being negligent before you can see the opportunities that you are letting slip by. So ask yourself if you are becoming lazy; ask yourself if you are letting things be disorganized or incomplete too much.

PROVERBS 10:5 - *He who gathers in summer is a son who acts wisely, but he who sleeps in harvest is a son who acts shamefully.*

This proverb reminds us of a crucial truth: there is a time to act. When that time comes, then you should act. It is possible to wait too long; to do too much planning; to keep putting off to the future the opportunities that are here right now.

I was just reading a report that a high percentage of people who retire thought they would have had more, but they just never got around to saving. It was summer while they were working and now that it is time to live off of what they harvested, it is gone.

This principle is true in relationships. There are times when one can connect; when it is summer in that relationship – whether it is romance or parenting or friendships or networking. One has to seize the day when it is harvest time. Our culture has warned people so much to look before they leap that many never leap. In many of the cases, every week it is summer in some aspect of your life. Don't sleep during the moment. Be assertive and try and get the benefits out of that moment. It is better to have tried and failed than not to have tried at all. By far the vast majority of people let opportunities with God, in their marriage, with their family, monetarily, vocationally, with friends slip by them.

Take stock this week of the opportunities that God has given you to make significant strides in some area of life. At any given time it is summer and time to act in that area of our life. Spend the time harvesting when it is appropriate. There will always be reasons why you can't or shouldn't. There will always be a little less certainty than we would like; but if there is an opening, probe and see if it will open more. If there is a chance to do something good and harvest a great personal and public good, then go after it.

The proverbs talks a lot about planning and seeking counsel, but it also wants us to move when the time is right. When it is harvest time, act with strong and consistent strokes. Remember that it is relationships that you are trying to build up. It is relationships that are the goal of life – a relationship with God and relationships in the other major areas of life. The two great commandments are love God and your neighbor as yourself. It is also important to say that one should not strengthen one relationship at the expense of all others.

Remember, harvesting is not just physical blessing – it is relational connection. The richest person is the one who has the deepest relationships across the relational spectrum.

In what area should you be harvesting this week?

What is holding you back from harvesting in that relationship at a new clip?

PROVERBS 10:6 - *Blessings are on the head of the righteous, but the mouth of the wicked conceals violence.*

It is worth it to live life God's way. It sometimes seems like the people who break God's rules have all the fun, but this is not the case. In this proverb Solomon gives us a reminder of what happens when we live God's way to the fullest.

The word *righteous* is the Hebrew word *sedeq* which means justice, righteous, conformity to a standard or norm. It is best to understand this as staying within the boundaries of the Ten Commandments and not just staying away from the violations of the standards but doing the opposite – really living out the life of faith. Blessings are actual spiritual, emotional, mental, physical, and material progress in life – additions and pleasures and encouragements. These are waiting for the people who will understand what God wants and move toward them. Being a righteous person meant that one would live out the meaning of the Ten Commandments by going in the opposite direction of the negative ones and doing the intent of the positive ones. For instance, it is not enough to not steal; one must work hard to produce a valuable product or service so that they can have abundance to share with others. The opposite of stealing is generous abundance. It is not enough to not murder; one must look for those whom God wants you to love by meeting their needs. It is not enough to not covet other people's possessions; one must embrace their lot in life with a deep level of contentment. It is not enough to not bear false witness; one must speak truth and blessings into the lives of others.

PROVERBS 10:7 - *The memory of the righteous is blessed, but the name of the wicked will rot.*

The choices that we make do not just last for our lifetimes, but they create a legacy that in a sense lives forever. We have been trained by our culture that our choices only count for right now, so please yourselves.

The destructive power of wickedness is demonstrated in a thousand lives all around us just as the constructive power of righteousness is demonstrated in lives all around us.

The word *wicked* means those who live outside the boundaries of the Ten Commandments: those who chose other gods, those who misrepresent God with an idol, those who dishonor parents and authorities, those who commit murder and adultery, those who steal, etc.

When living beyond the boundaries of God's moral law is the norm in a person's life, then they are biblically a wicked person. Our culture has tried to restrict wickedness to rape and murder of children and the like. But God has not changed the standard.

Ask yourself the question: Do you know people who have committed adultery and blown up their marriage and who have permanently altered the course of their children's lives? I do. Do you know those who have, through stealing from a company or the government or others, brought a plague upon their own family? I do. Do you know families that allow the children to be disrespectful and rebellious to the parents and who, therefore, have little or no reason to hang together as a family? I do.

These and many other examples of condoned wickedness have caused the legacy of a family to become rotten, damaging the potential and insights of the children and themselves.

Conversely, a practical definition of righteousness in the book of Proverbs is living within the boundaries of the Ten Commandments.

These people do not purposely or knowingly commit actions that would leave them outside of the moral boundaries of the Ten.

I was just witnessing a graduation of friends and their senior daughter from high school. The positive legacy of this father and mother's faith is wonderful to behold. The daughter who was graduating was recognized as having an extra measure of Christian joy. I was commenting on how marvelous it must be to be building a legacy of strong Christians in their family. I watched as a legacy of righteousness is being built. Discipline, courage, faith, love, and joy in the Lord – these qualities are a part of the blessing of righteousness.

One of the things that righteous people do is have a prioritized life so that they make sure they have time for their children. In our culture it is common to pursue success so hard that we run right past it when it is available to pursue. Life is relationships. A righteous person must slow their lives down enough to develop real relationships with family, friends, and others.

The word *memory* here is the idea of remembrance of that which triggers the memory of an event, person, or place. This proverb states that the righteous cause this type of positive trigger mechanism. Righteousness also brings blessing to the family as an individual and eventually a family and then an extended family learn how to live their life within the confines of the clearly revealed, ethical guidelines.

Do you want to build a lasting memory to the good name that you carry? Then work righteousness. If the answer is that you do not care about leaving a lasting legacy, then commit wickedness with gusto and you will create a lasting trail of wreckage into the future.

the name of the wicked will rot

This means that rottenness or decay will follow the wicked. There is a very true sense that the wicked bring decay and destruction. It is rottenness and parasitic to selfishly pursue wickedness to the exclusion of all else.

We must help parents understand that how they live their lives and how they parent will build a long-term environment in which their children will dwell. Choose wisely – others will have to live in, with, or down your choices. You are not alone when you make choices. You're a complex web of relationships that define who you are.

PROVERBS 10:8 - *The wise of heart will receive commands, but a babbling fool will be ruined.*

On the face of this proverb it seems to be about the need for submission. The person who is wise will be willing to submit to the commands of others – first God and then those who are in positions of God-given authority.

the wise of heart will receive commands

The wise of heart have learned that the commands or the commandments are the way that the Hebrew literally reads. It is the Septuagint translation of the Hebrew text that reads *the wise-hearted takes or receives commands, injunctions, or orders.*

The person who is wise – who really is looking for God's choice in the decisions of their life – is willing to receive God's commands and other's. If there is no ability to receive commands – but only the ability to give them – then you are a fool. If you must be in control and are unwilling to be a part of a team in which people smarter, faster, and better work with you and above you, then you will be ruined.

Commands is the Hebrew word *mitswah* which is the word for commandment, command, and precept. It is used most for commandment.

but a babbling fool will be ruined

The Septuagint version reads *the homeless or roofless lippy person is crooked or perverted.*

The Hebrew reads *the fool or perverse person who is full of speech or talk has been thrust down or cast aside.*

There is an element in this word *fool* that means one who has not done anything but is only talking a wonderful story. This person does not have anything to show for their theories or concepts, etc. They are all talk and nothing accumulated to show that it really works. This is the person with lots of degrees in marriage and family but with a bad marriage and rebel kids. This is the person who tells others all about God but does not actually pray or practice their faith.

This demonstrated wisdom would fit well in this section of the book of Proverbs where wisdom has hewn out her seven pillars and invites people to her banquet table.

PROVERBS 10:9 - *He who walks in integrity walks securely, but he who perverts his way will be found out.*

walks

This is the Hebrew word *halik* which means to walk, to travel, to move in general. Clearly in this case it is a word that means to live one's life. Solomon is saying that if you live your life with integrity, you will be fine. But if you do hidden and deceitful things in order to profit personally at the expense of others, you will eventually be found out.

integrity

This is the Hebrew word *tom* which means integrity, complete, and completeness. Solomon is trying to point out a crucial lesson that will tempt everyone. The temptation is to live the majority of one's life with honesty, fairness, kindness, righteousness, faithfulness, etc., and just in one small insignificant area indulge a sinful, selfish pleasure. The idea will always be: no one will notice and will look at all the other parts of your life – this is such a small thing.

Solomon wants to warn us that no matter how small and seemingly insignificant your little dip into unethical or illegal behavior is, it will eventually come out. He is wanting to make sure that you know that these little compromises will be found out so that you will walk on by when these temptations are offered – temptations to pad your expense account, to cheat on your timecard, etc.

perverts

This is the Hebrew word *maaqas* which means crooked or twisted or perverse. The idea is to live your life like everything will one day be written in a newspaper for all to see. If you can handle this level of scrutiny, then you will be fine.

Remember the joy in life does not come from the hidden or sinful stuff. It comes from the depth of relationships that you build throughout your life. Work on the relationships. In this case be honest with yourself. If you are concerned about some things that you are doing, ask someone to see if it is okay to do what you are doing. If you know that it is not, then stop and do the right thing. Live a life that you do not have to look over your shoulder about anything.

PROVERBS 10:10 ~ *He who winks the eye causes trouble, and a babbling fool will be ruined.*

wink

This is the Hebrew word *qarats* which means to nip, compress, pinch, wink, narrow. This word is used to describe a tendency by those who do wickedness and violence to others that brings a narrowness or even squinting to the eyes.

Proverbs 6:13 is a parallel passage which reads: *Who winks with his eyes, who signals with his feet, who points with his fingers.* There is clearly a signaling going on with one's eyes and/or a natural reaction when intensity in some form or manner is involved. A narrowing of the eyes or squinting or compressing of the eyelids is an involuntary response to intensive thinking. It is also true that those who are involved in wickedness on a consistent basis do not retain a wide-eyed look to their faces. We have all heard of the squinty-eyed person being up to no good. This seems to be the general idea in this part of the verse.

The Septuagint translates this word *enneuon* which means to signal. This word is used of the signs that people made to John the Baptist's father as to what name he would name the boy.

Solomon's point seems to be to show his students where the landmines of life are hidden. Two of the places are outlined in this proverb. The person who squints or signals a lot with their eyes is a landmine that will explode and bring pain and trouble to those around them. Therefore, the strategy is to get away from this type of person. When you identify this kind of person, steer clear of them for they cause trouble. The Septuagint says they bring pain. They are a landmine that will explode. Too often we do not heed Solomon's advice, and we continue our business dealings or social interaction with a person who draws trouble.

babbling

This is the Hebrew word *sapa* which means speech, lip, language. The idea in this verse is that the person is a speaking fool. The selfish impulsiveness comes out of them through speech. They allow all their selfish thoughts to come out of their mouths. This type of person just keeps talking until their selfishness is evident to all. They do not know how to keep quiet. Peter, on the mount of transfiguration, would have qualified in this regard. As Jesus was transformed, all he could think to do was talk. Finally God the Father had to say, "'This is my beloved Son, Hear Him." In other words: shut up, Peter.

A person who cannot keep quiet about what they notice or think about will be humbled, if not humiliated. They will put their foot in their mouth. Don't say all that you think you know. People assume that you are much smarter when you hold back instead of always having to say what you think about a situation. I certainly have been humiliated by jumping into a conversation with my two cents when I should have just stayed silent.

If people cannot be around you without hearing your opinion or your observations, then you are becoming a babbling fool. Let people talk about their stuff and only bring up your stuff if they ask.

PROVERBS 10:11 - *The mouth of the righteous is a fountain of life, but the mouth of the wicked conceals violence.*

Notice the contrast between the results of the righteous' words and the results of the wicked's words. The righteous person produces life and that which is positive. The wicked person's words hide what they are really doing which will destroy. Somewhere they are forcing their way or inviting violence. This is very important to realize that words have real impact and can change the course of someone's life. Wise righteous words bring life and increased harmony with others. Wicked words impose one person's will on another often through violence or its threat. Wicked words destroy harmony and creativity because it desires rigid conformity.

fountain of life

This is the Hebrew word *maqor haya*. One must realize the significance of fountains in the biblical time period 1,000 years before Christ. There were no decorative fountains as we know them today. A fountain meant that there was a spring pushing water out of the earth. This type of water was a fresh water source of pure water. Sources of clean, pure water were incredibly valuable in an arid place like Israel. Life could be sustained and developed around a spring. In fact, whole villages were birthed around springs because the water was so important. Solomon is saying that same thing about words that come from a righteous person. Others draw life from the positive comments and encouragement and direction that come from the righteous person. People want to be near this source of life. Is this true for you? Do people find so much encouragement and positive help that they just hang around you? Is your desk, your home, your table a place where people find encouragement and hope?

One of the things that Solomon is implying is that righteous people have a positive impact on their environment. Things and people get better around them. Is that true for you? What types of things could you say to the people you know that would speak life, encouragement, and hope into their life? This is what happens when righteous people speak. Do people have hope when they leave you?

conceals

Clearly what Solomon is suggesting is that when a wicked person speaks, they are all about winning for themselves. What advice and direction they give usually results in someone else being moved out of the way, pushed aside, defeated.

violence

This is the Hebrew word *hamas* which means violence or forceful wrongdoing. A different word is used for force applied to do right. It is interesting that this is the word for the Palestinian group that uses violence in an effort to overthrow the nation Israel. In the Scripture wickedness and violence are together. The one brings the other; the one uses the other. Just as the Mafia has to use violence to accomplish its protection rackets and enforce discipline, the violence comes with the desire to profit through sin. This is a way to see wickedness from a distance. Is their violence needed or integral to the activity?

It is interesting that here Solomon says that the words of the wicked are hiding violence. There is implicit force and pressure in the words of the wicked person. There is no hope, encouragement, or blossoming in the words of a person who has given themselves to wickedness. There is "I want my way and I am going to get it even if I have to take, shove, oppress, afflict you to do it." Some people cover their wickedness in respectability and the violence is concealed, but it is still there. "I want you to do what I want that profits me and damages you." This orientation is wickedness no matter how "respectable" it may be portrayed.

When people are empowered to do good things, to enjoy righteous relationships, to make beneficial choices, to develop healthy relationships, this is evidence of life and is the result of righteous words. When people's dreams are crushed for someone else's greed or goals, when people are being blocked from having necessities, when people are kept from pursuing beneficial goals to serve other's selfish goals, this is wickedness and grows out of the commands and words of a wicked person.

Do your words bring life? Hope? Relational health? Joy? If so, great. Keep going...

Let me say a word to teenagers at this point. You may be tempted to apply this to your parents and not to yourself. That would be a mistake. Your reaction to your parents' rules, directives, commands, and the like will live out this verse also. Your words can bring life or conceal violence. Now if your parents are seeking to oppress you for their clearly evil and wicked purposes, then your appealing to a higher authority for help is appropriate and needed. But if your seeking of your own selfish purposes cause you to conceal a seething violence just below the surface of your responses to them, then you are one who is bringing death to your home. You can bring harmony to your home. Become a fountain of life. Realize that your parents want the best for you, not the worst.

PROVERBS 10:12 - Hatred stirs up strife but love covers all transgressions.

This is a very interesting descriptor of what internal emotions do to the external actions. When a person hates you no matter what they say they feel about you, they stir up strife in relationship to you. They don't want to have anything to do with you. When a person loves you and wants your best and is willing to pursue you and have you pursue them, then they will be willing to overlook your faults and transgressions. They are covered.

When you have apologized for a transgression, it is often helpful to test and see if the other person is really willing to cover the problem or they still hate you. If they will not engage in another conversational topic or will not let you touch them (hug, touch, shake hands, kiss, arm around), then they are still closed toward you and the hatred is still there and will derail your relationship.

hatred

This is the Hebrew word *sinah* which means hating, hatred. The clear idea is that some form of bitterness and extreme negative feelings have attached to a person. Interestingly Solomon asks us to look inside of ourselves and look at who we have developed an extreme dislike towards. Sometimes it is for silly reasons. Sometimes it might be for legitimate reasons. But if we allow that ball of hatred to stay within us, it will cause strife with that person and potentially with lots of people.

This is why the message of the Old and New Testament is that we must learn how to forgive. We must learn how to love greater than our hate. We must learn to hand vengeance to the Lord and not try and exact our own revenge.

stirs up

This is the Hebrew word *awr* which means to awaken, to start, to move, to agitate. Clearly the idea in this verse is that Solomon tells us if you are harboring hatred for another person for some reason, it will come out. Your hatred awakens a need to be at odds with that person or potentially someone else. It is your hatred that does this. Until you deal with the issue or person that is causing the bitterness or hatred, you will go around stirring things up.

I have watched people who cannot help themselves from saying the volatile thing. Their face says, "I have been hurt and I will strike back." So many people change the trajectory of their life because they do not want to give up on their hatred of a particular person. If you allow hatred to live inside of you, then you will begin to cause strife with others even when you are not meaning to. You can learn all the people skills you want, but you need to deal with the hate in your heart.

Now I know it is not easy to let go of your hatred towards a person because of what they have done. In fact what they have done may be truly evil in the highest sense of that word. But if you let your reaction to what they did live inside you too long, it will change you.

strife

This is the Hebrew word *medan* which means contention, strife, controversies, discord. The clear idea is that hatred in your soul will make its way out in your conversations and relationships. We have all seen this and most likely been a part of this ourselves. We are angry at someone at work, but we can't get mad at them openly so we gripe or complain at someone else or are on edge with our spouse at home.

When we are asked why we are so on edge, we declare,

"It's not you."

"I am just upset."

What the other person wants to say is,

> "Fine, I am glad you are not mad at me but stop being so grumpy or critical or irritable."

> "Get over it."

> "Because right now you are a pain to be around."

Now what this verse gives us insight into is if there is a person at work or in your family or in the neighborhood who is just always picking a fight or taking a contrary position, then they most likely have hatred in their heart that is not completely resolved.

Solomon's solution to the hatred in your heart and the strife you may be experiencing from someone else is...

love

The Hebrew word translated love here is the word *ahabah* which does mean love. To love someone is to meet their needs, to pursue their soul, and/or to please them. When someone is ornery or always picking fights, loving them can be difficult; but it still is the solution. Sometimes what this person really needs is to have a no-holds-barred conversation about how they are coming across. I have had a number of tough love conversations with people in which they really thanked me for the honesty.

Also some times the love that needs to be expressed is towards the person that is the object of the hatred in your heart. This may be the real aim of Solomon's advice here. We must get over the hatred. The only way to do that is to overwhelm the hatred you feel with some form of real love. It may be that you need to meet a need in them that is causing them to act the way they do. It may be that you need to pursue their soul through listening or relating. It may also be that you need to exercise some tough love by meeting their need for reality or justice. But somehow you must deal with the hatred that is creating the fuel for the strife you are causing in the rest of your life.

In almost all of our lives there is someone who hurt you or wronged you in some way. What they did can stay with you unless you deal with it. Find a way to love them so that what they did is no longer the dominant thought you have about them.

I will say that sometimes one of the greatest acts of love is to hand them over to God for any justice that needs to be meted out. Romans 12:17 - If we are still trying to handle the justice, then it never gets handled and the hatred is still there.

For offenses of a personal or less than criminal variety, find a way to bless this person, to help this person. You will find that this diffuses your hatred and therefore diffuses this general irritability that affects you other relationships.

covers

This is a Hebrew preposition *al* which means on, over, opposite and because of those meanings it is usually translated in this type of sentence as cover, forgive, or conceal. The idea here is clearly that your love for a person that you once hated would be so strong that it would cover over or be on top of the hatred and eventually dissolve the hatred. You want the best for that person even in spite of what they did to you. You want that person to have what they need, so they will not continue to act in a way that caused them to hurt you. Cover over your hatred with love so that your life is not filled with unneeded strife.

all transgressions

This is the Hebrew word *pesa* which means crime, offense, wrong doing. Love is the acid that is strong enough to dissolve hatred. There is a need Solomon notices to stop hatred from twisting your soul. It is inevitable that you will be hurt in this world. The most successful people expect this to happen, but they do not hold on to the hatred that they may initially feel. They cover over their negative feelings with a desire to bless others, meet their needs, and pursue them. Yes, I know that the other person doesn't deserve it, but do it anyway. It will result in a much better life.

Let me wrap this up with a few observations that Solomon is making. First, if you are having a lot of trouble getting along with others, you need to look and see if there is hatred in your heart that needs to be resolved. Second, if you have someone in your family or at work who is just disagreeable and always causing strife, you can be sure that they have hatred in their soul that is fueling the whole mess. If you cannot get them to overcome their hatred, they will damage if not destroy their potential. Third, love is strong enough to dissolve hatred if it is used properly. Love in the right doses and in the right way can overwhelm hatred and bring back your life to the fullest. Don't let your hatred of a person rob you of the relationships and joy you could have.

PROVERBS 10:13 - *On the lips of the discerning, wisdom is found, but a rod is for the back of him who lacks understanding.*

Chapter 10 starts a section of proverbs that is designed to teach general principles of wisdom. Notice that chapter 10 verse 1 restates who wrote these proverbs. These are the ideas that wise people have tucked in their minds that control the actions that they take. This section is just a series of what seems like random statements that are bits of wisdom. They are actually thought-rhymes that are connected from one thought to the next.

This particular proverb is about where to find wisdom and the consequences for a lack of depth in your soul. It rhymes with the verse before it through the connection with the mouth in verse 11 and stirring up strife in verse 12.

discerning

His is the Hebrew word *bin* which is most commonly translated *understanding* in the NASB translation. It means the idea of careful pondering, understanding the connection between things, and realizing what will happen when something is done what the results will be. The 'discerning' person grasps many of these factors. The 'undiscerning' person does not.

Solomon is saying that if one is going to find wisdom, it is going to be in or stated by a person who has a grasp of the material and understands the results of particular actions. One does not find wisdom with the person who says, "Well, let's just try this and we'll see what happens."

In other words, wisdom has an accurate predictive element. This is what will result from that action and here is how long it will generally take. This predictive element is a crucial element in any philosophies truth claims. Can your philosophy of life accurately predict what will happen and tell you what to do about those predictions? Wisdom can. If you say this, then the other person will most likely act in this way... If you do this, then this will most likely be the result... If this is done, then it will typically cause...

When you find someone who really understands what will happen in the people dynamic business, then you find wisdom. If, however, you find someone who acts impulsively or without much foresight, then you are not in the presence of wisdom.

This is much like keeping your hand on the chess piece so that you can look at all the potential moves. Mentally this is the discipline of wisdom. If I say this, then that person will probably say that and it will result in this fight or this bizarre action or this development. It is this kind of thinking that the wise person does and the impulsive, foolish person does not do. Fools tend to evaluate things based upon whether they want to do them or not.

Ask yourself about the decisions that you are presently facing – today, this week. Do you really understand what will happen if you do what you are thinking about doing? If not, do some more research. You will never have 100 percent absolute certainty about what will happen, but wisdom has a high level of success in predicting what results from certain behaviors.

rod

This is an overall symbol correction that brings about a change in behavior. It is negative and difficult, but it does not always involve an actual rod. God disciplines us in various ways. The problem is that we are not always paying attention, and we endure the pain of the chastisement but do not learn the lesson.

The proverb is saying that the person who consistently engages in selfish pursuits at the expense of others really needs strong, firm, and negative correction and training. It has to stop. Often the only way to make a person stop being destructive and selfish is for the negative feedback loop to get significantly higher until there is a willingness to move in a new direction.

understanding

This is the unexpected word *leb* and not the word *bin*. It means that the person who is unwilling to ponder and think deeply with the whole of their soul will need to be forced into a level of contemplation and training for a new course.

PROVERBS 10:14 - *Wise men store up knowledge, but with the mouth of the foolish, ruin is at hand.*

wise

Again wisdom is the application of knowledge for the result that will glorify God, cause others to win, and you personally to win. This is called the triple-win. Its opposite is the foolish action or choice which is selfish, impulsive, and rebellious. It usually results in a completely different result than what you wanted or it entails other issues or consequences than you anticipated. In this case Solomon is talking about behaviors that wise people take. They store information.

knowledge

This is the Hebrew word *daat* which means information, skill. Both accumulated data and practiced skills are considered knowledge in the Old Testament. What Solomon is saying here is that people who are wise are constantly curious for helpful and righteous information and skill. They constantly grow. They don't graduate from school and then stop learning. They are always looking for more information and learning new skills.

Someone said when you are green you grow and when you are ripe you rot. You are either doing what the wise person does or you are going backward. Do you have a chance to learn a new skill or gain some new information? Do it. Some people hold back taking classes or going back to school or taking lessons because of cost or time or difficulty.

Invest in yourself is what Solomon is saying. Keep growing; it is the pursuit of wisdom. A rule of thumb is that you should try and add some significant new area or skill each ten-year period of your life so that you are able to grow into new responsibilities. Keep growing or you will start slipping backwards and life will become boring. It doesn't matter how old you are; keep growing. Invest a little money, a little time, and a little energy in yourself over the length of your life and you will have a richer life. Don't give into the temptation that you are too old to go back to school. Don't tell yourself that you are too tired or don't have the time to take lessons or read a book. Keep growing.

but with the mouth of the foolish, ruin is at hand

This is an interesting opposite or contrast to the first part of this verse. These are more central characteristics of opposite types of people than there are contrasting actions themselves.

One of the key characteristics of the foolish person is that they believe that they can talk their way out of anything or into something. It is their mouth that gets them into trouble. They don't have any real information behind it, but they have selfish rationale for everything.

foolish

This is the Hebrew word *ewil* which means fool, foolish. The key idea of foolishness is selfishness. It is all about me. It is time to focus on me. When they talk, it is about them. When they see the world, it is only from their own perspective. Their myopic point of view consistently will bring destruction to them.

All of us have foolishness as a part of who we are which is why it is best not to keep talking because eventually we betray our own selfishness. Solomon is saying to get a handle on your tongue; don't just say what you are thinking; don't just let a thought come in and a thought go out. Collect wisdom so that you can evaluate that thought; you can filter that thought; you can see where that thought is going to go and what its impact will be on other people.

Look at this week and see what you can add that will increase your knowledge and how you can talk less so that you do not increase or betray your foolishness?

PROVERBS 10:15 ~ *The rich man's wealth is his fortress, the ruin of the poor is his poverty.*

This proverb is about security and a place to hide.

fortress

This is two Hebrew words *qirya* for city and *az* for strong. The idea is that the surplus of the rich person is a place to flee when things are going bad. It is their refuge and security. This idea of security against attack and problems is what controls the rest of the proverb.

ruin

This is the Hebrew word *mehitta* which means destruction, terror, or ruin. Solomon is saying that while the rich man has a place to hide from disaster and mistakes and oppression, the poor person is exposed. They have no such place. There is nothing backing them up when they make mistakes or when a powerful person seeks to dominate them or a disaster strikes.

There is an interesting implied idea here which is that the poor person should have been saving some measure of what they received, so that they would have some to bridge them over the tough spots. The clear implication is that you don't want to be poor so do something about it. Spending all that you have exposes you. It leaves you vulnerable to the issues of life. It leaves no room for mistakes. Get yourself out of this situation by saving a little bit every day.

poor

This is the Hebrew word *dal* which means one who is low; one who has nothing. The image is between one who has surplus and one who does not. One who has planned ahead for the contingencies of life and one who has not.

One person feels secure (even though they may not be) and one feels exposed. Solomon is saying you have a choice as to which one you will be in this life, for the most part, unless injustice is at work.

poverty

This is the Hebrew word *ris* which means poverty. It has reference to those who have no surplus; those who live day to day and have nothing to give to others or to rely upon when things are difficult.

One of the lessons of life is that it is lived through generosity and the ability to give – having surplus time, energy, money, resources, etc. Therefore, if you are the person who is always taking and never have anything to contribute or give, then you are ruined.

Now if I can apply this in an interesting way that is the opposite of what one might expect. There are people in our society who, in a desire to have surplus money, give away all their time, energy, and other resources so that they are completely spent. They are deeply impoverished in time, energy, and resources and when others need these from them, they have none to give and they are ruined. This is what happens when parents give all their time and energy to money-making or lifestyle-acquiring and have nothing left for their children. This is what happens when the job consumes every minute, and we have no time for hobbies and friendships. This is what happens when we give all to impress others with our stuff and have no time for God. Our poverty of time, energy, and resources is our ruin for we have no relationships except in the pursuit of money, prestige, or lifestyle.

PROVERBS 10:16 ~ *The wages of the righteous is life, the income of the wicked, punishment.*

the wages of the righteous is life

A person earns or receives – as compensation or consequences – a particular type of life. The type of life that the person who is righteous receives is full of relationships and blessings.

the income of the wicked is punishment

On the other hand, the compensation that the wicked receive is punishment. These are those who have pushed the limits of their selfishness until it has become morally reprehensible. "It is all about Me" is their motto. They live beyond moral lines. They lie, steal, cheat, slander, intimidate, rebel, etc. The irony is that they think they are pursuing what they want, but instead what they gain is really a whole lot of people who secretly or openly hate them.

This proverb states that selfishness has consequences and it is not a great life. It is actually a life full of people against you. It will feel like everyone is against you when you choose a life of wickedness.

PROVERBS 10:17 - *He is on the path of life who heeds instruction, but he who ignores reproof goes astray.*

instruction

This is the Hebrew word *musar* which means discipline, chastening, correction, reproof, punishment, instruction. These often indicated hard lessons; ones that were not easy to absorb. There is clearly new information here, but it comes in the form of a setback or something done wrong that could have been done differently.

Solomon is trying to get us to pay attention to what happens to us and see it is as a lesson. He wants us to realize that God does not waste our experiences but wants us to learn from what we go through.

What are the things right now that are not going the way you want them to go? These areas are the prime candidates for this kind of instruction that Solomon wants you to pay attention to in this verse. What could have been done differently? What choices could have been made so that this negative result could have been turned to a positive result? What have you learned from this situation? If you do not learn from these types of things, then you are largely condemned to repeat them.

ignores

This is the Hebrew word *azab* which means to leave, forsake, let loose, abandon. All these carry the idea of ignore which is the word that the translators used here. The good is contrasted with the bad. Both people have negative consequences happen to them when they mess up or don't calculate correctly, but the person who is on the path to a great life pays attention to why it might have happened, other ways of handling it, and choices that could have been made differently to minimize or eliminate the problems.

The fool here just lets the rebukes of life come and go in their life with little evaluation. That is just the way life is to them. They just accept rebuke, difficulty, and problems as the fare for living. The idea of God engineering consequences into the society doesn't fully enter their thinking. If it does, they wonder why would God have wanted anything bad to happen to them.

God has made the rules for life, and we would do well to pay attention to them.

PROVERBS 10:18 - *He who conceals hatred has lying lips, and he who spreads slander is a fool.*

conceals

This is the Hebrew word *kasa* which means to cover, conceal, hide.

This is the Hebrew word *saneh* which is a strong emotional word which means oppose, detest, despise.

Solomon is trying to say that someone who has this kind of emotional response to a person will lie about them if they try and conceal that they have such a negative emotional reaction to them.

slander

This is the Hebrew word *dibba* which means defaming, evil report. The idea is either emphasizing the negative or using the negative to ruin another person's reputation.

Solomon declares that a person who would ruin another person's reputation through slander is a person who is extremely selfish. Look out for that selfishness. It will turn on you.

PROVERBS 10:19 ~ *When there are many words, transgression is unavoidable, but he who restrains his lips is wise.*

words

This is the Hebrew word *dabar* which means words, speaking, talking. Solomon is trying to help people understand that when you tell everything you are thinking or everything you are feeling, you will offend, you will be selfish, and you will exalt yourself.

transgression

This is the Hebrew word *pesha* which means transgression, rebellion, breach of trust. Usually this is seen as rebellion against God so, therefore, a transgression; but the underlying idea is rebellion against the direction and rule of God in your life.

Reason this through with Solomon. He is saying that if you talk a lot and disgorge all your feelings and thoughts consistently, then it is inevitable that you will be rebelling against God's will for you. You will make your life all about you instead of all about Him or others. If you are the one talking all the time, you missed His prompting to stop and to focus on the other person who is listening to you.

There is an appropriate level of self-disclosure and appropriate times, but too much focus on you will always lead to saying to God: NO, I don't want to love others; I like all this focus on myself.

unavoidable

This is the Hebrew word *hadal* which means to cease, to stop. There is a "not" that precedes this word in the original language. Therefore it says that if you are a person of many words, it is not possible for you to stop the coming rebellion. God will be saying stop and you will push right on through because you enjoy hearing yourself speak so much.

Let me suggest an exercise that you try every day so that you do not violate this proverb. At least once every day don't talk about yourself; just ask questions of the other person and be focused on them. Do not open your mouth to reveal what you think or feel; only use your mouth to ask questions or to compliment them. You will be surprised and delighted by what you learn and people will be delighted with the love for them that you are showing.

restrains

This is the Hebrew word *hasak* which means withhold, keep in check. This verb means to hold something back, to stop the normal or desired direction of an object or person. Our sinful nature wants to have others focused on us. It wants to drone on and on about what we think and feel. But God, through Solomon, says if we keep talking, it is inevitable that we will rebel against God's plan for that person and that day. Be ready to say no to yourself. Be ready to hold back all that you want to say about yourself and all you are feeling. Yes, there are times to tell it all to a trusted friend, pastor, or counselor but be prepared for the gentle nudge of the Holy Spirit saying: "Enough Ask a question about them."

One person suggested to me that I say NO to something every day just to stay in practice. If we are going to achieve God's will for us, we will have to say NO to ourselves at least once every day.

wise

Those who do not say everything that is in their mind or heart are allowing everyone to win. Those who dump out all they feel and think for public consumption are often an extremely selfish people. They win but a number of others lose.

I have a good friend who will always bounce any attention upon himself back to another question about you. You have to demonstrate that you are really interested in him with repeated questions before he will tell you how he is doing. He is an expert at focusing the conversation about the other person. I believe that he has the philosophy that if you really care about him, you will ask again about him; but if you are just being polite in your questions for him, his questions will love you and he will not have answered questions you really don't want to hear. When I am with him, we play this very interesting game of "can I deflect questions about me and focus the conversation about how he is doing or will he deflect questions about him and focus the conversation on how I am doing." Wherever this man goes, he is universally loved because he has somehow learned to heed the advice of this proverb: Don't talk too much; you get in the way of what God wants to do. Be alert to what God is prompting you to do.

PROVERBS 10:20 - *The tongue of the righteous is as choice silver, the heart of the wicked is worth little.*

tongue

This is the Hebrew word *lashon* which means tongue. This clearly refers to the spoken words of the righteous, not the physical tongue of the person. The things that this kind of person says is of extreme value. Pay attention when they speak.

righteous

This is the Hebrew word *saddiq* which means just, righteous, in right standing with God. The idea in the Jewish context was that if a person was keeping the covenant between them and God, then they were considered righteous. They were not hiding their rebellion; they were seeking to do as God asked them to. It is these people who are in relationship with God by faith, trusting that the commands that He gave would bring them to a position of right standing with Him.

When you find a person who is speaking who is actually living for God, then what they have to say is very valuable. It is as choice silver. However, if they are simply living for themselves in spiritual garb or pretending to live for God while really living for themselves, then it is doubly bad.

choice

The word *choice* is the Hebrew word *bachar* which means to choose, select, prefer. The idea is that if there is a purer silver, a more valuable silver, then each person would choose that silver. So the words of the righteous person are like that. When one needs counsel and direction, it is best to go to people who are righteous.

The tendency is to go to people who will tell you what you want to hear instead of people who will tell you what you need to hear. This tendency to talk to people who will agree that you need to be selfish is prominent when you are young. Look at the basic worth of each group.

heart

This is the general word *leb* which means the inner man or the soul of the person. In this case Solomon is saying clearly that a person who has feasted on selfishness and made their life a pursuit of a few selfish desires has a vacuous soul. There is nothing worth extracting from what they are saying, thinking, feeling, and doing.

wicked

This is the Hebrew word *rasha* which means wicked, criminal. This means that this person has pushed the boundaries of selfishness to the place where they consistently go beyond societal limits to get what they want. If a person does this, then they will become a worthless soul. Selfishness will eat up the value of the choices they could have made.

You will be able to find people who believe that you should do whatever you feel like doing. Follow your heart, be selfish. But that road will not end where you think it will end. It will not end in success and rich relationships and joy. It will end in loneliness, strife, distance, and brokenness. Selfishness always ends this way.

little

This is the Hebrew word *meat* which means little, few, scarce. The idea is clearly that the internal ruminations of the wicked person render them worth very little to others. They can only really think about themselves. Be very careful about this. Make no mistake; they are out for themselves.

PROVERBS 10:21 - *The lips of the righteous feed many, but fools die for lack of understanding.*

righteous

This is the Hebrew word *saddiq* which means just, lawful, righteous. It means conforming to a standard, being straight, ethical. What is the standard that is being conformed to in the economy of God? It is the Ten Commandments. It is the Golden Rule. It is the first and second great commandments. These all depict the righteous person as making a positive contribution to others, not being marked by selfishness and not being involved in harming others for personal gain.

The basic nature of the righteous person is explained in this proverb. The righteous person is not selfish but seeks to benefit others as much as, if not more than, any personal profit.

The righteous person stays within the boundaries of the Ten Commandments in terms of their morals, but righteousness is more than resisting strong levels of selfishness. Righteousness is embracing the Golden Rule: *Do unto others as you would have done unto you.* This is a positive statement of benefit to others and not just a negative statement about what you should not do. It includes the negative but is not restricted to the negative.

In this proverb the righteous person makes sure that even what they say benefits many people. They do not just say whatever they feel. They do not give an opinion without thinking through all the ramifications of the statement. They speak in a way as to benefit others. It is the benefit to others that is the key aspect of the righteous person. They actually do love their neighbor as they love themselves.

but fools die for lack of understanding

Clearly this is meant to be a contrastive proverb. The righteous person is like one thing and the fool does not comprehend that way of thinking.

fools

This is the Hebrew word *ewil* which means fool. The idea is not one who is mentally stupid but morally stupid; one who is selfish, impulsive, rebellious. The point of the whole book of Proverbs is to have you recognize foolish tendencies in yourself and move away from them to great wisdom. Wisdom is clearly an acquired taste. You must learn how to bless others as much as yourself. Our natural inclination is to only be interested in blessing ourselves.

understanding

This is the Hebrew word *leb* with is the standard word for heart or soul. The translators felt that putting the word heart or soul in this verse would not be as helpful as using the word understanding. In one sense they are right, but in another sense they have obscured some of the meaning of what God was saying through Solomon.

Solomon is saying that fools follow their impulses and therefore do not develop depth of soul. It is this lack of a fully developed inner person that eventually kills them. They live on a lower plane than the wise person who has a rich inner life. The fools only know what pleases them on an immediate level. They are like a child who can be entertained by keys and bright shiny objects. They want to be entertained now. They are easily distracted by the next shiny object or loud thing.

Solomon says that the selfish person will pay a high price for a lack of a reflective life. They will follow the shiny objects and bombastic people until they are separated from what would give them real life.

Do not follow the baubles of this world. Don't allow your life to be about following the next shiny object whether that is a sports team, a sensual experience, a quick buck, the rush of gambling, the feeling of drunkenness, the buzz of a party, or whatever. Develop an inner life. Allow yourself to think. Develop wisdom. Look to benefit others as much as yourself. Life is actually found there It is a much richer and more rewarding life than just playing with a new set of toys each month.

PROVERBS 10:22 - *It is the blessing of the Lord that makes rich, and He adds no sorrow to it.*

Solomon is saying that there are many ways to get rich, but only one of them doesn't come with sorrow mixed in. That is through following the blessing of the Lord. Where the Lord is guiding, you build an abundant life. It may not involve abundant amounts of money, but it will surely involve building abundant relationships of love. This is the best kind of riches

blessing

This is the Hebrew word *berakah* which means a blessing, a benefit, a gift, blessings, present.

This verse has been misused numerous times. Some have suggested that this verse means that an evidence of God's blessing in your life is material abundance, but that is not what this verse is saying. This verse is saying that one of the results of following the Lord and living His way is that He might give you riches as a gift and if He does, then it will not result in destruction and sorrow to you or your family.

We are watching the riches of the world be destructive to people. I read somewhere that over 70% of large lottery winners are bankrupt in a few years and that over 90% of large lottery winners are divorced in two years. What was supposed to be a great blessing turned into destruction for these people. Many who have looked into setting aside large trust funds for their children and grandchildren have concluded that there does not seem to be any way to avoid the trust fund being a degenerating issue in the children's lives.

There are all kinds of ways to get rich from cheating – to illegal goods, to mortgaging your family to put in more hours, and many others. But they end in great sorrow along with the riches. Solomon is saying that when your God gives you wealth because you followed His plan, it doesn't come with sorrow.

rich

This is the Hebrew word *asir* which means rich or rich man. The idea is abundance beyond day-to-day or paycheck-to-paycheck. Solomon is clearly pointing out that the goal of many people is to pile up extra so that they are secure, but what good is that if the sorrow is added to the pile? The riches of God do not come with the sorrow of unrighteousness and greed.

sorrow

This is the Hebrew word *eseb* which means sorrow. Notice that God says, through the mouth of Solomon, that He may let you have wealth without Him; but He will add sorrow to it so the enjoyment over the long haul is not there. Do not love money and pursue riches. Pursue instead God and His kingdom and all these other things will be added to you.

PROVERBS 10:23 - *Doing wickedness is like sport to a fool, and so is wisdom to a man of understanding.*

sport

This is the Hebrew word *sechoq* which means laugher, sport, derision, enjoyment. This word is the key analogy in this proverb. Solomon is comparing the main themes of the whole book to sport: wickedness, foolishness, wisdom, and understanding. It seems that this word is used for its playful nonchalance in this context.

Solomon compares the fool wandering into the moral darkness as if it meant nothing or was not a big deal. And in the same way the person who has understanding just instinctively and playfully chooses the wise course. It is not a big deal to him. The idea in both cases is that it is playful, laughable; not a difficult choice – the fool to wander past the boundaries of ethics and morality and do wickedness; the man of understanding to choose to glorify God, meet the needs of others, and meet his own needs. Solomon sees this intersection between both kinds of people. They both act to change their destiny in a playful nonchalance. These actions have become their destiny through prior choices and now there is no agony or struggle or prayer or deliberateness about what they are doing. They are doing what they are – either wicked or wise.

The question is: Which are you playful at? Which of these two options would characterize your destiny: playfulness in doing wickedness or playfulness in doing wisdom? The answer is your destiny. All of the consequences flow from the path in which you choose to reside.

If you find yourself playfully living beyond the moral boundaries of God, then repent and take the difficult step of seeking God's face and pleading for forgiveness. Ask Him to remake you into a person of wisdom instead of a person of wickedness.

The good news from this proverb is that if you become a man or woman of understanding, then wisdom will be easy for you. It will seem like child's play. Wisdom starts out as difficult and hard to know what to do, but it ends up being playful enjoyment because it is so obvious.

PROVERBS 10:24 - *What the wicked fears will come upon him, but the desire of the righteous will be granted.*

wicked

This is the Hebrew word *resa* which means one who lives outside of God's moral boundaries in the Ten Commandments. These people are so selfish that they will do whatever they have to to accomplish what they want. They no longer respect God's moral boundaries of private property, of marital faithfulness, of truth, of honor for authorities, or of focus and worship of the one true God. These boundaries are to be broken if it means that they can get more of what they want.

fears

This is the Hebrew word *megora* which means fear or terror. Selfish, wicked people are always fighting a rear-guard action to protect their selfishly obtained pursuits. They are always concerned about losing what they have gained. The level of their selfishness bends all thoughts back to their own desires. It therefore causes them to be afraid that what pleases them will be taken.

This verse is a truism in that the selfish people dwell on what they fear and can spot the weaknesses in their defenses. They are consumed with themselves and not having what they want is a great fear. It becomes a self-fulfilling prophecy. They gain these fears through watching the natural consequences of others like themselves.

The difference is striking between the wicked and the righteous. The wicked are self-consumed; the righteous think of others and are God-oriented. One group is longing to benefit others; the other group is trying to gain more to consume themselves. One is longing to accomplish something positive for people; the other is fearful of losing what they have.

desire

This is the Hebrew word *taawa* which means desire. This is an interesting word in that it is most often used as something bad. It refers often to lust, selfish desire, covetousness. It is what a person deeply wants, dreams about, lusts after. In this context Solomon is using it to speak about the godly achievement or goal that those who are righteous want in their life. Their goal or dream is a godly one. It is a good one that has powerful positive impact. It is the goal that God births in the heart of the person. They have sought to love God and benefit their fellow man, and they can see a specific benefit they want to be a part of or accomplish for God or others. It is this benefit, goal, dream that God gives them or, in many cases, allows them to accomplish for Him.

It is important to not see this as though it will drop out of the sky like a Christmas package. God will allow the path to that goal to be pursued. It will take hard work. It will require all your prayers, abilities, involvement, etc. But it has been granted. If you don't act, it won't happen. Do not see this as the idea that if you live within God's standards, He will drop your desires in your lap. No, He will not block you from accomplishing the dreams He has put on your heart. He will aid you to accomplish the dreams that He has given you.

righteous

This is the Hebrew word *sedaqa* which means conformity to an ethical standard. Practically speaking, to be righteous in the Old Testament was one who lived within the boundaries of the Ten Commandments while doing the first and second great commandments. In other words, they did not willfully violate any of the Ten Commandments and they pursued, on the positive side, loving God and loving their neighbor.

It is important to say that righteousness must have this positive dimension. One is not righteous by what one does not do. People are righteous by the love they express within God's moral boundaries.

257

There are a number of religious people who are declaring themselves righteous or believing that they are righteous because they do everything in their power to live in the Ten Commandments box; but they are bitter, angry, hateful, judgmental, spiteful people. This is not righteous.

It is also important to say that one must be loving from within God's moral standards. There are people who are selfishly wicked and pursue what they want, in any way they want, and then they throw a little money at the hurting or homeless and believe that they have been righteous. They accept all kinds of deviant behavior as tolerable as long as it doesn't personally and negatively impact them; and they call this tolerance of sin, love. It is not. It does not meet the needs of others to allow deviants to practice their craft on others.

In the ultimate sense of righteousness there is no one righteous; no, not one. But in this general more practical sense, it is possible for people to fit this description and to be "righteous." It is this definition that was meant when it was said about Mary and Joseph that they were righteous. They lived their lives within the boundaries of the Ten Commandments. They did not blatantly trespass across those moral boundaries nor live in violation of those standards.

granted

This is the Hebrew word *natan* which means gift, reward, bestow. The idea is that God blesses the righteous with the fulfillment of what they desire because what they desire is righteous. He can give it to them without destroying them. It is all grace and unmerited because none is righteous; no, not one. But God delights to shower down on those who seek to follow His rules.

PROVERBS 10:25 - *When the whirlwind passes, the wicked is no more, but the righteous has an everlasting foundation.*

whirlwind

This is the Hebrew word *cuwphah* which means whirlwind, storm. It could be thought of as a tornado of destruction or a hurricane. These are the storms of life that come to test the type of materials and construction that you have used to construct your life. These storms or tornados come in all kinds of forms. They could be business cycles where the normal downturn in customers that happens after a big expansion tests whether you have really been operating your business on sound principles. These storms could actually be storms, which destroy a building, a factory, a home, or a business, and this tests your resolve and your plans before the storm came. These storms, whirlwinds, or tornados could be health related such as a disease or accident, which lays you low. If you have been operating on wicked principles or constant growth being your salvation, then your poor foundations will be exposed. The storms could be investigations by the authorities that audit or charge or investigate some aspect of your life. These storms could be terrorists or robbers who destroy parts of your life and maybe culture. In biblical times it was not uncommon for raiders and enemy agents to destroy families, farms, towns, and regions. These whirlwinds could be natural disasters, which bring life back to its basics.

Solomon is saying that these various testing agents will expose those who have built their life in shabby and wicked ways. Problems always expose folks like this. Do not build your life for the short term. Build for the long term. Build your life on a foundation of righteousness. There are and will always be these kinds of whirlwinds passing through a culture, a region, a family. The more solidly you build your life on righteous choices, solid relational wealth, and Godly prosperity, the more you will survive these testing agents.

In this proverb the whirlwind is the judgment of God – either directly or indirectly testing life and culture. This has been seen down through history as various things, which bring back balance and punish those who play too fast and loose with the freedom that God has given us. We must recognize that God has given humanity incredible room to design their life. Our choices can make a real difference in how our life goes. We can choose to do righteous and wise things and have a stable life built on a solid foundation as Jesus says. We can choose to lead a selfish life, grabbing and cheating our way to what we want with little regard for others – either those who are around us or who will come after us.

It is clear that our culture in America is moving away from righteousness and moving towards sexual impulses, greed impulses, and power impulses being king. We have the freedom to choose this sinful path, but our society will not survive when the whirlwind comes if we continue down this road. We need revival and a wholesale turning to God before it is too late. It has happened twice before in our country's history. The first great awakening under Jonathan Edwards and the second great awakening under Charles Finney were significant turning points in the history of America. Before those crucial revivals, America was on the same selfish, immoral path that it is on today. If we continue down this road of licentious and selfishness, we as a culture will be wrecked when the whirlwind passes. It may be that God will use some whirlwind of judgment to turn us back to Him, but it is clear that we cannot keep moving down the immoral path we are own without doing great damage to many people.

PROVERBS 10:26 - *Like vinegar to the teeth and smoke to the eyes, so is the lazy one to those who send him.*

vinegar to the teeth

Vinegar wine – which the grape-growing Israelites would be familiar with – has an especially irritating flavor and sting when applied to the teeth or inside the mouth.

smoke to the eyes

Smoke – when it is blown in the eyes – is particularly irritating to these organs.

In just this way Solomon is saying that the person who is lazy will be particularly irritating to the person who is trying to get work done through the lazy person. It will be a major stinging and irritating aspect of work. Don't do this. No matter if the person needs a job, is a relative, promises that they will do better than the last time. Do not use a lazy person. Do not count on them to do a particular thing. It will not happen that way.

lazy

This is the Hebrew word *atsel* which means sluggish, lazy. This is the person who does not want to work. This is the person who is slow in his/her work. This is the person who does not do portions of his/her work.

Solomon is trying to point out what happens to those who try and do a good deed by hiring the lazy person. He says it is like putting vinegar on your teeth or having smoke blown in your eyes. This is one of those leadership-lessons proverbs. Solomon is saying that as a leader you cannot afford to hire or use the lazy person because you will be the person who pays.

PROVERBS 10:27 - *The fear of the Lord prolongs life, but the years of the wicked will be shortened*

The phrase *fear of the Lord* has been explained in this devotional commentary as both reverence and actual fear. We serve a huge, immense, and transcendent God who is capable of all kinds of actions. He is more powerful than any power of nature that we fear. And we cannot control Him as we seek to control nature.

Many times we lose sight of the Awesomeness of God.

Following God's way pays off. We can live longer if we do not harm our bodies through sin and rebellion. When we stay within God's boundary structures, it does prolong life. I was reading a statistic the other day that the vast majority of cervical cancers come from a sexually transmitted disease. Therefore if you fear the Lord enough to not commit adultery in any form, you will most likely not get that kind of cancer.

but the years of the wicked will be shortened

We tend to forget in our day of antibiotics and advanced medical care that when you disregard God's boundaries, you do significant damage to your body. Being wicked means that you live outside of God's prescription for life. You lie consistently; you live in adultery; you hate and are angry regularly; you swear, curse, and blaspheme constantly. All of these activities inevitably expose a person to diseases, weaker immune function, and dangerous relationships. The idea in this verse is that the wicked introduce into their own life what causes their bodies to break down.

Remember that it doesn't seem that wickedness is anything but pleasure. But it will do harm to you and to those around you.

It is worth it to live the good life with the Lord.

PROVERBS 10:28 - *The hope of the righteous is gladness, but the expectation of the wicked perishes.*

hope

This is the Hebrew word *tocheleth* which means hope, expectation. This is much stronger than a wish or doubtful desire. It is an expectation built on the faithfulness of God. The righteous know that God will come through. They have built their life on the faithfulness of God and the rules He has built into the universe. They have seen Him act both in their lives and in the Scripture. They are not wishing for material wealth or desiring power that may or may not come. They do pursue full development of their lot in life, but that is not their hope.

righteous

The righteous is one who lives within the boundaries of the Ten Commandments even as the wicked live outside of them, but the righteous is far more than just not doing sin. They are positively loving God and others. This is why Jesus says the two great commandments are to love God and to love others. The righteous person gets it. They allow themselves to be filled every morning with God and then they dispense His love and grace everywhere they go.

The righteous do not define themselves by what they don't do. They define themselves by the good they were able to do.

gladness

This is the Hebrew word *simchah* which means joy, gladness, delight, mirth. The firm expectation of the righteous is that they will have joy in the depth of their being and will be able to share that with others. God will meet and/or exceed their expectations for the relationships of their life. This brings joy to their soul. Their expectation is not selfish pursuit but instead deep connected, positive relationships with those around them. In this expectation they are not disappointed and because they add so much to every relationship, they are a self-fulfilling prophecy of their own expectations.

The question: Are you a positive, righteous person injecting joy, delight, and gladness into your relationships? Or are you a negative, self-centered individual? Which has the better life? The positive, righteous person who seeks to bless every person with whom they come in contact.

The classic biblical example is Joseph. Everywhere he was he injected positive benefit and met or exceeded the expectations of those around him. His father loved him and had great joy in his presence. When his brothers hated him and were jealous of him, they chose to be wicked rather than emulate his example. But when he was sold as a slave, he was positive and exceeded the expectations of Potaphar. Then when he was thrown in jail, he was positive and exceeded the expectations of the jailer. Then when he was introduced to Pharoah, he was positive and exceeded the expectations of the ruler. In each case Joseph was the definition of a righteous man – not just for what he did not do but for what he did.

expectation

This is the Hebrew word *tiqvah* which means hope, expectation, longing. The wicked that live outside the Ten Commandments grasping and clutching after what they want in the end will find that their selfish desires cannot be fulfilled. They will grow old and die.

perishes

This is the Hebrew word *abad* which means to perish, to annihilate, broken, destroy. The idea here is that the selfish desires of the wicked fade as they cannot find the way to accomplish them. Their hoped-for dreams and aspirations crumble in their shriveled soul. It is a terrible thing to realize that you will not be able to accomplish your desires.

But the contrast with the righteous is extreme. They just want to be a blessing to all the people they meet. They want to bring gladness, love, and connection wherever they go, and they are fulfilled in this function and gain so much more on top of that. All they want to do is be a positive light of God's love to the people they will meet that day. The rest is in God's hand. But God can powerfully use a person who is willing to be a channel of His love to each day.

PROVERBS 10:29 - *The way of the Lord is a stronghold to the upright, but ruin to the workers of iniquity.*

the way of the Lord

The word *way* is the Hebrew word *derek* which means path or road or way. The idea is that God has a path to live on in this life. It is bound by certain kinds of behavior. Outside of this path of the Lord are types of behavior that are ruinous to your life but appear to be shortcuts to your goals. To get off of God's pathway is to pursue intimacy through sexual unfaithfulness; to pursue money through lying, cheating, and/or stealing; to pursue power through deception, witchcraft, anger, or violence; to pursue prestige through cursing, swearing, and lying; to pursue fulfillment through lust, greed, and pride. All of these appear as viable choices as we go through life, but only the way of the Lord – God's right way of living – keeps us from the destruction that comes from these shortcuts. With God's way, we reach our goals and also have the blessing of God.

stronghold

This is the Hebrew word *maoz* which means safe place or refuge or means of safety. Solomon's father David – when fleeing from Saul – found strongholds in the caves of Engedi where Saul's men could not find him and his men. They were safe there even though they were being hunted. It is this sense that Solomon is talking about – the stronghold here. When the world is against you and people are assailing you, it is the path of the Lord that will act as a refuge and stronghold to protect you. When you live the world's way, you offer places to attack you. But when you live God's way, He protects you. Living for God and not for yourself offers a layer of protection that is important.

Are there areas in your life right now where you lie, where you are greedy, where you are sexually unfaithful, where you are violently angry, where you scheme to take another's position or property? It is in these areas that you are exposed. Repent and stop. Change your ways. Flee into the stronghold that is the Lord's way of living.

ruin

This is the Hebrew word *mehitta* which means destruction, ruin, terror. Solomon is saying to those who have made their way in life through lying, stealing, cheating, anger, and scheming that it is terrifying to live in a place where that is not the way one gets ahead. It is a terror to live in a righteous place.

workers of iniquity

This is the Hebrew word *awen* which means trouble, idolatry, wickedness, iniquity, etc. The idea of this word is that which lives outside of God's moral boundaries given in the Ten Commandments. The workers of iniquity are those who get by in life through these nefarious means. They only know swearing, rebellion, anger, violence, lust, stealing, lying, and scheming. They would not know how to act if they could not do these things.

Make sure that you run into the stronghold of the Lord which is His way of life. It is like hiding in plain sight surrounded by the grace of God for the life of God.

PROVERBS 10:30 ~ *The righteous will never be shaken, but the wicked will not dwell in the land.*

righteous

This is the Hebrew word *sedaqa* or *tsaddiq* which means just, righteous, blameless.

Too many people believe that going to church makes them righteous. No, connecting to God through repentance, faith, service, worship, study, prayer, and love is what righteousness in this context means. It is a righteousness given by God through faith; but it is also a participatory righteousness that interacts with God and lives out His will, drawing on His grace and power.

It is important to point out the positive quality of righteousness in the Old Testament. Righteousness is not just a person who stays away from certain things, living inside the Ten Commandment boundaries. Righteousness is one who is full of God's love, spreading it around to all those who know him or her. The righteous person is one who fulfills the servant leader/lover role in the relationships of their life. One would not see the negative legalistic Pharisee as a righteous person because nothing of love, beauty, dignity, and compassion is produced out of his life. His life is all about what you can't do instead of doing good things for others that you can do.

A truly righteous person is one who is a positive source of energy, encouragement, help, service, and benefit to those who they meet. The good Samaritan in the story that Jesus told – this was the righteous person.

shaken

This is the Hebrew word *raash* which means to totter, shake, slip, fall. Those who have discovered the wonder of making a positive difference in the lives of others through holy love will not be shattered by misfortune or trouble. They expect that in a fallen world there will be selfish people who devise schemes, devices, and deception to oppress others.

God is still in heaven. He has created a world in which the free choice of sin of His creatures does not change His plan and does not derail His plan for mankind. He knew all of the selfish choices that we would make. He knew all the evil that our nation would perpetrate on others. He knew the devastation of allowing Adam and Eve to plunge the world into sin, and yet He still executed the creation of the universe. The finding of worshippers who will worship Him in spirit and truth was worth the hardship of a fallen world.

Those who are righteous are not destroyed by difficult times because they are connected deeply to the One who is outside of time and space. This does not mean that the righteous aren't discouraged or depressed or struggling with doubt from time to time. But they will not be shaken so as to fall completely. Their house of faith will not crumble under the earthquakes of a sinful world.

Are you ready today to make a positive difference in the lives of those you meet today: the waiters, airline attendants, other drivers, colleagues, family members, etc? The glow of the love of God within you must shine out or you are not a righteous person – someone who appears as a light shining in a crooked and perverse world. This is how the Christians turned the world upside down. They energized themselves with the love and grace of God so that they could make a positive difference everywhere they went.

but the wicked will not dwell in the land

wicked

This is the Hebrew word *rasha* which means wicked, criminal. The idea, as we have discussed elsewhere, is these are people who have allowed selfishness to become the controlling impulse of their lives and they no longer recognize normal moral boundaries like the Ten Commandments. They live in the jungle of do unto others before they do unto you. They can expect to eat or be eaten.

dwell

This is the Hebrew word *shakan* which means to settle down, abide dwell. The idea here is that Solomon notices that those who have embraced selfishness as their guiding principle with no moral boundaries are unable to really settle anywhere. They are restless and hounded from within and from without. The internal impulses to selfishness drive them to keep moving. The jungle no-rules world that they have joined means that they are always on the edge of disaster. They will not make a long-term stay. They will not exist over generations. When down times come, they will be swept away. When pressure builds, their relationships will break under the strain. They will not survive the pressure of a fallen world.

If you are living a wicked life outside of the moral boundaries of God or of the government, repent and stop right now. Go in a different direction. There will come a time when all your gain will be washed away and you will need to admit that you live in somebody else's world under somebody else's rules. The sooner that you repent and come back inside the moral boundaries of God, the better it will be. Even wicked people can repent and find forgiveness in God. Never forget that.

Solomon says that they will not dwell or abide in the land; their selfishness will cause them to keep moving.

PROVERBS 10:31 - *The mouth of the righteous flows with wisdom, but the perverted tongue will be cut out.*

This is the second in the series of insights into the righteous person's conduct and life. Solomon chooses to contrast the righteous with the wicked in each case. These two types of people are moral opposites. The one is all about self and the other is all about God and others.

mouth of the righteous

This refers to the speech of the person who is righteous. Now what is interesting is that Solomon sees the words, conversation, and manner of speech as a major characteristic of the righteous person. "How do they speak?" He would ask. "Do they criticize, share their pessimistic view, withhold the wise solution from others?" These are the actions of a wicked person. The righteous person uses their speech to uplift, encourage, and offer wise solutions.

wisdom

This is the Hebrew word *hokmah* which means wisdom, skill, information, applied information. In this devotional we have understood a shorthand version of all that wisdom stands for as the triple-win choice or action. That choice or action brings about a win for God, a win for others, and a win for yourself. If you leave out any of these wins, then it is not wisdom. The only group that it is permissible to fashion a loss for is the wicked – those who have crossed the line of moral behavior and refuse to repent and return to basic ethical boundaries.

Ethical boundaries are defined by two questions: Who does your action benefit? Does your action harm anyone? If the only person who benefits is yourself and it harms others, then it is an unethical behavior no matter how strongly you like it or desire doing it.

This particular proverb deals with the righteous desire to benefit those around them with triple-win wisdom. They want to help people get life right. They continually talk of God's solutions to life's problems. They talk about how to live life God's way.

perverted

This is the Hebrew word *tahpukah* which means perversity. In older translations of the Scriptures it was translated by the word froward rather than perversity. Froward has a different meaning than perverse. It means habitually disposed to disobedience and opposition. This is the rebel orientation.

cut out

Are we to understand that the person who is rebellious, obstinate, and disobedient will have their tongues literally cut out? No. But rather the person who has this frowardness or obstinate, disobedient, rebellious speech and attitude will find that people will tune them out. Their influence will be over. When they speak, no one will listen. So, effectively their tongues have been cut off.

Have you run into this type of person before? When you make a suggestion or even a direct order, they resist it or change it or completely disregard what you said. It does not take very long in these kinds of situations where this kind of person is just shut out of decisions. The obstinate and disobedient person will cross the wrong person and have their speech cut off. They will no longer be heard. Their ability to be heard and give influence will be at an end.

Be a righteous person whose mouth flows with good things and positive solutions.

PROVERBS 10:32 - *The lips of the righteous bring forth what is acceptable, but the mouth of the wicked what is perverted.*

This is a continuation of Solomon's insights into the results of a righteous or wicked way of life.

Notice what is said about the righteous person. The righteous person brings forth words that are *ratson* or full of good will, full of favor, full of acceptance. These are words that bring encouragement, help, and comfort to the hearers. The righteous person is alive with the glow of God's love, encouragement, and blessing. Sometimes it takes the righteous person a while to find what they can say that will be full of good will and favor to some people, but they find it. Now righteousness does not sugarcoat sin or evil; but righteous people do not look for the negative, the wrong, or the mistake. They are positive and full of love for others.

It is Solomon who is saying this. Too many times we have suggested that the most legalistic, condemning, and negative person is the most righteous. "They can find something wrong with almost anything." But this is not God's definition of a righteous person. The righteous person speaks blessing and comfort and encouragement into the other person's life.

Who are you going to meet today? What positive, encouraging, accepting, and comforting words can you speak into their life? What negative rumors do you need to not say today about the people you know?

but the mouth of the wicked is perverted

Notice that the words that flow out of the wicked person are *tahpukah* which means twisted, perverted, distorted. The wicked person always has a selfish agenda. They take a stab at the truth but twist the meaning or implication so that they benefit and gain in the process.

This is a very instructive lesson in discerning a wicked person. Does someone you know twist the plain truth of a situation, discovery, and interaction to suit their benefit? Then they are living outside of God's moral boundaries in other areas also. Build a wide margin around this person. They are a law unto themselves. They worship at the shrine of themselves and if pushed will violate any law or cultural norm that gets in their way.

If this describes you, then stop lying. Start telling the truth. Even today. It will be hard, but it will serve you better as your relationships will become real relationships and not sham dances. Stop lying.

Proverbs 11

PROVERBS 11:1 - *A false balance is an abomination to the Lord, but a just weight is His delight.*

The essence of wisdom is contained in this little proverb. If others have to lose for you to win, then it can't be wisdom. The only exception to that is that the wicked will often lose when the righteous and the wise win.

Stealing through deceptive business practices means that one party is the winner and other parties are the losers. This is not the basis of a healthy economy. A healthy economy is the transfer of goods for a certain value that is agreed upon where everyone agrees on the worth of the item.

If a business is built on trickery and deception, it may prosper for the short term; but it will not make it in the long run. It will be discovered and cease to exist or pay a heavy price for its win-lose strategy.

When a person has an everybody wins philosophy in its business, then it is the delight of the Lord.

PROVERBS 11:2 - *When pride comes, then comes dishonor, but with the humble is wisdom.*

pride

The basic idea is pride, a sense of self-importance, which often is exaggerated to include defiance and even rebelliousness.

What is interesting about this proverb is that it proclaims that the one thing the proud person wants is exactly what this person will not receive. The person who is proud wants to be noticed and to have attention focused on them for who they are or what they do. This person wants their accomplishments trumpeted; they want even just their presence at an event or place trumpeted. They must be noticed. They want honor – the added value that is given to the truly deserving. Their pride, however, causes them to seek attention in a disruptive and obnoxious way.

When the aspect of any person's personality shows up that has to be noticed or on top, etc., then dishonor is on its way. Hold back those impulses that make you want to focus attention on yourself - that moves you to want to be noticed just for being there.

dishonor

This root signifies the lowering of another's social position. When we seek to elevate our social position or standing through power plays, rebelliousness, bizarre attention, getting devices or stunts, we may get what we seek; but it will come with a lowering of our social position. In other words, the very thing we seek we will not have. This is a pulling away of social esteem and favor. When we seek to be noticed or gain attention for ourselves, we are moving into a place of foolishness and away from wisdom. You can't find wisdom clamoring for the spotlight. When you seek to be noticed and attention on yourself, you will be devalued. Your goal is negated by the search. Honor is a by-product of a loving life.

humble

The verb means to be modest or humble. The Septuagint translates this Hebrew word with a word that means low-lying. This could be taken to mean calling attention to ourselves – a notice-me spirit. When we seek after the acclaim, fame, or attention of others rather than doing a great thing for the simple sake of its needing to be done, we will find it brings shame. A test in a sense is set up. Can we do something and not demand notice or point out that we did something? If you make too big of a deal about yourself or what you have done, then it will be your downfall. It seems to be that God would have us be noticed for what we truly do, not what we do to be noticed. It is not wrong to be noticed and even to be strong or forceful in our personality. But when we seek out the fame, attention, power, and prestige that accompanies real honor, then we get the opposite of what we wanted. To seek after the results of doing something positive without doing the deed is the essence of pride. It will result in dishonor. I may not know my great-grandchildren at all, but I do want them to know that whatever the world looks like at that point, it is still God's universe and pride will not help you for long and it will eventually hurt you. Do good things that really help people and the honor you seek will come to you.

wisdom

Wisdom is again that triple-win choice. What type of choices are you making? Are they choices where everybody wins? Does God win? Is He pleased? The fear of the Lord is the beginning of wisdom, so start looking for the wise thing to do by asking what would please God in this circumstance. That is a much better starting place than starting with what would please me or others.

PROVERBS 11:3 - *The integrity of the upright will guide them. But the crookedness of the treacherous will destroy them.*

The word *integrity* means wholeness or undivided oneness. The idea in this verse is that if you are always the same person in every situation and every relationship, that oneness – that undivided type of thinking – will tell you what to do in each new situation.

If you would not cheat in business, then you should not and will not in golf. If you would not utter swear words in the family, then you should not when your team loses the game or you hit your thumb with the hammer. It means when you don't know what to do, you look at the decision before you and ask yourself if you would do this kind of thing in another context. If the answer is no, then don't do it. If the answer is yes, then move ahead.

There are too many people who are duplicitous – people who act one way at church or around friends and a different way in business and sports. What is amazing is that even though people try and play a deceptive game of "I will only be like this in one area of my life," it always bleeds over and they cheat, lie, steal, swear, are unfaithful, and angry in every relationship.

Strive for wholeness... be the same way... always aim to stay in the Ten box – INSIDE THE 10 COMMANDMENTS

will guide you

The interesting thing is that this phrase *will guide you* can be understood in two ways. It could be the idea that when a person does not know what to do and is righteous, he/she should look to that which is full of integrity and in line in every way with the Ten Commandments. This is a reasonable application of this idea. What is consistent with righteousness is the right question when one does not know what to do and then do that particular thing.

The second way of looking at this phrase is what will happen. Your integrity will guide you. In other words, that which you do consistently will guide you. The only question is whether you will be guided by the best advice. I have watched person after person do what seemed right to them or what was consistent to them even though it made no sense. This is the principle that we make a series of choices and then those choices begin to make us. It is the accumulation of our choices that determine what we will do in almost every case.

Notice that integrity and crookedness are parallel to one another in this proverb. One either acts in a way that is consistent with the path of righteousness or one acts consistent with twisted or crooked, selfish dealings. It is the accumulation of these choices that will guide each person and seem right to them.

Ask yourself the question whether your typical solution to a problem results in good being accomplished. Does it have the ring of what is inside of the Ten Commandments? Or does it come out wrong consistently even though it feels like the right thing? You are either being guided by what is outside the Ten Commandments or what is inside the Ten Commandments. This guidance is either building your life or it is tearing down what is really wonderful about life.

PROVERBS 11:4 - *Riches do not profit in the day of wrath, but righteousness delivers from death.*

This is referring to the Day of Judgment – the time when God evaluates your life. Righteousness is not what you stayed away from but what you accomplished in terms of loving God or loving others.

Were you able to demonstrate your love for God through acts of faith? Too often people think of righteousness as negative things or what was not performed.

It is the righteousness of Christ that will deliver us from death on that day; the righteousness that comes from faith as Paul proves in Romans 3 and 4; the righteousness that only comes from obedience to the Word of God out of faith.

PROVERBS 11:5 - *The righteousness of the blameless will smooth his way, but the wicked will fall by his own wickedness.*

This is a contrasting proverb designed to show the stark difference that choices make. There is a multiplying effect with good and bad choices. Every good choice opens up more good choices and the blessings that result from good choices. Every bad choice results in more bad choices that were not available before the bad choice was made, and then the consequences of that bad choice come along also. So there is at least a four-fold multiplying effect for every choice.

Let me spell it out this way. If I choose the right choice then, first, I gain the blessings of that good choice; second, I have new good choices available to me; third, I do not have the consequences of the bad choice I could have made; fourth, I do not have new bad choices available to me.

the righteousness of the blameless will smooth his way

There are results from choosing wisely. All of us believe that, but we need to be reminded of that from time to time because at times it seems that the wicked get all the good stuff. But this is not true. Their way is hard and full of difficulty.

The word righteousness *sedeq* means conformity to an ethical or moral standard. What is that moral or ethical standard in the Scriptures? It is the Ten Commandments. So if you make choices to stay within the boundaries of the Ten Commandments, then you have made choices to be righteous.

Let's just review what these are...

- *You shall have no other gods before Me*

- *You shall not make for yourself any idols*

- *You shall not take the name of the Lord your God in vain*

- *Remember the Sabbath Day to keep it holy*

- *Honor you Father and your Mother*

- *You shall not murder*

- *You shall not commit adultery*

- *You shall not steal*

- *You shall not bear false witness against your neighbor*

- *You shall not covet your neighbor's goods*

These ten mark the edge of acceptable behavior. They each also point to a much deeper, ethical behavior. Instead of playing around the edge of what is allowed, we want to please God by being in the center of His will. Let's take a look at the hoped-for opposite behavior that each commandment implies.

You shall love the Lord your God with all you heart, soul, mind, and strength.

Understand and contemplate the wonder, infinity, and transcendence of God and never reduce Him to something in this world.

Let your actions match your words and become a testimony of the integrity of a person who walks with God. Do what you say you will do.

Live a balanced life full of work, worship, rest, and relationships.

Add value to everyone around you, especially authorities who keep watch over you.

Develop a flexibility in the face of life and opposition that does not strike back or seethe, instead looking for a new option in the face of the reality of the situation.

Work hard to build abundance that you can generously share with others. Be honest in your dealings with others.

Enjoy the blessings and relationships that you already possess, maximizing their contribution to your life.

This verse claims that when we make choices to stay within the boundaries of the Ten Commandments, our lives will smooth out and not have many of the obstacles, difficulties, and problems of those who live outside of these moral boundaries.

the wicked will fall by his own wickedness

We need to hear that wicked choices bring difficulty. Unfortunately the TV, movies, and magazines hide the difficulties of those who live outside of God's boundaries. We see mob bosses who don't have problems. We see sexually promiscuous men and women who never get diseases or are deeply lonely or have multiple alimony payments or emotionally break down under the weight of their broken relationships. We see thieves who live in rich houses and never get arrested or have to deal with unsavory characters or get cheated themselves. We see envious people who always get what they want instead of destroying what they are after in the lives of others and their own life in the process of pursing the great prize they must have. We see foul-mouthed hero types whose verbal filth does not limit job opportunities, earning potential, relationships, or team cohesiveness. All these unreal images are constantly driven into the minds of our children and ourselves until we really believe that there are not consequences to wickedness.

Do not believe that; limit your exposure to these lies and remember that wickedness brings consequences: spiritually, emotionally, mentally, physically, relationally, and in a whole host of ways beyond this.

It is important to say, at this point, that this verse points out that it is not God who curses the wicked; it is their own wickedness. Their own choices bring consequences. Many people will scream at God and ask, "Why are you against me?" I believe that He answers, "I am not against you; you are against yourself. Repent and come to me that you may live and enjoy My blessings."

Too many people want to continue to make the choices that they have been making and that they are comfortable with and get a different result. It won't happen.

What trips up those who make bad choices? The bad choices that they make.

PROVERBS 11:6 - *The righteousness of the upright will deliver them, but the treacherous will be caught by their own greed.*

This is another in this series of proverbs that reminds us what righteousness fully-embraced in a person's life is able to do.

Notice that Solomon separates righteousness from the person who acts righteously. He acts as though it is a separate entity. It is your righteousness that will speak to you. It will deliver you. It will smooth your way.

Basically he is saying that righteousness – when embraced as a lifestyle – does generate its own power in your life. It steers you around many problems and protects you from those that come to destroy you.

It is actually extremely realistic in its portrayal of problems coming to the righteous person. Too many other religious epics seem to suggest that the truly righteous person is excused of all problems. Notice that God gives it to the believer straight: You will have problems – even if you are righteous – but you will be shown a way out of the problem. It is the process of agonizing for a solution that is guaranteed. God will send, through righteousness, a solution to the dilemma.

Now it is often thought that it is outside of strict righteousness that deliverance is to be found. But this is not so. When a person asks themselves what is the truly God-honoring right thing to do, they come up with a way that will deliver themselves from unseen troubles and a proper solution.

but the treacherous will be caught by their own greed

It is the desire more for selfish gain that does not allow the treacherous person to escape from the scam. The con man always gets the sucker to make a little illegal money before he moves for the big score. It is the greed of the person that draws them into the trap.

Be careful and do not be sucked into something that is just a little on the sly or just barely illegal. If the product or service does not really help people or it is illegal to do it, then one should move away from it no matter how lucrative it is.

PROVERBS 11:7 ~ *When a wicked man dies, his expectation will perish, and the hope of strong men perishes.*

This is a very interesting proverb speaking to the temporariness of the desires of those who live outside of God's moral boundaries. They may get what they want, but what they want is so fleeting. It never outlives them. And in many cases, it does not even last till they themselves die.

The word *wicked* is the word in the Old Testament for the person – man or woman, young or old – that lives outside of the Ten Commandments. They don't just sin and then try and live a moral life. These people continue to practice and engage in sinful acts over and over again. They steal and keep stealing. They commit adultery and keep being adulterous. They blaspheme and keep slandering God. They rebel and continue rebelling from authority. They wound and harm people – even murdering them – and they keep getting what they want that way. They covet other people's goods and take action to seize them. This is the definition of the wicked person. Our society is making more and more people who live in this way. They refuse to respect God's boundaries or even their own society's boundaries.

The word translated *expectations* in the NASB is really the Hebrew word meaning hope. The rough idea of this phrase is that the person who lives outside of God's moral boundaries hopes for more selfish things to go their way; and when they die, all they hoped for comes to an end. They don't hope for good things that live beyond them. They don't strive for those things that others will carry on after they are gone. Even if others carry on with their traditions, it will be only for their own selfishness and not reflective of honor on the original wicked person.

So, as the proverb says, the wicked person has no enduring hope. What they have here is all they get. There is a strong desire in American culture today to get this kind of live-for-now focus to be the dominant view of everybody. Some do not realize that this is the wicked person's perspective. They live constantly for the moment with no thought for the future or eternity. It is the righteous person who builds for the future that will outlive them. It is the righteous person who builds for endless time in eternity.

There will be times when you are doing the right thing when there is no payoff right away and, sometimes, even in this life. It is just the right thing to do. If you want to build a lasting legacy, don't follow the road of wickedness. That is only a temporary stop in a pleasurable place before being herded on the path of loneliness and pain. If all you live for is yourself and the now, then you will have nothing to show for your life when it is over.

If, however, you are constantly doing good things for others and glorifying God with your words and actions, then you are building up a true reward and a lasting legacy.

I want to stand before Jesus on judgment day having been forgiven by Him for my sins with a whole pile of selfless acts and good works that bring honor to His name. I do not want to be empty-handed with nothing to show for my life except a lot of memories of selfish and sinful pleasures that profited nobody but me.

and the hope of the strong men perishes

The same idea of hope and the future is repeated in another person who will lose what he built his life around. In this case it is the muscled person who built his whole life around being strong and muscular. That is not where your body is going. There will be a time when no matter how strong you were, you will not be very strong.

Think through what the proverb is saying. It is trying to point out the temporariness of what the world says is all important. Notice the two items that Solomon, under God's inspiration, picks as temporary – the very things that every society highly values: the pleasures of a sinful life and the power of strength and violence. Every young man and woman is taught to value these things. They internally are drawn to and impressed by these things But the proverb teaches us that we should not be impressed by these actions and qualities.

What is interesting, also, is that this proverb does not say what will last; but it is trying to get you to think about building your life for and on something that will last – by not mentioning them. It gets you to question: What should I aim at with my life? What should I invest my time, energy, and money in? What should I try and get the most of as I live my life? It is interesting that the answers are not in this proverb, but they are throughout the book of Proverbs and the whole Bible.

The answer is given in the two great commandments: *Thou shalt love the Lord thy God with all thy heart, soul, mind, and strength and thy neighbor as thyself.*

What should we aim at? What should be try and build a whole pile of? What should we invest our time, energy, and money in? Relationships – especially with God and also with the other people God puts in our lives: parents, mate, children, church members, workmates, community, finances, friends. When we are going through life, it is the quality of our relationships that determine the quality of our life. At the end of our life it is the quality of our relationships that determine the value of our relationships. The hope of the righteous is that those who are important to them would be able to live out their dreams and prosper and that God would receive worship and glory through the world that He created.

How much time are you investing in stuff that doesn't matter? How much time have you spent investing in the relationships in and around your life? When a person has a near-death experience, they always realize that every day is precious and the people in their lives are the most important.

PROVERBS 11:8 ~ *The righteous is delivered from trouble, but the wicked takes his place.*

This is clear evidence that one's destiny is not sealed. The fact that trouble is coming is undeniable, but your preparation and choices determine whether you are in it or away from it.

The choices of a righteous man keep him from trouble. He does not experience the kind of consequences that come on those who live in the jungle of wickedness.

It is interesting that just as Jesus says, it is inevitable that trouble comes but woe to the one through whom it comes. You may not be able to stop trouble, but you can keep it from coming through you or affecting your family.

PROVERBS 11:9 ~ *With his mouth the godless man destroys his neighbor, but through knowledge the righteous will be delivered.*

This proverb declares false the child's saying, "Sticks and stones may break my bones but words can never hurt me." Words can be some of the most powerful and damaging weapons. This is a discouraging and encouraging Proverb at the same time.

Notice that it states that godless people will try and attack your reputation. And they will succeed unless you are righteous and equipped with knowledge. So we must define who is the godless person. What are the two antidotes to this person's desired destruction: Righteousness and Knowledge.

godless

This is the Hebrew word *honep* which is usually rendered hypocrite; the phony; the one who puts on a mask to hide their real intentions. It has the idea of looking like the person is doing right while their internal motive is to break rules, laws, and commandments to get what they want. The translators draw out the idea of this person not remembering judgment day and therefore call this person godless. But it is important to realize that while this is clearly what they are, the predominant characteristic is that they are phony. They really don't believe or live the way they say they do.

There is an understanding in what Solomon is teaching here in that this person wants to maintain their pleasant position and good situation and will step on anyone or anything that might cause people to see what they really are all about.

The warning is to watch for phony people – not people who make mistakes and aren't perfect but phony people who want everyone to embrace a glittering image of themselves.

Sometimes this person is the con man who will try and suck good, gullible Christian people into some scam or scheme.

Notice the instrument of the hypocrite is their mouth. They are trying to smooth talk you. Watch out for the person who is the incredibly smooth talker and appears too good to be true. How many different times do we have to hear of people who have been bilked out of their life savings or drawn into a romance and then bilked?

righteous

This is the Hebrew word *sedaqa* which means righteousness or justice or doing things the right way. One of the things that con men do is they try and get a person to make a small break with legality to set them up for a bigger break later. If you refuse to compromise on what is right or what is legal in trying to gain money or promotion or some other desirable thing, then these people cannot trap you.

Con men can only trap people who will compromise on God's laws and on legal issues and who do not check into things enough, getting all the facts.

knowledge

This is the Hebrew word *daat* which means knowledge. The one thing that phonies can't stand is the truth. The light of facts and inconsistencies exposes these kinds of people. The word here is never enter into a deal or relationship with a person or a company until one has sufficient facts that this is completely legitimate. If there is any question, make several phone calls and/or go online to check out the deal or plan. If the person will not wait as you check it out, then they are some level of phony.

Solomon continues his unique training into wisdom through this penetrating insight into the world of con men and phonies. His solutions – although given over 3,000 years ago – are still valid and effective.

PROVERBS 11:10 ~ *When it goes well with the righteous, the city rejoices, and when the wicked perish, there is joyful shouting.*

Is it the responsibility of the civil government to create a climate in which it goes well with the righteous? In other words, where righteousness is rewarded with favorable laws and wickedness is punished with punitive measures? Is it the responsibility of the civil government to create a climate in which the wicked perish or do not survive? In other words, to pass laws that discriminate against the wicked and that certain behaviors are regulated, discouraged, publicly shamed, and even punished?

Unfortunately we are currently living in a culture that has forgotten what basic righteousness is. It is defined in two ways in the Scriptures. On the positive side, it is loving God and loving others. On the negative side, it is defined as that which is outside of the Ten Commandments. When a civil government permits or encourages people to live outside of the Ten Commandments, then individuals, families, businesses, and the community as a whole suffers. We have seemingly forgotten these basic ethical lessons. It is not just about whether the person feels pleasure doing something; it is about whether a person, family, business, or community is harmed by condoning or encouraging a behavior. We now exist in a culture where civic leaders do not want to tell anyone NO. We would rather just try and clean up the mess from the condoned wickedness. We are seeing individuals, families, businesses, and communities be damaged and destroyed because our cities are not holding up the standard of righteousness.

The wicked are those who seek their own selfish ends by any means even if they have to harm or damage others in the pursuit of their goals. This has always been called an ends-justifies-the-means strategy. As long as we condone this idea, we will have growing amounts of human damage in our communities. The sad thing is that we are becoming so lost in regards to righteousness that we do not even know where the lines and laws go. When righteousness and basic ethics are upheld, then a community rejoices because it is safer and does not have as much "random" harm occur in it.

We know where a society tips over into unrighteousness:

- When it allows the worship of false gods, images, and occultic practices

- When it allows cursing, breaking oaths, and slander

- When it does not allow for and even require people to rest and prioritize God, family, and health

- When it promotes rebellion and insubordination in the family, the education system, and community

- When it allows violence, intimidation, bigotry, and murder to be a means to accomplish anyone's goals

- When it allows sexual pleasure to be a worthy goal apart from a lifetime commitment to one opposite- sex partner

- When it allows or promotes stealing, dishonesty, and vandalism to exist without punishment

- When it promotes or allows lying for personal gain

- When it encourages scheming and plotting revenge, takeovers, and personal pleasure at the expense of another

PROVERBS 11:11 - *By the blessing of the upright a city is exalted, but by the mouth of the wicked it is torn down.*

The Scripture declares clearly that there are blessings that attend to the actions of righteous people. These blessings are spiritual, mental, emotional, physical, monetary, relational, and societal (Proverbs 10:6). It is this societal blessing that is often overlooked in our day and age. When people do the real intent of the Ten Commandments, it blesses not just them as individuals but the whole of the community in which they dwell.

We need more people who will do the opposite of violating the commandments – people who seek to delight God and bring blessing upon themselves and others by doing selfless actions of love, worship, compassion, and generosity. Remember that in the Ten Commandments there are not just boundaries for selfish behavior but directions about selfless behavior.

The word *upright* is the word which means within the confines of morality – the Ten Commandments – but it also means doing positive actions within those confines. We have forgotten to mention and teach that people bless the whole community when they act in an upright way. Uprightness is not a negative; it is a positive. A man who is upright does not just refrain from adultery but instead builds a strong, vibrant marriage. A man who is upright does not just refuse to steal but instead develops – through hard work – knowledge, insight, and wisdom, a pile of resources that he can generously share with his loved one and his community.

In our culture we have become under the direction of those who are consumed with pushing out the limits of what is permissible by law. It is this desire to be able to do more within the boundaries of legality that has consumed our culture. Why is this outlawed? Why can't we do this? This is the cry of the last fifty years of western civilization. As we have quickly dismantled the morality that has been handed to us by the accumulated wisdom of three millennia, we have seen an increase in divorce, murder, unwed pregnancy, suicide, gangs, stealing, psychosis, and now disease, corruption, sexual deviancy, and the like. We have moved the lines of morality and have watched a society and culture disintegrate.

This proverb is so true that we need to have politicians pay attention. The blessing of the upright exalts a city and not the debauched conduct of those that live outside the boundaries of right and wrong. Unfortunately much of our media have tried to magnify those cities that permit the most sin. This is tragic and misleading.

but by the mouth of the wicked it is torn down

A city can be destroyed through the permissive musing of the wicked. Those who are wicked give hearty approval to those who flaunt God's rule, the apostle tells us in Romans 1. It is this promotion of expanded moral boundaries that destroys the fabric of a city.

A return to old-fashioned morality has been good for the towns that have embraced it, and flaunting morality has meant that the citizens of a town are less safe and secure.

This is all well and good but what does this have to do with the individual – with you? Solomon is trying to cause you to realize that you present your city with a gift when you act righteously. When God blesses you, that blessing spills over to the whole of the city. Even though the newspapers will not necessarily cover your righteousness, it will make a difference for the whole city: volunteering at the Rescue Mission; serving at the retirement home; welcoming an unexpected baby home rather than aborting it; building a loving marriage and family rather than having the affair; teaching the underprivileged; serving at your local church a couple hours a week; building wealth enough to be generous rather than cheating, stealing, and defrauding to get ahead; treating people as individuals, not labeling and categorizing people because of one trait about them; by enjoying the blessings and relationships that you do have rather than coveting and longing after other people's blessings and relationships.

PROVERBS 11:12 - *He who despises his neighbor lacks sense, but a man of understanding keeps silent.*

despises

This is the Hebrew word *buz* which means to hold in contempt, to scorn, to despise to the point of rejection. What is clearly interesting is that God states that we have a choice whether we will allow ourselves to feel this emotional reaction toward someone. Our society generally feels that we do not have control over whether we feel contempt or not. Contempt is a nursed emotion that starts out as a slight irritability and only with continued care and nurture does it become scorn or contempt. I talk with many people who have allowed themselves to feel this emotion for their spouse by constantly focusing on their weaknesses and shortcomings. If you focus on what the other person is not doing or what they do wrong, you will end up with a healthy crop of disgust, scorn, and contempt.

In marriage counseling I have asked individuals: What would it take to really live with this person and enjoy it? Usually they come up with a list of actions or behaviors that are not difficult but which they refuse to do because they are so mad or bitter or hurt by the other person over wounds of the past. This seems tragic and silly – holding a great future hostage to the mistakes of the past. I am not saying that major wounds or immoral conduct should not be dealt with, but I consistently watch as people nurse their hurts until they live in a cesspool of relational crud and then blame the other person for it.

The advice of 1 Corinthians 13:4-8 is worth looking at. Love must overlook a lot if it is going to be effective. If you want your life to be full of love, then you must be patient with others, be kind to others, endure others, believe others, etc. Strong relationships do not allow scorn to grow.

his neighbor

This is the Hebrew word *raa* which is the word that means friend, companion, neighbor, associate. It often means one in close relationship or close proximity. It is the word that is used in Leviticus 19:8 in the second great commandment: *Thou shalt love thy neighbor as thyself.* Many people have often restricted this word to those they live next to as that is its somewhat restrictive definition in English. But God is not saying to love those you live next to, but that we must meet the needs of those who are within relational proximity to us. These are the toughest people to love (meet needs). God wants us to escape the gravity of our selfishness and look out for the needs of those around us.

lacks sense

The word *lacks* is the Hebrew word *haser* which means to have a need or be lacking. It represents a poverty of something. In this case, it is a complete poverty or lack of depth in the soul.

The word translated *sense* in the NASB is the word *leb* or heart and means mind, soul, understanding, etc. The idea is clear that the one who despises a person they are in constant relationship with has a shallow soul – a fairly complete orientation toward self. A person with a deep soul or heart is one who can overlook small offenses and even large ones (with interaction and apology). It is work to overlook the wounds that others cause and to keep giving to them what they need, but it is through this process that we dig out depth in our soul and thereby can enjoy life to the fullest.

This idea also clearly has the meaning that the person who scorns those closest to them does not have a proper understanding of the way life works. They need to think through what happens if they push forward with the selfishness of scorn and contempt. It will come back to them as a diminished relationship which is unwise. They will then only have more fuel for their contempt and escalate a downward cycle in the relationship. That is why another proverb says to abandon the strife before it breaks out.

You can't improve a marriage by nursing your hurts. You can't improve a family by increasing your contempt for your parents or your children. You can't improve your work environment by increasing your scorn for your boss. All you do is foul the stream that you are standing in. This makes no sense.

All of us are tempted to keep score of how many times a person is thoughtless or hurtful or inept, but this type of scorekeeping does not improve your life. Instead, all loving relationships must develop daily forms of amnesia which allow you to start fresh with a person each day.

understanding

This is the typical word for understanding – *bina* – which means insight, discretion, discernment; especially about the connection between things. This is the person who sees the connection between what will happen if he says all that he is thinking and what is happening now. So many people just do not think about what will happen if they clear their chest of all that they feel. These people just spew their feelings about everyone and everything, and then people are just supposed to forget and forgive what they said. This is just nonsense.

Solomon is saying that the person with real wisdom sees the unbroken line between the future state of the relationship and what they say right now

keeps silent

This is the Hebrew word *charash* which means to be silent, dumb, speechless. Clearly the idea is that feelings of hatred and dislike are fleeting and changeable. How many times have we congratulated ourselves for not saying something that we felt like saying when we discovered that it would have been completely wrong?

Yes, you will have strong feelings about your boss, about your neighbor, about your spouse, about your pastor; but if you do not broadcast them, then they will pass and you will have given them and you time to change.

Take Solomon's advice and keep your feelings silent except to trusted confidants who can really listen and care for you in the midst of your emotion. Do not take your emotions for/or against this individual as permanent. Be mature and do not be driven by your emotions.

PROVERBS 11:13 - *He who goes about as a talebearer reveals secrets, but he who is trustworthy conceals a matter.*

One of the principles or axioms that you must begin to live by if you are to be trusted with "what really happened" information is that you must not tell people all the things that are revealed to you. The only exception to that is if they have a real need to know for a moral purpose.

You can either be known as someone who tells what they know or as someone who can be trusted. You can't be both. It takes a maturing person to realize that it is better to know the real facts and information – even though you can't tell anyone that you know – than be a person who spreads all the rumors, gossip, junk, and secrets that they hear.

The wise person is the one who does not need to be noticed for what one knows. The wise person does not need to be known as one who knows – knowing is enough. If you are to be a confidant of others, you must be confidential.

talebearer

This is the Hebrew word *rakil* which means slander or slanderer or talebearer. This is a much more negative word than is conveyed by the English translation. It is much more about slander – a libelous destruction of a person's reputation through the rumors, secrets, lies, and truths that are spread about the person. The intent is clearly to increase self and decrease the object of the slander.

So if you are sitting listening to a person bad-mouth someone else, realize that they will be doing the same thing about you in other situations. It is their form of foolishness. Do not reveal secrets you don't want known to a person who you know regularly slanders others in order to look like they are "in the know."

secrets

This is the Hebrew word *sod* which means counsel, intimate plans, secret, consultation. It seems to have the idea of something that is closely held or intimately known.

Realize that Solomon is trying to cause us to wake up and notice that there are types of fools who derive their importance by dishing dirt and intimate details to others. It is their way of being important. They will act in whatever way they have to in order to hear new information so they can keep their importance up. DO NOT TRUST THIS PERSON WITH SECRETS.

trustworthy

This is two Hebrew words *aman* and *ruach*. The first word is the word we get our word *amen* from, and it means so let it be true or it is true; it is faithful; even it conforms to reality. The second word is the word *ruach* which means spirit or breath. It often refers to God's Holy Spirit, but it also refers to the immaterial part of a person. In this case it seems to stand for the motive and general nature of a person. Are they faithful and trustworthy to do what they say and commit to, or are they people who will sell you out for a little public adulation?

matter

This is the Hebrew word *dabar* which has a wide range of meaning but largely refers to one's way or path in life but also speech, word, acts, direction, etc. The person who can be trusted conceals more than facts; in fact, they might not conceal facts. They would conceal possible motives and directions of the person.

A friend does not sell out a friend or a client or a spouse or a child just to seem more important. One who has character resists giving up the secrets of another. If you are going to be trusted with real secrets, you must demonstrate yourself confidential first.

PROVERBS 11:14 - *Where there is no guidance the people fall, but in abundance of counselors there is victory.*

Solomon is helping us understand in this proverb two things: the need to get outside wisdom and counsel and the balance between keeping everything to yourself and telling everybody everything.

The proverb right before this one is about being a talebearer or someone who tells everyone everything they are involved in and all of the juicy details. You don't want to be this but in avoiding this, some people don't seek counsel and advice which is what this proverb is about.

guidance

This is the Hebrew word *tahbula* which means good advice, wisdom, guidance, counsel, direction. Clearly what Solomon is saying is that you should not be the only person determining the direction for your life. Other people should be able to see the wisdom of what you want to do. Also, you should seek out the counsel of others so that enough different options have been considered that the one chosen is clearly the right one.

This requires that you have a number of people who are clearly wise that you can run things past. What do you think about this? How would you handle this? What are some options that are available that I have not seen? This does not take long, but it is essential if you are to stay away from ruin.

fall

This is the Hebrew word *naphal* which means fall, ruin, fail, rot. The idea is that what has planned did not work and the person is destroyed, ruined, died, and did not accomplish what was desired, etc. The plan did not work because it was the work of only one person. It did not take into account enough variables and contingencies. It did not work through the counterattacks and the other various interactions that might spoil it.

but in abundance of counselors there is victory

Solomon is in favor of running your ideas through numerous filters to purify them and refine them.

counselors

This is the Hebrew word *yaas* which means advice, counsel, purpose, devise, plan. This is interesting in that the word in the Hebrew text is a verb – advise, counsel, plans, etc – but the translators have chosen to translate it as a noun. But the part that Solomon is pushing for is the advice and not the people who give it. He wants you to get an abundance of advice, not to get a bunch of people to agree with you. This is very interesting. It is the opposing, different perspective – even unique advice – that Solomon wants you to hear and grapple with. Do not just get a group of advisors who will tell you what you want to hear or who come from the same philosophical point of view.

There is a way of leading and managing that is sometimes used where subordinates are allowed to debate an issue from various sides while the leader is watching, listening, and judging the various streams of thought and merits of the arguments. Then he will make a decision after hearing this kind of debate. This carries some of what Solomon is talking about. Make sure that you have enough counsel and advice, not just what you think is the right thing to do.

In fact, impulsiveness is only checking with yourself before you do a thing even if you check with yourself for a long period of time before acting. If the only person you check with is yourself, then your actions are defined by impulsiveness. This does not mean that you need to check with others on every decision you make but clearly the major decisions in life – business, family – need the advice of more than just yourself.

victory

This is the Hebrew word *tesuah* which means deliverance, salvation. In this case the translators have chosen the word victory. But it seems more certain that Solomon's perspective is that there are numerous enemies and dangers that will be coming at you and unless you get enough advice and counsel, they will win and you will lose. If you get the advice and counsel that you should, then you will be delivered from these destructive results. You will delivered; you will be saved. Left to your own way, you will be destroyed is the orientation of the Old Testament. Life is a dangerous place but with the help, advice, and consent of others and a desire to become wise, you can live a great life and enjoy the fruits of wisdom.

Be constantly aware of the fact that since sin has entered the world, there are numerous ways that the world will destroy you if you are not careful. You need a guide; you need wisdom; you need counsel. There is stuff that will come at you that is too much for you, but if you seek wisdom and the God of wisdom as well as the counsel and counselors that He has placed along the way, then deliverance from many of these problems is possible.

Take the time right now to just pray a prayer of surrender to God and our Lord Jesus Christ, telling them that you are willing to listen and do what they want. You will not be stubborn, proud, and rebellious insisting on your own way. Look for His direction and His advice. It may look different than you might expect, but it will clearly be a win/win/win.

PROVERBS 11:15 - *He who is guarantor for a stranger will surely suffer for it, but he who hates being a guarantor is secure.*

The word *guarantor* is the phrase to strike hands with. It means that the person has made an arrangement or a deal. In this case it means that they have said that they will vouch for those they do not know. They have made a business arrangement to cover the debts of someone who is not family. This is not wise.

It is bad enough when you become the guarantor for those who are family, but those who make these kinds of deals for strangers are really jumping in the deep end.

Solomon is really saying that we should not tie our future to the performance of another through debt. You need to avoid debt and especially debt that seeks to predict the actions of others.

Debt threatens your security. It presupposes that you know what will take place in the future. It is this "I know what is going to happen in the future" that is poor judgment.

PROVERBS 11:16 ~ A gracious woman attains honor and ruthless men attain riches.

This is one of the delightful proverbs that tells us about the real world. It says that if you want honor or value in the eyes of lots of people, then be gracious. It would seem to be an interesting irony that in order to get people to value you publicly, you must be a person who dispenses favor to others.

gracious

This is the Hebrew word *hen* which means favor, grace, charm. The idea here is a woman who always celebrates the best in the other person; the one who sees you in a favorable light and also gives favors to those she meets. She is a giver not a taker. Who are the people that you want to spend time around – those who are selfish and focused upon themselves or those who consistently give and grant favors? The idea of gracious here is to grant a favor or put a person on a pedestal of importance. We all think that we have strength which should cause people to be impressed with who we are, so it is wonderful when we find people who are willing to focus on that aspect of our personhood that is our strength and not our weakness.

honor

This is the Hebrew word *kabod* which means abundance, honor, glory. Solomon wants to point out the fact that this woman is always granting others grace and favor and giving herself away to help and promote others' lives in abundance of what she gives away. How do you gain true honor in the eyes of others? Serve others and stop trying to protect your prestige, value. and/or reputation.

It is absolutely true that a woman who does not air other people's dirty laundry will be thought of very highly, while the woman who climbs the social ladder by knowing and dishing dirt on others will be universally despised.

and ruthless men attain riches

This word *ruthless* is a word that means mighty, aggressor, and the like.

Solomon's insight here is unexpected. It is not what we would expect in this "religious" book, but Solomon is a realist with his wisdom insights. He basically says that those who are assertive and aggressive are those who will amass greater levels of wealth. Those who wait and demur will be passed by as the goods are gobbled up by the assertive and aggressive men.

Do not miss the point in this proverb. Women who want to be highly valued for their charm and grace must give away grace, favor, and compliments to others. Men who want to have riches must have a single-minded focus and assertiveness or the goods will be gone. Do not dawdle, Solomon says, in business it may be gone.

It is important to say that the attainment of earthly riches may be gathered this way, but heavenly riches are not collected through assertiveness or ruthlessness. These are gained by seeking first the Kingdom of God and His righteousness.

PROVERBS 11:17 - *The merciful man does himself good, but the cruel man does himself harm.*

merciful

This is the Hebrew word *hesed* which means lovingkindness, love, mercy. This is the main word for love in the Old Testament. It is one of the most significant words in the Old Testament: God's *hesed* or love for His people. The people were to *hesed* God and each other. There has been a modern attempt to focus on this word in connection with the covenant between God and Israel and emphasize loyalty as a dominant theme in this word. It is best to take the older view and translate this word as love or lovingkindness.

In this proverb Solomon is reminding us of two truths that seem like the opposite would be true. The natural feeling is that when one is aggressive and demanding and disregards anyone's needs except his own, that person gets ahead fastest. There may be a short-term gain in this way, but long term it does not work.

It is the person who looks for the needs of others and meets them who is really benefiting himself as well as others around him. Love means meeting needs. It is the ability and willingness to meet other people's needs that sets you up to be blessed.

Our natural inclination is to be selfish. These impulses are the foolish impulses that suggest themselves first to our soul. In every situation and each decision, we sense the selfish thing to do. If we are to grow wise, we must begin to resist these impulses and instead look to love others. This is the Golden Rule: *Do unto others as you would have them do unto you.* It runs counter to what we initially feel is right.

One person said it this way, "You can get everything that you want if you help enough other people get what they want."

If you will work hard at meeting the needs of others, then you will be doing yourself a lot of good.

good

This is the Hebrew word *gamal* which means to recompense, to ripen, to reward, to deal bountifully.

The first part of the verse actually reads: *the man who loves ripens or deals bountifully with his soul.* Solomon is appealing to our natural self-interest to get us to love others. He is saying that the path of wisdom lies through loving others and there is a personal benefit to living this way.

cruel

This is the Hebrew word *akzar* which means cruel, fierce. The idea is that this person does not care about what happens to others; they just want what they want.

It is interesting that it is here contrasted with the person who expresses *hesed* to others. The one person uses others and has little regard for their concerns, needs, wants, or well-being. The other person seeks to meet their needs, helps them achieve their desires, and alleviates their concerns. These two kinds of people take different paths – both hoping to get to the same place. It is the loving person who will get there because if you arrive at your destination without relationships, then there is no point to getting there.

harm

There is another interesting contrast in this phrase which literally reads *troubles his flesh*. The person who loves others and meets their needs enlarges and benefits his soul, but the person who has no concern for anyone but himself troubles or harms his flesh. Almost everything in this proverb is the opposite.

Solomon is trying to make the distinction as great as possible. The life is lived out of and through your soul. If your soul is enlarged and ripened and benefited, then you will have a richer, fuller, and deeper life. If you are cruel and fierce and overtly selfish, then you will shrivel your soul; but you will also trouble your own physical body. Your selfishness software has an effect in your hardware. It will bring troubles to your body.

With a contrast this great, which one of these options will you take today? Take action to love someone else today. It may be a family member, it may be a colleague, it may be a neighbor, it may be a stranger – but actually do something today that meets the need of another.

PROVERBS 11:18 - *The wicked earns deceptive wages, but he who sows righteousness gets a true reward.*

wicked

The word *wicked* is the Hebrew word *resa* which means one who will not conform to God's standards for conduct and covenant living. This is the person who decides to live beyond the boundaries of the Ten Commandments in biblical shorthand. They live in adultery, they lie regularly, they deceive, they steal, they scheme to take other people's goods and claim them, they blaspheme God, they gain through violence or the threat of violence. They do not just commit these actions, but they consistently do them and excuse their conduct. The wages of the wicked are the pleasures of selfishness: I want to get what I want and then I will be truly happy. It is true that the pursuit of selfish ends feels like the right thing, but it is accomplished on the backs of others and especially in the case of those who live outside the moral boundaries of the Ten Commandments which ends in relational alienation rather than connection. So they may gain the things they want but end in the relational disconnection that leaves their soul alone.

deceptive

This is the Hebrew word *seqer* which means lie, deceptive, deceive. The idea is that it is not what it seems. Solomon is saying that the gains that the wicked achieve through their moral shortcuts do not amount to what they hoped. They thought that the things would satisfy when they stepped on people and froze their hearts to the needs of others. Now they have the things – and maybe even a host of shallow people to go along with them – but they do not have real soul connection or, even in some cases, the ability to understand how shallow their own heart has become.

sow

This is the Hebrew word *zara* which means to scatter seed or sow. It is a farming term to mean spreading that which is good; hoping for a good harvest. In this case that which is sown is righteousness or covenant-keeping or love for God and love for neighbor. This person does the right things in small amounts. They really care for people and do not make a splashy show of it. It is the little caring and living within the boundaries that respects the other people that builds the basis for good relationships and a rich life.

true reward

This is the Hebrew words *emet seker* which means true or real or "as advertised" wages or earnings. One is rewarded with real life and real things when they are gained through righteousness. It may be slower but it will be a bigger payday in the end. And, more importantly, the relationships will be real and the joys will not be masks for deep pain.

PROVERBS 19:19 - *A man of great anger will bear the penalty, for if you rescue him, you will only have to do it again.*

anger

The opening of this sentence reads in the Hebrew *gadol chemah* which means great anger or rage. The focus of this proverb is the anger, fury, or rage. The person who uses it is assumed. The great anger is the focus because of what it will do. Anger is a reaction to expectations not being met. When we build expectations of what should happen or should not happen in our mind and then those expectations are not met, anger is a common reaction. It would seem that anger is a part of motivation to act and to fix what can be corrected on our end. But many have used anger as a bullying tactic to get what they want. They do not use anger as motivation to fix their side. They allow anger to build beyond a little internal fire to a wild, uncontrollable fire that bullies others into action to appease, change, correct, and act. It is this kind of bullying anger that is being talked about here in this proverb. Anger as an internal motivational tool to move you to action, change, correction, or development can be a good thing. But some have discovered the power of anger, and they let the fire out and use it to control people.

penalty

This is the Hebrew word *onesh* which means penalty, fine. The idea is that there is a price to be paid for getting what you want through anger. That penalty is not named because it takes many forms. It may take an emotional form, a spiritual form, a psychological form, a physical form, or all of the above.

Notice that in this verse Solomon talks about rescuing a person from the penalty of their anger. The idea of rescuing is another form of responding to a person's anger by your acting instead of their acting. The word *rescue* in the Hebrew is the word *natsal* which means to deliver, snatch away, rescue. The people who regularly use anger to get their own way must feel the blow back from their anger, or they will continue to use it on other people.

Solomon is trying to continue our lesson in types of people and how to handle the various types of people wisely. His lesson today is about the angry person: the bully. He gives us great insight into this kind of person. They are used to having others adjust to them; others rescue them. They are used to getting what they want. But if you are wise, you will stand back and let the natural consequences of their intimidation, anger, and bullying land on them full force. This type of person will try and drag you into the mix. Resist rescuing them. They must learn that controlling others through anger is not an acceptable lesson. Anger can be used as an internal motivational tool but not a consistent external prod for others.

If young children are allowed to get their way because they got angry or might get angry or might get angry again, then you are violating this verse and creating a lifetime of pain for these children and those around them. Children and adults must be told "no." They don't always get what they want. Creating a bully is easy; let them get their way through anger. Anger then becomes the magic wand through which they get their way. They will have learned how to change circumstances, change people, and demand that their selfish demands be met. They have the weapon of anger. They will, most likely, use this weapon for selfish purposes and not righteous purposes.

Solomon is saying: Don't become an angry person's latest slave. If you are acting out of fear of what someone will do to you, you are rescuing an angry person. If you are intimidated into doing something that is not righteous, then you are rescuing an angry person. If you think of things to do so that so-and-so won't be angry, then you are violating this verse and the angry person won't learn.

At some time or another, angry people will bear the penalty of their anger. Notice that Solomon says: *You will only have to do it again*. If the angry person can get you doing their bidding through the weapon of anger, then they will keep using it until it no longer works. That is why Solomon says to step out of the line of fire of their anger. Stop being motivated to act, appease, change, and grovel because of their anger. Stop rescuing them from the troubles they are in and stop doing the bidding of their selfish demands.

This verse is also about how when the angry person finally is about to be clipped because someone is strong enough, do not keep them from feeling the sting of real authority and real justice. Let them feel it. They have to internalize that they cannot allow their anger to go to the lengths that it has gone in the past. The sooner that a young person learns this lesson, the better.

PROVERBS 11:20 - *The perverse in heart are an abomination to the Lord, but the blameless in their walk are His delight.*

perverse

This is the Hebrew word *iqquesh* which means twisted, distorted, crooked, perverse. The idea is that which is beyond the normal and against something's function. In the moral arena it is the use of something or someone which is beyond the normal or a bizarre twist of or on the item – usually to the detriment of someone else for the individual's selfish gain or desire.

Some action or thing becomes perverse when it is used for a different function than it was intended or when it is a selfish pursuit of a gain through the twisting of a person, place, object, or function. This is why homosexuality has been consistently labeled perverse in the Scripture because it is the use of your own body and another's for that which it was clearly not intended.

This became a way of expressing aspects of wickedness that were not just beyond God's boundaries but those which twist or change the function of a person, place, or object.

abomination

This is the Hebrew word *toeba* which means abhor, detest, loathe. Notice that Solomon is giving a value judgment on the certain behaviors that are selfish pursuits of desire.

blameless

This is the Hebrew word *tamim* which means complete, blameless, perfect. The idea here is one who makes "perfect" decisions. Notice that our culture has a hard time representing righteous behavior except by what it is not. It means to live in such a way as to not be blamable about anything. Some have taken that to mean that you don't do anything wrong but that only deals with the negative side of this. The idea is that you do a lot of things right. You make decisions that are not selfish but instead wise. You take actions that meet other people's needs and not just your own. You bring delight to God and those around you with your maturity, inclusion, and plans. This is the opposite of people who are perverse in their selfishness. They push the envelope of how to please themselves until it involves direct harm to others.

delight

This is the Hebrew word *rason* which means pleasure, delight, favor. The idea is that God is pleased and delighted with the actions of those who display positive righteousness. Those who are wise and loving are not just unblamable; they actually bring Him joy.

It is the same when parents watch their children loving their siblings or choosing the mature or wise thing over the selfish action. It is amazing how much joy we receive from watching our children make the right decisions even though their decision does not affect us. I am filled to overflowing when I watch my daughter love her sister. I can remember when I was building a playhouse for her and she came to me and said, "Dad, I think that my sister is going to get more use out of it than I will. Why don't you build it for her?" Her statement just filled me with joy. To watch her make a sacrifice for the good of her sister blessed me at a level that is hard to describe. It is this that takes place in the heart of God when we make the right decision rather than the selfish decisions that we are so prone to.

PROVERBS 11:21 - *Assuredly, the evil man will not go unpunished, but the descendants of the righteous will be delivered.*

At first the contrast that is mentioned here seems odd and misplaced. How do punishments and blessed descendants fit together? This is one of the understanding connections that Solomon does not want us to miss. Evil people will be punished in this life and/or in the life to come. This is an iron-clad connection. If one decides not to become immoral, then there are huge downstream benefits for our descendants. Solomon is helping us see that we are not making a decision between the gain of immorality and the lack of righteousness but the eventual punishment of the wicked and the blessed descendants of the righteous.

We are connected to our descendants. The choices that we make radically affect them whether we realize it or not. It is clear from history that when an individual decides to become immoral, he alters the choices that will be available for his children. It also increases the likelihood that they will choose the wrong path also. There is the classic illustration of descendants of Jonathan Edwards and an imprisoned thief alive in the same era. Jonathan Edwards produced, down through the generations, many righteous men and women who made a positive difference in their world. The thief produced a train of misery and human collateral down through the generations.

In one of the congregations that I served, one of the men who seemed righteous began embezzling from the church offerings. This allowed his family to live well above the standard of living that his job could provide. It took years, but eventually it was discovered and he went to prison. His daughter became a part of a greedy murder plot a decade later and is now in prison. Countless examples could be cited.

It is not just you that your choices are affecting. Your choices affect the spiritual, mental, emotional, physical, and relational choices of your progeny. It is the height of arrogance to believe your selfish, sinful choices only affect you. This is the mistake Adam made, and we are all now suffering under his delusional thinking.

evil man

This is the Hebrew word *ra* which means evil, distress, or bad. The idea is of malicious selfishness. When a person conspires to make another person lose so they can win, it is selfishness at a whole new level beyond just wanting yourself to win and doing everything in your power to make sure that it happens.

Evil is that which is beyond the boundaries of the Ten Commandments. Those behaviors – past no other gods, idols, swearing, no worship, rebellion, murder, adultery, stealing, lying, and scheming for another's goods – are malicious forms of selfishness that will take a great toll on those who pursue them and on the society around them.

Solomon is expecting that any forms of malicious selfishness will bring their own forms of punishment rather than blessings.

unpunished

This is Hebrew word *naqa* which means clear, innocent, free, cut off. The idea is one of innocence or unpunished future. The problem is that people who pursue evil see it as the shortcut to what they want. They bend the rules to gain what everyone wants, but they do not realize that they will not be innocent and without consequences in their life.

descendants

This is an interesting contrasting phrase because it promises benefit to the righteous man's descendants rather than predicting harm to them. The idea seems to be that one can expect that what you choose to do will have significant effect downstream. This is true whether your choices are maliciously selfish or not. I have heard countless stories of young women who watched their fathers look at the "Playboy" magazines admiringly and thought that this was their father's ideal of feminine beauty and achievement. They then moved down the road of "sexy" girl hoping to impress their father. They did not understand why he was so upset and restrictive when they were just living out the ideal that he was adoring. His choices to allow pornography changed the course of his daughter's life and untold heartaches with it.

righteous

The righteous person is the one who looks for God to get glory and for others to profit and themselves to gain all within the boundaries that God has laid down.

delivered

This is the Hebrew word *malat* which means save, escape, be delivered. People who do not cut corners or become maliciously selfish to get what they want will escape from the problems and traps of life. They will escape many problems that cause many others to stumble.

Evil people's greed for their own gain is what sucks them into a troubled spot. It sets up a series of consequences.

Are you facing the temptation to gain through cheating, lying, immorality, or violence? Don't do it. Punishment is assured and your choices now change the future for your children.

PROVERBS 11:22 - *As a ring of gold in a swine's snout so is a beautiful woman who lacks discretion.*

beautiful

This is the word *yapeh* which means fair, beautiful. This refers to outward appearance. The physical beauty of a woman is of high value.

Beauty is something of high value. It is, in this proverb, parallel to the ring of gold – something of value; something that one wants to bring close; something one wants to look at and possess. But then it is attached to something of incredible ugliness and distain. In the human case, it is the lack of discretion; in the animal parallel, it is the swine. Solomon is comparing a lack of discretion with the ugliness and emotional reaction to a swine.

Now both in our day and in Solomon's day people did not have this kind of strong reaction to a lack of discretion. This is why Solomon uses this word picture. He thinks we should. It is a great travesty of what is right in the world. We should not allow a person – any person – to grow up without discretion, or Solomon says it will turn that person into the most ugly, reviled thing in culture. Without discretion people become spiritually, emotionally, physically, and sociologically ugly.

swine

This is the Hebrew word *hazir* which means swine or boar. This was the symbolic unclean animal. Therefore Solomon chooses this animal that is the ultimate symbol of ugliness. It was spiritually ugly, physically ugly, and it liked to live in filth. In this culture there would be absolutely no conception of a pig as a pet. They were not even allowed to raise them as food. It was emotionally, mentally, spiritually, and physically reviled. So the mental picture that he is painting would be severe.

A completely ugly, reviled animal with a beautiful ornamental piece of jewelry with high value placed in its nose – this is the height of contrast.

discretion

This is the Hebrew word *taam* which means taste, discretion, discernment. This word is very interesting and is clearly the key to the understanding of the lesson in this proverb.

Since the root meaning is to taste and evaluate with the tongue, Solomon is saying that when a beautiful woman is impulsive and unwilling to evaluate the various things that she is being led into, it will render her despicable. She will ultimately be a joke. Her impulsiveness and unwillingness to evaluate will destroy her beauty and make it of no value. We have all witnessed this.

Solomon is saying that the high value of beauty must be coupled with that ability to make good judgments, or you will end up being reviled. If you are drawn to people because of their handsomeness and beauty but they have no ability to make good judgments about what they do, where they go, and who they are with, then they will become reviled. Beauty attracts flies just as it attracts productive bees. So a beautiful woman must have the ability to discern and to evaluate the who, the what, and the where or they will become a pig with a ring of gold.

Beauty is a given quality but discretion is a learned skill. Make sure your sons and daughters learn this or they will become a source of constant sorrow to you. We live in a culture that elevates folly and that tries to convince the most handsome, the most beautiful, and the most gifted to use these gifts for selfish pleasure and impulsive desires.

We must train our children to think. Where does this path go if I walk down it? What will be the typical result of taking drugs, of going to these parties, of cheating on my tests, etc?

The classic example of this verse is the movie and television industry that takes beautiful people and leads them down a destructive path in which almost all of them develop a drug and/or alcohol addiction and need therapists to recover from what they did in the early stages of their career. They become swine with a ring of gold because they did not evaluate where the road of fame was about to take them. Some have escaped this path and when they are interviewed, they always show a high degree of judgment, foresight, and critical thinking. They all talk about where they didn't want to end up. They usually had a mentor who helped them evaluate the choices before them. They also usually kept the Hollywood industry at arms-distance.

When you are handsome or beautiful, you will have options and opportunities that will come streaming towards you. You must evaluate them. Just because it is offered to you does not mean it is good. Just because it means a lot of money or fame or power does not mean that it is a healthy thing to do.

Don't become a swine with a ring of gold.

PROVERBS 11:23 - *The desire of the righteous is only good, but the expectation of the wicked is wrath.*

This whole chapter of the Proverbs has the theme of judgment day running through it. This is a very interesting theme that runs through this chapter, and we catch a unique glimpse of judgment day through the Proverbs.

The desire of the righteous is only good

They seek the benefit of others constantly, and they will receive benefit and blessing from God. What the righteous person wants is that others would be benefitted. This is what good is – the benefit of others. The righteous person loves God and loves others.

The hope of the wicked

What they can expect and what they will receive is wrath: the unrelenting presence of God's justice on their continuing and confirmed selfishness. It is the selfishness of sin that continues to twist them and renders them unusable.

Solomon is clearly telling us that you can tell the righteous from the wicked in that the righteous wants to benefit others – they want to have people beyond themselves gain. The wicked are only out for their own gain and usually expect to be caught at some point. They expect judgment. Make sure that you do not stray over to the wicked side of the fence by only wanting what allows you to win and forces others to lose. It is always easy to think of your own personal win, but you must ask if this allows others to win and God to get glory. If your best personal win does not cause others to win and God to get glory, then it may be wickedness.

PROVERBS 11:24 ~ *There is one who scatters, and yet increases all the more, and there is one who withholds what is justly due, and yet it results only in want.*

This proverb is one of a string of proverbs that deals with wealth. Solomon comes at this topic from a number of different angles. But he wants his students to understand what they must do when they actually acquire wealth. Too many people focus their attention so much on the acquiring that they do not know what to do if they attain it, or they never think they have attained it because there is always more.

scatters

This is the Hebrew word *pazar* which means to scatter. What is interesting here is that Solomon does not say what is scattered. He assumes that we will know what it is. The biggest clue is the two contrasting agents: more and want. One who scatters his wealth and one who hoards his wealth seem to be in view here.

withholds

This is the Hebrew word *chasak* which means to withhold, refrain, to hold back. Solomon is saying that those who use their wealth generously will have more wealth. Those who are hoarders and misers will have less wealth.

justly

This is the Hebrew word *yosher* which means straightness, uprightness. In this case it is clear that there is a certain generosity or sharing of one's wealth that is required of those who have been able to acquire it. One cannot shut their heart to the cry of the poor and afflicted. There is a just obligation to scatter parts of one's wealth to charities and things which will seemingly have no personal benefit to you. This is not a sound financial investment, but it is a wise soul and community investment. It allows you to be freed in your soul from the grip of money, and it allows your community to care for those who are disadvantaged.

want

This is the Hebrew word *machsor* which means a need, a poverty, a want. It doesn't say what the poverty is regarding. Solomon is saying that there are some people who do not recognize this community responsibility to share some portion of their wealth with others. They just want to hoard their money and make more. He says that this will create in this kind of person, want. Hoarding and not sharing one's accumulated wealth will not give you more but will create a hole in your soul and your life that will be incapable of being filled. This person may stuff all kinds of things and excessive practices into this hole, but it will not be filled up.

This is why those who are well adjusted with great wealth have a generous mindset and a service mindset. This is the only way to stay sane when the normal motive of feeding the family and getting by is taken away. One needs to have an internal driving motive that is not selfish. When the motive of feeding and caring for family is taken away, one needs to have other needs that drive one's daily life.

Do not just consume the wealth on yourself. Realize you have an obligation to share some portion of your wealth with others.

Do not develop a selfish focus on wealth as though that will solve all your problems. Selfish possession of money creates more problems.

PROVERBS 11:25 - *The generous man will be prosperous, and he who waters will himself be watered.*

generous

This is the Hebrew word *berakah* which is usually translated blessing, benefit, gift. The idea seems to be that this is a person who is full of blessings and is constantly blessing people. So the translators decided to use the word *generous* to convey this idea. This is okay, but it tends to suggest that the person gives away money rather than all types of blessings. There are emotional, spiritual, physical, mental, relational, financial, and many other kinds of blessings. It is the person who is looking to bless others that is being talked about here in this proverb.

man

This is the Hebrew word *nephesh* which means soul. This is the word for the invisible interior part of a person's life. It is your soul that you are trying to add to through the acquiring of wisdom. You are trying, as Moses says in Psalm 90, to present a soul full of wisdom to the Lord at the end of life.

In this case Solomon is saying that it is the person who is always ready to bless others in some way who will have the enlarged soul.

prosperous

This is the Hebrew word *dashen* which means to be fat or grow fat. The idea is that one has abundance or over what is needed. The way that the Hebrew mindset conveyed this was through being fat. The person who was overweight had abundance. In fact, in their culture this was a somewhat desirable thing. We see this idea expressed in the movie *Fiddler of on the Roof* when the main character sings that he dreams about having a proper double chin.

Remember that this is not being applied only to the physical body but metaphorically to the whole of life through the application to the soul. You want a fat soul, laden with wisdom and blessings to give away. The more you give away blessings to others, the more your soul will be enlarged and prosper.

The danger with this translation of the proverb is that it makes it seem to be about money and financial areas. This is, however, not what it is about. It is about becoming a better person with an outward focus towards others and seeking to meet the needs of others. This verse is a different way of saying what Jesus said when he said, "Thou shalt love thy neighbor as thyself." Giving a blessing is looking for a need, an encouragement, or a want that you can give to another person. It is an outward focus rather than a selfish one.

waters

This is the Hebrew word *ravah* which means to be saturated or drink one's fill, to drench, satisfy. The idea is the same as the first phrase in this proverb but spoken from a different angle. If you seek to satisfy the needs and concerns in others, you will increase the needs that are met in your life.

This outward focus is the way life works. Let me add what is not spoken in this proverb. This is a general rule of thumb. There are people who, no matter how much you meet their needs, their selfish leech-like parasitic thinking knows no end. These people are the exception to these verses and will suck you dry if you try and fill them up. They have psychological dysfunctions that do not allow them to live out the truths of this verse. They would have you give and give until you disrespect yourself in the amount you give to them. Do not do this. Their behavior is covered by other proverbs. I say that so that you do not think that this verse is not true because you found a person in your life where it does not work. It works as a general rule, but there are people who are so self-focused and/or damaged that they are an exception to this verse because of their selfishness or victimization.

PROVERBS 11:26 - *He who withholds grain, the people will curse him, but blessing will be on the head of him who sells it.*

This language is strange to us but Solomon is talking about the common business practice of creating shortages in order to drive up prices. In Solomon's day the crops of wheat and corn were usually the commodity which farmers would hold back to make it more scarce, especially during times of high demand.

Solomon is instructing those who would be wise that when they are in a situation to exploit a shortage even more than it is so that prices can be driven upwards, this will be perceived as price gouging and corruption – even if it is legal. People will curse you for your business acumen. They will not celebrate how smart and clever you are. They will see that you took advantage of a crisis of some kind to drive profits.

Now what is interesting is not that he says it is wrong; he doesn't. He says it is stupid. It is the way to permanently damage your reputation. Yes, you can make a lot of money; but you will alienate a lot of people.

This principle carries over to a lot of different relationships:

- When a spouse withholds what the other spouse needs; such as, respect, intimacy, conversation, companionship, etc., so that the other person is more pliable to your way of thinking.

- When a Christian suggests that they will withhold giving to their church until things get straightened out.

- When a person withholds what another person needs at work in order to make their contribution to the project more visible or more valuable.

Be very careful, Solomon says, that you are not reputationly stupid. Yes, lots of things are personally profitable, but they are relationally ignorant.

Do not withhold a good from someone when it is in your power to do so.

PROVERBS 11:27 - *He who diligently seeks good seeks favor, but he who seeks evil, evil will come to him.*

If you go looking for evil, then it will come upon you. This is the message but there is a deeper more subtle meaning. If you keep allowing yourself to be tempted by that which is outside of the moral box of God, then all kinds of evil that you cannot imagine will attach to you and come upon you. You will get far more than you can possibly imagine. The definition of evil in the Scripture is much different than our definition of evil. We seem to understand by evil that which is violent, radically deceptive, and morally reprehensible. God, however, sees evil as anything outside His Ten Commandments box which prescribes the boundaries of loving God and loving others. When we pass His moral boundaries, then we are pursuing evil and doing it. There are far more consequences than we can possibly imagine.

The opposite of seeking evil is diligently seeking good – that which is morally good. This is the heart of the first and second great commandments: *You shall love the Lord your God with all your heart, and with all your soul, and with all your mind. You shall love your neighbor as yourself.*

When you seek what is good, you seek the delight of God. To be delighted with God and to delight God is the highest moral good. This type of activity is the way to beat back the pull of temptation. If you are seeking the good, you are not and cannot be seeking evil. While it does not say it in this proverb, the consequences of seeking the good is also far more than one can envision when the pursuit began.

PROVERBS 11:28 - *He who trusts in his riches will fall, but the righteous will flourish like the green leaf.*

This is a very interesting agricultural comparison: the leaf that trusts in how big and full it is versus the leaf that still is drawing off the nutrients of the root. Solomon is painting the picture of the leaf at the end of the summer: proud in how big, full, and self-contained it is. It does not need to draw any more off the branch or the root. It trusts in itself. That leaf is in the early stages of death and will fall soon. This is like the rich person who trusts in how wealthy they are, how much they have planned for the future, and how they have insurance to cover everything. They no longer are openly dependent upon God, but they are self-contained. Just like the leaf at the end of the summer that no longer draws off the branch and the root, so this person and family will fall.

On the other side, the righteous person who realizes how dependent they are on God and those whom God has placed around them is like the leaf in the spring which keeps drawing nutrients from the branch and the root and thereby grows and flourishes. Solomon may even be making a comparison between the trees that lose their leaves and the evergreen. The person who has a dependent attitude on God is like the evergreen which keeps growing and flourishing because there are always more people to serve and minister to.

Which are you? Are you self-contained and pretty proud of what you have obtained? Are you dependent upon God, waiting for who He will have you bless or love today? It doesn't matter how much you have; it matters how much you are willing to help.

PROVERBS 11:29 - *He who troubles his own house will inherit wind, and the foolish will be servant to the wise hearted.*

The key here is to understand this as talking about changing the family legacy. Each person can change their family legacy by their actions. If they invite sin to be a part of their lives, they create a sinful stream in their lives. If they act out of the obedience of faith to be loving and generous and giving, they will also create a legacy.

When you trouble your own house, you change the destiny of the people who come after you. This proverb reminds us that the decisions that we make do not only affect us, they affect all of our progeny: our children, grandchildren, and great-grandchildren. It is so easy to be in the pursuit of selfishness and forget that we are troubling our children when we do.

You turn what could be kings into servants. Be careful what you choose and pursue; it could change everything.

PROVERBS 11:30 ~ *The fruit of the righteous is a tree of life, and he who is wise wins souls.*

fruit of righteousness

This means the results of righteous living. Also, in Hebrew, understanding of the biblical era fruit was the sweetest thing one could have other than honey. To be enjoying fruit meant that one was having dessert. One was rewarded for their perseverance, work, and patience.

tree of life

The Hebrew understanding of the tree of life was that which prolonged life, sustained it, and gave it a quality of existence that was beyond mere biological existence.

In this case the fruit of the righteous life is not just a dessert or extra element but instead what sustains life and allows it to be life beyond just biology.

Solomon is saying that the positive way of living that is righteousness produces a kind and quality of life. Do you want to have a higher quality of life, give up on the selfish route, and instead find ways to be a positive benefit into the lives of those around you so that they expect good and not evil from you?

Remember life is relationships.

No matter how much you possess, if you do not have close people to share with, then your victories are hollow. Life is lived at a higher plain with soul-to-soul contact and connection.

wise

This is the person who applies knowlege in a way that is mutually beneficial to others, yourself, and glorifying to God – the person who is not after their own selfish ends but the good of the family, the good of the society, the good of the business, the glory of God.

wins

This is the Hebrew word *laqach* which means to take, to accept, to capture, to seize, to win.

Solomon is giving us the clue that we should focus on the person's soul and not their body or material possessions. The person who focuses on connecting and influencing the soul – which is the real person – is the wise person who has a much easier time in life.

souls

This is the Hebrew word *nephesh* which means soul, living being. It is what happened when God breathed into Adam and he became a living soul. The soul is the inner part of the person – the real you which is the collection of your experiences, education, skills, etc., and the software that is you running on the hardware called your body.

The fool tries to win bodies through power, authority, seduction, deception, and the like. But the wise person tries to capture the soul of the person for the project and the relationship.

Have you been focusing on getting people to do what you want instead of winning their soul to your way of thinking?

PROVERBS 11:31 - *If the righteous will be rewarded in the earth, how much more the wicked and the sinner.*

This proverb maintains the basic principle of cause and effect in this world. Galatians 6:7 says it this way: *Do not be deceived, God is not mocked; for whatever a man sows, this he will also reap.*

Solomon is stating that those who live within the boundaries of the Ten Commandments and seek to fill their lives with love by filling other people's lives with love will be rewarded for that behavior in this world. He also maintains that those who choose to go outside of the boundaries of the Ten Commandments to achieve the victories and rewards of the righteous will be "rewarded" for their actions also.

What typically seems to happen is that the wicked become involved in a game of diminishing returns. The more they achieve, the less they can enjoy the spoils that they seek. There is an emotional, spiritual, mental, and often physical deprivation. On the other hand, the righteous who seek to fill their lives and others with love are filled to overflowing with rewards. Their little is made much by God while the much of the wicked is made little by God.

Jesus said it this way: "What does it profit a man if he gains the whole world but loses his soul?" The answer is that the immaterial deprivation is greater than any material gain!!!

Yes, it may look like the criminals and oppressors have all the material rewards, but they will be and are being rewarded for the means that they used to obtain those material gains.

Solomon, Jesus, and Paul all remind us that it is worth it to be righteous. It pays to love God with a whole heart and others as ourselves. A life filled with love has a reward deeper and richer than the latest technology or gold-plated toilet seat.

Proverbs 12

PROVERBS 12:1 - *Whoever loves discipline loves knowledge, but he who hates reproof is stupid.*

How much do you love to learn new ways to improve? How much correction can you stand? Do you really want to get better at your job, parenting, marriage, and living for God? Then you must be willing to be corrected so you can make progress in those areas.

It is not possible to make progress without change and realizing that there is a better way.

There are an awful lot of people who want better marriages, families, careers, and connections with God. They just don't want to change anything. If they are willing to change something, they are willing to add something. But they are often unwilling to eliminate anything. We act as though maybe we aren't doing something we should but never that we are right now doing something we shouldn't.

This proverb says that whoever really loves knowledge also loves correction, rebuke, chastisement, and instruction in the proper way. It is the willingness to be corrected that tests our real love of knowledge.

whoever loves discipline loves knowledge

The Hebrew word translated *discipline* here in the NASB is the word *musawr* which means instruction, correction, chastisement, rebuke. In this context it seems to carry with it the idea of contrary information because of the parallel idea given in the second half of the proverb: *but he who hates reproof is stupid.*

In other words, the person who really wants to display that they are interested in knowledge and not just getting their own way will be open to contrary knowledge - knowledge that is a rebuke to the way that you have been living; knowledge that means you must change.

Think of instruction as feedback. All of us use and enjoy feedback. When we drive and turn the steering wheel, we need the feedback of where the car actually goes to give us feedback and what to do with the steering wheel next. When we are trying to convince someone of something or sell them something, we need the feedback of what they are thinking about what we are saying. Without the feedback, we will keep doing what we think is right even though it gets no results. There are all kinds of feedback experiments where people have been hooked up to monitors and they get to see how their stomach responds to particular stresses and thoughts. People have learned how to overcome their fears and the like.

PROVERBS 12:2 - A good man will obtain favor from the Lord, but He will condemn a man who devises evil.

This proverb is the essence of moral living, but it also hints at at least one of the problems of viewing moral living from a foolish perspective.

This proverb says that the person who does the good thing – the morally helpful thing and not just abstaining from the selfish and/or morally reprehensible thing – will receive favor, blessing, and grace from God. At the same time, the person who plots and schemes to accomplish selfish and sinful ends will be guilty and receive a compensation or consequence because of it.

One needs to spend some time thinking about the idea of goodness. This is the opposite of evil. Evil and wickedness in the Old Testament is behavior that is beyond the Ten Commandments; therefore, stealing, lying, adultery, blasphemy, idolatry, rebellion, murder, coveting others property are all forms of wickedness. Much of morality has been discussed and framed as stopping before one commits these violations of the Ten Commandments. That is true but it is not being good. Good is a positive, not the absence of a negative.

One could make a case for the boundaries of morality being in the place they are because it is at that point when the selfishness-track that the person is on begins to do significant societal damage. The actions that are being perpetrated at that morality point are now going to collect damage and difficulty to the person and others at a point where it begins to destabilize the individual's life and the peace and security of the society at large.

Goodness is doing the opposite of the negative and, thereby, benefiting society and another person. Being good or doing good is worshipping God and putting Him first. Goodness is speaking blessings into others' lives. It is adding value to authorities rather than rebelling. It is meeting the needs of others rather than being angry and violent. It is developing a strong and loving marriage rather than being selfish and unfaithful. It is being generous and charitable rather than stealing. It is being truthful instead of lying. It is being content rather than covetous of others' blessings.

We must make sure that we do not begin to define being a good person as one who didn't do really bad stuff or being a nice person. That is not a biblical definition. Goodness is doing really good stuff. This means that we need to set out each day to do positive things into the lives of the people that we meet that day. I am amazed at how many well-meaning Christians never escape thinking about themselves every day. They somehow have not gotten this idea of being good – doing something positive and need-meeting into the lives of people. They believe that if they are nice and not overtly evil or selfish that this somehow is okay and good. It is not; especially for the person making a claim to godliness.

Pour into the lives of the people and relationships of your life positive, helpful, need-meeting activities, words, and attitudes so that people will know you as a biblically good person.

One must also realize that this is not good in the ultimate sense as God is good. That would require perfection in goodness. No one but God has that level of goodness and because of that, no one but Jesus Christ has ever earned a place in God's presence with their life.

One of the hints or subtle truths of this verse is how long it takes for the favor of the Lord to show up. This is not talked about in this verse directly but think through the process of goodness and foolishness. The fool is one who lives for self and immediate gratification. They want what they want right now with no waiting. If they do not personally see a benefit to an action immediately, they will rarely do it. This is the opposite of the person of wisdom. They are motivated not by self but to glorify God. They are able to be patient and wait for the personal benefits that come from righteousness and goodness. Because of how the wise person and the fool approach benefits and results, it is obvious that the favor that the good person receives will not come as a candy motivation to keep doing good things. Instead, the favor the Lord bestows on those who do good and slowly builds up and envelops the good person. They may not even be able to point to specific benefits as to why they came; they just surround the good person. For while God rewards those who live righteously, it is not a Pavlovian reward but instead a higher more patient benefit.

In other words, realize that the benefits of the good actions you perform will come to you over time and by the hand of a good and benevolent God who knows how to reward those who seek Him. Do not do something good and then look heavenward for where the candy reward will fall.

PROVERBS 12:3 - *A man will not be established by wickedness, but the root of the righteous will not be moved.*

What an encouraging insight. It seems in our day and age that any business can go out of business; that no one's pension is secure; that no one's marriage is safe; that even one's convictions can come under assault.

But this proverb declares that one never really built a lasting enterprise on the violation of God's law or basic selfishness. Understand that wickedness is living outside of the Ten Commandments. Solomon is stating a truth that many do not think about: You may go outside of God's moral boundary structure to establish your life, but it will not lead to much for your family, your legacy, and the society as a whole. The gaining by wickedness is a short-term proposition.

All of us would like our lives to have a lasting impact and count for something way past when we are alive. This is possible when your life is built on righteousness. This is how you build a lasting legacy. It is not quick nor necessarily fancy, but it is an unmovable root. You bless generations when you begin today to be righteous.

Too often we do not think about what we are doing to ourselves ten years from now; our children or grandchildren twenty years from now; or society thirty-plus years from now. But we need to do this kind of thinking. When anyone voluntarily lives within the boundary structure of the Ten Commandments, they begin at that point to establish a righteous root and develop a legacy.

It is your decision. Are you going to start a legacy today by living by God's grace righteously or are you going to continue making the same selfish choices that you have been making – living largely only for yourself at the present time. Only thinking about today is a fool's choice. Be righteous.

PROVERBS 12:4 - *An excellent wife is the crown of her husband, but she who shames him is like rottenness in his bones.*

This verse deals with a forgotten subject in today's Christianity – the conduct of wives and its effect on their husbands. There are actions of a wife that can mightily bless or curse her husband.

The word *excellent* is the Hebrew *hayil* which means mighty, powerful, able, virtuous. It has been translated *excellent* in the NASB. The word moves in the direction of virtue or moral mightiness – the actions of virtue and moral excellence that a wife can do to bring great honor and respect to the husband. If she searches for the positives in her husband and takes the morally high road in her interactions with people, this brings a whole new glow to his life.

We can understand the word excellent or virtuous also by seeing its results and contrasts in this verse.

The proverb is very interesting in that it intimates results and contrasts ideas that we would not.

crown of her husband

A wife's virtue causes a crown to be placed on her husband's life. Look at the possible implications or definitions of this crown on her husband's life: to potentially have more authority in his dealings with others, to carry a beauty and wonder not normally associated with that man, to adorn him.

These results would suggest that the word excellent or virtuous has to do with what she does to her husband directly and what she does to and for others.

shames him

One would not normally suggest that moral virtue is the opposite of shaming a person. But in this verse, this is the contrast. It means that Scripture feels that if a person is honest and trustworthy but shames others with their speech and conduct, then they are not a virtuous person.

Unfortunately, one of the regular habits of many wives is rehearsing all the bad, stupid, or ridiculous tendencies in their husbands. This expose' of his faults clearly comes under the title of shaming her husband, and it means he is viewed with suspicion by others. She has been sucked into the temptation to gossip and even slander. These are serious errors and undermine the type of marriage that she wants.

rottenness in his bones

This is an unseen disease. He remains largely unaware that his reputation and standing in the community is largely being corrupted by his wife's lack of virtue. She has crossed the line into gossip and slander. He pays the price through a diminished capacity to reach his full potential.

This means that virtue and moral excellence in a wife turns away from gossip and slander opportunities, especially when they involve intimate, negative details about her husband. It also means that a virtuous and morally excellent wife focuses on the positive, on building up her husband, on openly admiring her husband, and on steering clear of those who would engage in slam sessions on their husbands.

PROVERBS 12:5 - *The thoughts of the righteous are just, but the counsels of the wicked are deceitful.*

The word *thoughts* is the Hebrew word *hissabon* which means ideas, new thoughts. It largely has to do with using the mind to create something new.

The word translated *just* in this passage is *mispat* which means justice, judgment, ordinance. It carries with it the idea of practical application of right, holy, and good. It is also often used of a governmental function in which decisions must be rendered or judging between people or between competing interests.

Clearly this proverb tells us what the various kinds of people think about.

The righteous people think about how to make sure that the right decisions are made. How new ways of doing the right thing can be invented. How to make sure that that which is right is done rather than what is wrong. How to make sure that injustice does not win.

What is interesting is that this tells us about what righteous people think about; how more righteousness can be spread. The things that wicked people think about are deceptive.

The word translated *deceit* in this verse is the word *mirma* in the Hebrew which means deceit, treachery, fraud, swindle. It is used of a plan in which someone is clearly being defrauded or stolen from in a deceptive or secretive way. In other words, how to get away with something so that nobody even knows that something has been done. This is different from stealing in that the person or organization is to never know that anything was done. It is hidden.

What do you spend your time thinking about: How to make sure that your boss doesn't find out what you are doing? How to make sure that your spouse is not aware of how you are spending your time? How to hide your income from the IRS?

The question in this proverb is what do you spend your time thinking about or planning. This will tell you whether you are becoming a wicked person and/or whether you are interacting with a wicked or a righteous person.

All of us can move from thinking about promoting righteous things to hiding wicked activities. Emphasize the former and you will become a more righteous person.

One of the troubles in our world is that we do not have a clear picture of what righteousness is all about. One needs to think about two things: what is right and relationships. To promote righteousness one needs to promote that which is right for people. If you were to begin to think more righteously, you would begin to think about how you could draw closer to God and please Him. You would begin to think about how you could strengthen your marriage. You would spend some time thinking about how to connect with your family – parents, children, relatives, etc. You would think about how to promote positive and helpful interaction with people at church. You would think about making the workplace a more relationally positive place with less back-stabbing and gossip. You would spend time thinking about how to promote peace, safety, and security in the community and country. What we have to realize is that when people promote positive interaction between people, they are performing a righteous act. Righteousness involves people and what is done to people.

If you are not careful, you can find yourself thinking about how to become deceitful rather than how to promote righteousness. It is easy to fall into thinking only about yourself and how to promote your interests.

PROVERBS 12:6 - *The words of the wicked lie in wait for blood, but the mouth of the upright will deliver them.*

words

This is the Hebrew word *dabar* which means words or speech or speaking. The idea here is that Solomon says that the intent of the person who is wicked is for someone to lose, to be hurt. One of the characteristics of wickedness is that this person gains through the loss of others. It is the win-lose way of negotiating and living.

Remember that the wicked person – according to the Old Testament – is one who lives outside of the Ten Commandments as a way of life. Lying is okay if it gets you what you want; stealing is okay as long as you get what you want; intimidation, physical violence – even murder – is okay as long as you get what you want; pretending to worship other gods is okay as long as you get what you want; sexual unfaithfulness is okay as long as you get what you want; planning and plotting how to take other people's possessions is okay as long as you win; open rebellion against authority is okay as long as you are living the life you really want. All of these are the components of a wicked life.

This is why Solomon says that underneath the speech of the wicked person is a motive for them to win and you to lose. In their mind there is no looking for the win-win; they only focus on gain through other's loss.

The wicked use words to their advantage to get what they want; there are no boundaries to how they use words. They use them to serve their purposes and do harm to their opponents and others who have what they want.

Notice how carefully God says that the righteous person needs to be with what they say. The wicked person is trying to trip you up through their words or using your words. The righteous person will be delivered through their constant focus on what is right and good for everyone.

The righteous person will not participate in the schemes of the wicked. As soon as it becomes apparent that a plan is designed to rob others of their gains or possessions, then the righteous person is out. It doesn't matter how much the profit is or how easy it is or that someone else will just get the profit or gain. It matters that the gain comes by making other people hurt or wounded or lose.

When you are with a person, what do their words tell you as you read between the lines? Are they out for themselves? Are they twisting their words so that they profit while others lose? Is it clear that their intent is to hurt another or make them lose? This is a signal that you are dealing with a wicked person even though they may be a relative or close friend or respected person. If their words belie a waiting for blood, then the person is beyond the boundary of acceptable behavior in God's eyes. They are living a wicked life in some area or areas of their life.

You need to be extra careful with what you say and make sure you are looking for the triple-win. Does what you want to do really benefit the other person as well as you?

PROVERBS 12:7 - *The wicked are overthrown and are no more, but the house of the righteous will stand.*

The principle that Solomon is trying to establish is that the wicked are always looking over their shoulder to see if the justice that they are due has arrived. Wickedness is profitable in the short term, but it is not secure. Wickedness is taking shortcuts outside of God's moral boundary structure to gain abundance. You steal, you lie, you commit adultery, you covet, and you use violence and intimidation in order to get what you want. Taking moral shortcuts to the good life may produce some of the prosperity and pleasure that you are looking for, but there is a continuing element of uncertainty. When will "they" find out? When will I be cheated like I cheated others? If there is a God, then I am in big trouble.

Solomon wants us to build our lives on a safe and stable platform and that is righteousness or actions that are within the moral boundaries of the Ten Commandments. Yes, I know that it is not possible for anyone to keep the Ten Commandments perfectly and earn their way into heaven, but the moral boundaries of the Ten Commandments are the basis of righteousness between people. It is this moral high ground that will be safe and stable for the development of a great life without concern that it will all be taken away in an instant.

Solomon is saying that when the wicked are overthrown because of their wickedness, they are no more. There is nothing with which to rebuild. The obvious case in our day and age is Bernie Madoff, who swindled people out of 50 billion dollars of investments, and when it came crashing down has nothing for his family and his heirs. He said he knew it would happen one day and was just waiting until they came and got him. It took much longer than he expected because others were duplicitous in his wickedness, but his day of reckoning came and it will not be rebuilt.

Don't be like those whom Jesus says build their life upon the shifting sands of deception, stealing, anger, violence, and pride. Instead be among those who build their life on honesty, love, integrity, and diligence. Embrace the grace of Christ and your need for His mercy. Start living a life of integrity in which you have nothing to hide.

Who has the responsibility of overthrowing the wicked? Is it God alone or do individuals, institutions, and leaders have the responsibility to echo God's action in this?

Another principle lying dormant in this verse is the principle of the overthrow of the wicked and who is supposed to do it. There has been a fundamental misunderstanding over how the wicked are to be overthrown in this world. Many people believe that it is God's job to do it and for man to stand back and watch it happen. But clearly by what God says in Genesis 9:6 *Anyone who sheds man's blood by man shall his blood be shed!* is that He has delegated the majority of justice to mankind to police itself. It is when men and women look the other way at evil that wickedness is allowed to flourish.

There are a number of cynics, skeptics, and critics of Christianity and religion in general who ask questions about the goodness of God and the evil in the world. What they usually mean is the evil that humanity does to itself in various governments and spots around the world. They have the belief that if there was a good and powerful God that He would automatically put a stop to people doing evil to one another. But it escapes their purview that God has delegated much of this function to men themselves. He wants us to seek justice, to love mercy, and to walk in humbleness before our God. He is proving to us that we are not the gods that we think we are. He is proving that our confident superiority is not superior at all. He is giving us the freedom to destroy ourselves. We are commissioned with taking the blueprints that He has given us and what resides in our conscience to draw moral boundaries for the whole of the society, not just for ourselves.

I can remember when my father helped me see this truth. He was offered an opportunity to get a really good deal on some things that he had been looking for at a swap meet. He refused. I remember his telling me that he refused because he discovered that the items that were discounted were stolen items. The good deal was because the seller had ripped them off. He told me that if he had purchased the items, then he would be creating a demand for stolen items. He was aware that the price was attractive and he would have personally benefitted by this offer, but he would have created another level of demand for stolen merchandise. He had to look out for not just what was good for him but what was good for the whole of the society. We face this dilemma regularly. We can personally profit by going outside some moral boundary, but we encourage a consequence that we don't want in which others we don't know will be harmed or damaged.

In our day we are seeing a new level of human trafficking for sexual activity. This is universally deplored for the oppression, slavery, violence, emotional damage, and imprisonment involved; but most are unwilling to understand that when we encourage adultery in any of its seven unbiblical forms, we increase the demand for sexual activity which will encourage human trafficking. The Christian is not just against one form of adultery but all forms because it will end up in the enslavement of women and children for sexual purposes. It is on us as a society to draw the moral boundaries where they go and where a society is sustainable. If we encourage stealing, adultery, and lying, then we should not be surprised that we have a significant level of wickedness living all around us. We must seek good government that will move in the direction of justice for the poor, oppressed, and afflicted – not just the wealthy and influential.

PROVERBS 12:8 - *A man will be praised according to his insight, but one of perverse mind will be despised.*

The word *insight* is the Hebrew word *sekel* which means understanding. This is almost synonymous with the word *bin* which means to distinguish between and, therefore, to discern connections. This word also carries with it a penetrating analysis of the reasons a thing happened or was successful. This is the reason why the translators used the word *insight* to translate the word rather than understanding.

The word *praised* is the word *halal* which means to shine. This is the word we get our word hallelujah. When we sing praises to God, we make Him shine. When we use penetrating analysis to reveal the real reasons something took place or will take place, then we shine in the eyes of others.

The implications are significant. If we regularly do not have an answer for why someone would do this or that, then we do not shine. If we regularly give the wrong reasons or ridiculous or conspiracy type of reasons for the things that happen, we do not shine.

Each of us must try and make sense of the things that happen around us. Each of us must try and understand the reasons for why a particular thing happened to us or did not happen to us. We must come to some conclusions about why our life is the way it is. Too many people come to the wrong conclusions. They do not have the kind of insight that is mentioned here.

I watch people – who did not get the promotion or who did not get the sale or who did not get the girlfriend – refuse to look penetratingly at themselves and their behaviors for the reason. They would rather blame someone else or something else. Do not do this. Most of the time the penetrating analysis should begin and end with your own actions, attitudes, and speech.

There is another place I am watching the abandonment of the type of insight or understanding talked about here. In the political or social arena people are beginning to embrace fanciful or conspiracy theories about why tragedies and disasters take place. One of the difficulties about this is that everybody has different theories that fit their own prejudices. Do not fall for "Elvis is still alive and being hidden by the CIA" thinking. Penetrate the nonsense with sound reasons. Just because a person can ask some questions about a grainy photo or a coincidence does not mean that they have found a conspiracy. This does not mean that there are not conspiracies, but there must be hard evidence. Some people have allowed their whole lives to be changed by these types of bizarre theories about why a thing happened or who is out to get us.

Getting back to a more practical application of this idea is to think through: Why do our children act the way they do? There are reasons. Why do the people at work act the way they do around and to us? Why is our business doing good or bad? Why is our marriage or dating life in the state that it is? Why do we feel close or far away from God? Why don't we have enough money? All of these questions about our life have answers. Our willingness to really look for the answers and penetrate beneath the surface will allow us to win at life and shine.

Let me give you an example or two: My wife and I found, some time ago, that we were running low on money regularly. When we looked at what was actually happening, we were letting it slip through our fingers on little items that we did not even notice that we were buying. When we analyzed these patterns and put some control into this miscellaneous area, our finances changed dramatically for the better.

I have counseled enough marriages that have been about to split up to realize that many people just expect their relationship with their spouse to be good without any changes or work on their part. I have watched men and women act very selfishly and then be amazed that their spouse is upset. I have watched one or both spouses ignore the needs of the other and wonder what they are so upset about. If your marriage is not as enjoyable as it could be, then there are reasons. It usually means one or both of the partners is not meeting the needs of the other. It also usually means one or both parties are being selfish. It is your job to analyze and find the reasons and fix them. Do not just assume that everybody has these problems and it is the way it is or even worse and that it is time to get a new spouse.

but one of perverse mind will be despised

The word *perverse* is the Hebrew word *awa* which means twisted, warping, and is one of the words for iniquity. The word perverse is used to translate this idea because taking something good or normal and twisting its purpose or its use – especially in the moral sense – is what is connoted here.

Solomon is telling us that some people use a twisted analysis of the situation to recommend twisted solutions. Some marriage counselors recommend that couples view pornography to help their marriage; this is twisted. Some people come to the conclusion that they need a new spouse rather than working on their present marriage. Some people come to the conclusion that they need to hurt or kill or maim the people in their place of employment to make their point. Some teens come to the conclusion that the best way to really make it in life is to ignore all advice from the people who love them and make their life possible and instead listen to peers who are making nothing of their own lives.

Your analysis of why life is the way it is will either bring a level of glory and adulation to you or it will cause you to be despised. All of us have to analyze our life in at least nine areas – the nine relationships of life. If we are able to accurately figure out what is really happening in these areas of life and make them better, we will be praised.

Let's take a look at that in detail. We have to analyze whether our personal life is on track to accomplish the goals that we believe God wants for us and change the direction if it is not. We need to analyze our marriage and perceive whether it is where it should be or could be and what changes to make. We need to look at our family life and explore how we got here and how to make it better. We need to examine our career and employment situations to see if these are where they could or should be and what recommended changes are needed. We need to examine our church and our interaction with it. We need to look at our finances and see if we are accomplishing what we should in this area. We need to look at our friendships and see if we have the type, kind, and number of friendships that we would like to have or need.

Notice that this twisted analysis is with the same set of facts that insightful analysis comes from.

How insightful are you in analyzing the real reasons that something took place and then acting accordingly? If your analysis and actions do not change the circumstances, then you may need to rethink your analysis.

PROVERBS 12:9 - *Better is he who is lightly esteemed and has a servant than he who honors himself and lacks bread.*

This is one of the classic comparisons that Solomon sprinkles into the Proverbs for us to ponder. Every time he does this, it is to cause us to say "Really? I would not have thought that!"

The issue here is should you go around telling people all of the good things that you have accomplished or should you do good things, letting people find out about them on their own.

There is something inside us that wants to trumpet our good stuff; but when we do, it makes us come off like a pompous carnival barker. Most of us have found ourselves telling others about something we did that we thought would make us look good, and it just came out making us look like a fool. Solomon is telling us that there is an appropriate time for people to hear about the good things you did.

He is also making a contrast between someone who actually accomplishes something and one who just says that he does. Notice the *has a servant and lacks bread* contrast. In our cultural mindset, the person who has a servant is someone who has enough business taking place to have an employee. This is a measure of the person's business success. In that day it was common for the whole family to be engaged in the family business to keep food on the table. When a person was doing well enough with their family business that they needed and were able to sustain a servant to help them, it was a subtle measure of how well the family business was doing.

Notice that the person who is actually growing his business enough to need a servant to help, but doesn't brag about how well things are going, is the more valuable person than the person who keeps proclaiming how well he is doing or how valuable he is but they do not have enough food to eat.

In our day there are people who buy cars they cannot afford, houses they can't afford, and clothing they can't afford in order to look more successful than they really are – all the while putting themselves in debt to the point where they can't pay their bills and in some cases put food on the table.

Bread is, here, both a reference to what you eat but also the basic necessities. So Solomon is pointing out a phenomenon that we see in our day where people make themselves look valuable and successful through debt but really cannot meet their basic obligations.

In the fascinating book, *The Millionaire Next Door*, the authors explore this idea. The person who really has a million dollars in the bank rarely shows it off and lives frugally in a house far below what they could afford. They drive cars that are "lightly esteemed" even when they could buy status cars.

Solomon is accurately pointing out to us which path is the clearly better one. It is the one where you are actually successful but do not trumpet your success through clothes, cars, homes, speech, lifestyle but instead live a life of quiet humility, all the while continuing to do good and be successful.

PROVERBS 12:10 - *A righteous man has regard for the life of his animal, but even the compassion of the wicked is cruel.*

One of the distinguishing characteristics of those who are righteous and those who are wicked is how they treat the surrounding environment: animals, plants, air, etc. The wicked has a disregard for anything except what directly serves him.

righteous

This is the common Hebrew term for righteousness – *sedaqa* – which means to be in line with what is right; to do justice; to be straight. This is the person who is inside the boundaries of the Ten Commandments and the program of God. Since it is not possible for a person to live their whole life inside of the Ten Commandments and never sin, God has made provision for forgiveness. In the Old Testament it was the sacrificial system which looked forward to the ultimate sacrifice: the Lamb of God, Jesus Christ, who lived the perfect life and then gave up His life so that as many as believed in Him could be forgiven of their sins. So the truly righteous in our time are those who live within the boundaries of the Ten Commandments as a course of life and trust the death of Christ to bring forgiveness to them for their sins and selfishness.

regard

This is the Hebrew word *yada* which means to know. It suggests that Solomon is saying that the righteous person is really aware of the needs of his animals; he is not just using them up for his own purposes. Since there is life there, he respects that.

life

This is the Hebrew word *nephesh* which means life, soul, or even personality. It is regularly repeated in the Old Testament that certain levels of beasts have a life. They are not just alive but they have a life. The righteous person is aware of that. This distinction is usually what causes people to make pets out of certain types of animals; the fact that they have personality. They seem to have a soul and can respond to their owners. The righteous person does not just use the beasts for his own purposes but is aware of the personality and even needs of the beasts that he employs. They are not just tools to be used and then discarded.

The prime example of the contrast in this verse in our modern era is Adolf Hitler. He treated even humans as nothing more than consumable parts for his own ends. He and his henchmen calculated how much work they could get out of people with how much food and when these people would break down. They actually calculated how to get the maximum work for the minimum food before the person broke down or had to be killed. This same type of thinking takes place with the wicked in terms of their animals.

animal

This is the Hebrew word *behema* which means beast, animal, or cattle. Now it is important to realize that in the ancient world a person's animals were not pets but were their equipment for commerce. Animals were the tools for their ability to earn a living. Therefore, Solomon is watching how a different type of people treat the engines of commerce. He makes the observation that those who are wicked, even their compassion is cruel.

compassion

This is the Hebrew word *raham* which means to love deeply, to have pity or mercy, to be caring and compassionate.

cruel

This is the Hebrew word *'akzar* which means fierce or cruel. It is equated to wrath in Proverbs 27:4. This is interesting in that the wicked person's compassion is equated with cruelty and fierceness. This may mean that the wicked person does not take the time to really know the animal. He just becomes aware that they are broken down or in some way incapacitated and puts them out of their misery (he thinks) by killing the animal.

PROVERBS 12:11 ~ *He who tills his land will have plenty of bread, but he who pursues worthless things lacks sense.*

One of the things that Solomon continues to hammer home to us is that we must continue to be diligent. If we do not learn to work hard, then wisdom will be of no good to us. We must be willing to put lots of energy into our lives to expect that they will come out all right. There is no magic wand that will allow a person to escape hard work.

tills

This is the Hebrew word *abad* which is work or serve. Solomon declares that the key to having an abundance of bread is to focus on working your work. I am amazed at how many people want good grades for no work, want a great marriage with no effort, want an enjoyable family with no energy expended on the family, want a large paycheck for just sitting around. In order to have abundance of material and/or spiritual and/or psychological benefits, one must work that area.

plenty

This is the Hebrew word *sabea* and means satisfied, fullness, satiated. The key insight here is that to have satisfaction, enjoyment, and fullness in an area, one must work that area. Put some energy into it. If we want a satisfying paycheck, we must put time and energy into work. If we want a satisfying marriage, we must put time and energy into the marriage. In order to enjoy your family, you have to spend time and energy on the family. In each area that we want a satisfying life, we must put work into that area. Too often I think that we want someone to just give us a great marriage or a great family or a great big paycheck or a great church. We often want someone else to do the work to make something good or abundant, and we just want to pluck the flower without the work. Life does not work out that way.

but he who pursues worthless things lacks sense

pursues

This is the Hebrew word *radap* which means to follow, pursue, be behind. One is following after is the idea. Solomon helps us by saying that he sees people not putting in the energy to the places where it would matter but instead, putting in a lot of energy on things that will amount to nothing.

worthless

This is the Hebrew word *reqam* which means vain, empty. These are things that Solomon notices that one can put a lot of time into them but get nothing out of them. It is amazing that he notices this in ancient biblical times when it seems that our culture, in modern times, specializes in these things. We are a culture of innumerable worthless things. People can spend major portions of their life doing things that get them nowhere. The list is almost endless: movies, video games, clothing, shoes, sports, hobbies, etc.

One of the key insights that wise people internalize is that they will put their effort into arenas that have a payoff, not just an escape value. I have watched people live within the midst of a lousy marriage but have meticulous hobbies. I have watched as people know television shows and movies while they don't know their kids or their relatives. I have watched people plunge into debt in order to pursue a favorite singer or sports hero. God keeps screaming back through Solomon: Put your effort into working your land; put the effort into the arena where there will be payoff! You and I have nine relationships, and we need to put sufficient effort into those nine so that each is a vibrant healthy relationship. If we do this, then we will have a satisfying life. What are the nine relationships: God, Marriage, Family, Self, Work, Church, Money, Society, and Friends. Ask yourself if you are putting enough time, energy, and learning in these nine areas.

PROVERBS 12:12 - *The wicked man desires the booty of evil men, but the root of the righteous yields fruit.*

Solomon is trying to help us spot those who are wicked by seeing what they are going after. Those who live outside the lines of God's commandments are aimed at the people who have amassed great wealth through cheating, lying, and illegality. It is their pursuit that gives them away. There is an implied sense that if you have not gone after your pile using corrupt means, then those who are wicked will not go after it.

desires

This is the Hebrew word *chamad* which means to desire or take pleasure in. It also has been translated as covet or delight or that which is precious.

Notice the insight that we are given. It is the wicked person who has an interest in the treasures that come from evil. This would be ill-gotten gain, sexual unfaithfulness, power obtained through corruption, bribery, etc. In other words, what they want is what other wicked people are after.

Notice the connection and distinction between the desires or cravings of the wicked and the yield of the righteous. This is a steady, consistent harvest that comes from the natural results of being righteous versus the impulsive lustful hunger after what is outside the lines of morality. They want that which is perverted and gained by other's loss.

The righteous has yield; the wicked have cravings which they are willing to take shortcuts to obtain. Realize that those who are within the boundaries of God will yield a crop. It will be a righteous crop, and it will be real instead of constant cravings that either are not satisfied or not satisfying.

Be careful what choices you make for it will spell the difference all of your life whether you live with cravings or are satisfied with a fulfilling life.

There is nothing that evil can offer that is as rewarding as a great bond between husband and wife; between parent and children; between yourself and a job well done; between God and you; between a full display of what you were created to do, etc.

PROVERBS 12:13 ~ *An evil man is ensnared by the transgression of his lips, but the righteous will escape from trouble.*

A more literal translation of this proverb would read like: *In the transgression of the lips is an evil snare. But the righteous will come out of trouble.*

The idea here is not an absolute promise about what evil men will do but how lying seems to be a charm that allows you to escape from all kinds of trouble by deceiving people, but this powerful charm of deception ensnares people in a web of deceit that eventually collapses on them. Lies are like a path around the difficult truth or painful situation, but this path is guarded by a long rope with a noose on the end which you step into and it seems like nothing happens. You have escaped the difficult situation, the punishment, the pain; but sometime later that long rope will jerk you back and up and you will be swinging by the lie you told a while back.

Solomon says that the righteous person escapes or goes beyond or misses (Hebrew word *yatsa*) the trouble that was on that convenient path of lying and deception. The righteous person knows that while that path is tempting and offers temporary relief from troubles and difficulties, it also creates great difficulties, pain, and snares down the road.

The righteous person actually weighs out the various options in each situation and decides against the options labeled: half-truth, misrepresentation, lies, deception. It is difficult at times to stay within the smaller boundaries of righteousness, but it pays rich dividends in two directions: the pain, snares, and difficulties you miss and the blessings, relationships, and opportunities that are open to you.

PROVERBS 12:14 - *A man will be satisfied with good by the fruit of his words, and the deeds of a man's hands will return to him.*

Solomon sums up the two sources of a good life in this proverb: what you say and what you do. This is short and sweet and true. If you bludgeon people with your words or gossip, you will destroy your own life. If you are lazy or slow or have no surplus out of which to share with others, you will receive back a diminished life.

satisfied

This is the Hebrew word *sabea* which means to be satisfied; to be fulfilled. The idea here is to have a good life where it fills you up. Where you are enjoying life. One of the images I have used in the past is having a very satisfying meal and, therefore, being full and knowing that you also have a full refrigerator full of food for the future. This is what satisfied means.

Solomon says that when you use the right words and the right deeds, this is the kind of life that will be harvested.

good

This is the Hebrew word *tob* which means good or beneficial or pleasant. Solomon is using this word to say that how you use words and the ones that you allow to escape from your mouth will create either the benefit or cursings that you will live in. If you want to live in a relational sewer, then use words that point out the flaws, the mistakes, and the problems with everyone. If, however, you want to enjoy a picnic-like atmosphere with the people in your life, use words that will help people be around you. Focus on people's strengths and people's positive actions.

fruit of his words

Our words bear fruit. They go out from our mouth and plant themselves in the lives of other people and grow. They either grow thorns, weeds, thistles, or fruit. Ask yourself what kind of words could you use today that will grow fruit in other people's life. This is especially true of your loved ones. We are often so careless with what we say to those who are closest to us.

I heard one good man say that at one point in his life he made a commitment to never treat anyone better than he treated his wife and family. He had discovered that he was treating strangers with greater kindness and mercy and grace than he was treating his family.

Life is Relationships.

The quality and depth of your relationships is the quality and depth of your life, and how you talk about people and to people is crucial to building great relationships and therefore a great life. Not everything you think or flashes across your mind should see the light of day through your mouth. Not everything that is true about another person should be said.

I cannot stress it enough that you must focus on a person's strengths and positive qualities if you are to build a quality life. No one wants to have their weaknesses and mistakes pointed out. I realize that some of you see people's mistakes and problems with laser-like accuracy, but you must get past this. If a person has weaknesses, they also have strengths. These must be focused on.

The second part of this equation is equally true and will result in the life you live. The nature of your deeds: Are they half-hearted? Are they creative? Are they above and beyond what is expected? Are they complete? Are they accurate? Are they consistent? Are they helpful? Are they selfish? Are they rebellious? Are they impulsive? Are they planned? Are they strategic?

All of these – and many more – can describe the way you work. Your life will be the reflection of the payback of the way you work and the way you live. God has given you a cause-and-effect universe. Make the most of it. Live to glorify Him.

PROVERBS 12:15 - *The way of a fool is right in his own eyes, but a wise man is he who listens to counsel.*

fool

This is the Hebrew word *ewil* which means fool, foolish. The actions of a fool are what Solomon is trying to warn us to avoid. It is the natural inclination to selfishness, impulsiveness, and rebellion that will change our destiny and destroy our future.

In this particular case Solomon is pointing out that the foolish person uses the feel test to decide whether something should be done. Does it feel right to me? I hear this all the time. Why did you do what you did? It seemed like the right thing at the time. This kind of thinking happens all the time. A friendship or a romance is beginning and rather than check with family or friends about this person, you decide whether to go deeper based on how it feels to you. A business deal is presented and rather than consult with experts in that field or wise business men you know, you check with yourself to see how it feels to you. You are in the midst of a heated discussion with your spouse and you have some things you want to say to her/him and the only person you check with is yourself and you let fly with a lot of stuff that damages your marriage more. You get a new idea to try something at work and rather than run it past other people on the team, the more you think about it the better it sounds so you just implement it.

Solomon is pointing out that if any of us is not careful, we all fall into this way of living. Remember, foolishness is born into each one of us. Since sin entered into the world back in the Garden of Eden, all of mankind has been infected with a natural inclination to act like the fool that Solomon describes here. This is only counteracted by repentance, faith, discipline, diligence, and conscious decisions to choose wisdom.

PROVERBS 12:16 - *A fool's anger is known at once, but a prudent man conceals dishonor.*

The fool or selfish and impulsive person immediately lets people know in words, actions, and attitude that they did not get what they were expecting. This lack of expectation is the source of much anger. "My expectations were not met." As you grow in wisdom, you realize that it is not healthy for you to let everybody know that you had an expectation that was not met – that everything did not go your way.

As you grow in wisdom, you begin to realize that it is not healthy if everything were to go your way. Much of our expectations are selfish: I want to win all the time; I want to be noticed positively all the time; I want to make the most money; I want everyone to be interested in my ideas; I expect that everyone will feel sorry for me for a long time; I was hoping that I would be the center of attention at school. All of these types of expectation can trigger anger when they are not met. It is much more mature that a person realizes they should not play God or think that they could.

The wise or prudent individual realizes that there will be many times when what they want or expect to happen in their perfect world will not happen. So one's disappointment or anger should be hidden. When something other than what you wanted to happen happens, find a way to go with the flow rather than fighting it and insisting that it would have been better if things had completely broken your way.

It is dishonorable or devaluing to be angry because you did not get your own way. If people see you as a whiner or complainer when things don't go your way, then you will be devalued in their eyes. Just realize that God is God and many times He does not ask you what He will allow to happen. Go with it...

PROVERBS 12:17 - *He who speaks truth tells what is right, but a false witness, deceit.*

speaks

This is the Hebrew word *puach* which means to breathe, blow. The idea here is that the normal – almost unconscious – comments of a person should be evaluated for their truth content. If they are true, then that person is telling you what is right. But if the unexamined and almost unnoticed comments of a person are not true, then do not trust that person to advise you.

Does the person say inaccurate facts? Does the person exaggerate even when they don't need to? Does the person distort the truth to make themselves look good almost as an instinct?

truth

This is the Hebrew word *emunah* which means firmness, steadfastness, fidelity. It is translated *truth*, but it really has the idea of what can be counted on. When this person says it – even if it is a side comment – then you know it is true. That is the kind of person you can count on to guide you right.

right

This is the Hebrew word *tsedeq* which means righteous, rightness. There is in this word both accuracy but also positive in its presentation. Remember that the righteous action is not just the one that is inside the boundaries of what is wrong; but it is positive towards God, others, and yourself. So the person who worries about even their throw-away comments accuracy will work hard to shape their comments to be a positive influence and proper in their orientation. They will not spread that which is a lie nor will they use the truth as a weapon to destroy others or damage that which is good.

Notice that the one is a prerequisite for the other. Solomon is essentially saying you want to know who will steer you in the right direction. Who is saying the best course of action? Who is giving the advice that will make the most positive impact and reliable information? It is the person who obsesses over whether they are accurate and not the person who is into half-truths and manipulative deceptions to make themselves look good.

false witness

This is made up of two Hebrew words *sheqer* which means deception or falsehood and *ed* which means witness or evidence.

Solomon is saying that experience with people and the truthfulness of what they say trumps the words that are coming out of their mouth. If they have been a false witness in the past, they are deceiving you in the present. If they have bent the truth to their advantage, then they are most likely doing it again. Many times we get caught up in what they are saying – especially if what they are saying is what we want to hear – then our ability to be deceived is very great.

I hear this all the time. The gossip who has spread lies about others begins to tell you dirt about someone whom you want to hear dirt about, so you ignore the source of the information. The flirtatious boy or girl who lies to the right person to go with them is lying when they say that they love you – they only love themselves. They will deceive you.

deceit

This is the Hebrew word *mirmah* which means deceit, treachery. Solomon is saying to look at the obvious. The person who manipulates words for their advantage is manipulating words to their advantage. Don't get suckered in by what they are saying. Realize who is saying it.

He is giving us a lesson in real life. We need this lesson.

PROVERBS 12:18 - *There is one who speaks rashly like the thrusts of a sword, but the tongue of the wise brings healing.*

speak rashly

These two English words are really one Hebrew word *batah* which means to speak rashly or thoughtlessly.

Notice what Solomon is doing here. He is comparing some who use words to stab and wound and destroy and some people use words to bring healing and wholeness.

thrusts

This is the Hebrew word *madqarah* which is a piercing, stab, thrust. This idea is the key idea in this verse. People use words as weapons just as they use swords. They power into people with their words.

Solomon is declaring that this is not the work of a wise person. They may be successful because people do not resist them. But this kind of person is not what you think they are. We tend to think that the person – who always has the comeback, always has the ability to put another person down or in their place, or always has the ability to win the argument – is the winner. No, who really wants to deeply connect with the person who can and will leave them bleeding emotionally or psychologically?

Having the snappy comeback does not make you a better person. In fact, it is not wise to always be able to express what you are feeling right when you are feeling it. The winner carefully selects his/her words in order to do the opposite of winning the point at times. They use words to heal.

healing

This is the Hebrew word *marpe* which means a healing, cure, health. Clearly Solomon is saying that the wise person is in exactly the same situation that the fool is in. The wise person does not use words to strike out against the other person. The wise person seeks to bring a new level of wholeness and healing in the life of others – even those others that you would like to thrust the sword of your words into.

Who are the people you would really like to tell off and unload on, thrusting the truth at them and through them? Ask yourself: What do they need to be healed from?

The first step in wisdom with your mouth is to often close it. The second step is to say something positive or keep it closed. The third step is say something that meets a need, heals, and comforts.

PROVERBS 12:19 - *Truthful lips will be established forever, but a lying tongue is only for a moment.*

This is one of the most important but difficult truths to get teens to embrace – the idea that it is better to be truthful than to avoid punishment because of lying. Lying offers a magic wand when you are younger. People want to believe you and so they take you at your word and give you the benefit of the doubt. Some young people have been impressed by the power of lying in their teens and never give up the practice and become addicted to it. It is a shame because lying will catch up with you, and it will destroy what you have so carefully protected and collected.

It is painful to tell the truth at times. It often involves taking responsibility for mistakes and errors that you would just as soon avoid, but it will be a benefit to you over the long haul both in this life and in the one to come. We are hearing more and more cases of bizarre actions by young people where they murder their children rather than give them up for adoption; where spouses kill or seek to hire assassins to kill their spouse rather than walk away; where children brazenly harm or steal from their parents. In each case the people have a history of lying in which it seemed to them that they had always gotten away with their impulses through lying, and this was just one more impulse. Coddling lying is not helpful. It can set up a practice of deception and selfishness that is destructive to meaning, significance, and prosperity.

It is hard to get kids to embrace truth-telling but it must be modeled; it must be taught; it must be demanded; and it must be corrected when it is not demonstrated.

truthful

This is the Hebrew word *emet* which means firmness, truth, even faithful. It is the idea that this statement will stand up to the scrutiny of examination. It is the way things are – it is firm and sure. In this context it is about whether your statements can be said to be accurate and non-deceptive.

established

This is the Hebrew word *ken* which means established, prepared, fixed, certain. The idea is that Solomon is saying that because you can be counted on to speak what corresponds to the actual reality, then your life and reputation will be lasting.

It is clear that Solomon extends the effect of becoming a truth-teller into eternity. He sees a future beyond this world for those who tell the truth. Therefore Christians must be truth-tellers. They are forgiven by the Lord Jesus Christ for their sins, but they then must move forward and become truth-tellers even though it may be to their own hurt.

lying

This is the Hebrew word *seqer* which means lying or false. It does seem that a lie has great power and gets you out of trouble and gains you certain privileges, but those gains are only for a moment is what Solomon is asserting. And quickly the moment of the lie's power will fade and the destruction that it causes will be with you a long time.

PROVERBS 12:20 ~ *Deceit is in the heart of those who devise evil, but counselors of peace have joy.*

deceit

This is the Hebrew word *mirmah* which means deceit, treachery, deception. There is a clear sense of hiddenness. The person who is involved in deceit is hiding some huge piece of information that would change everything if it were revealed.

In this case Solomon exposes that in order to plan to go beyond the Ten Commandments. One has to spend time hiding something that is destructive, harmful, and would change everything if it were to come out. Notice that Solomon says that it resides in the heart of the person who plans evil.

A critical component of planning and executing evil is hiddenness. If you are planning to steal, you need to hide it; if you are planning adultery, you have to hide it; if you are going to blaspheme, you have to hide the fact that you talk that way to some people; if you are going to use anger or violence to intimidate, you have to hide that anger at times. There is hiddenness in order to plan evil. Evil plans cannot be exposed to the proper moral authority.

Ask yourself the question: Can I let people know what I am doing or what I am planning? If I cannot, is it because there is something about it that is unethical, immoral, or illegal?

counselors

This is the Hebrew word *yaats* and it means to advise or counsel. This is a most interesting contrast to the phrase that precedes it. It is not what we would expect. We might expect the phrase *but the one who does right is open*. But instead Solomon sees a connection to peace and joy as the opposite of deceit and evil.

The word *counselors* here means that Solomon is talking about those who advise themselves or others in the proper way will move them to peace rather than hiddenness or immorality.

peace

This is the Hebrew word *shalom* which means peace. It means the absence of war; it means a harmony between people that is positive, not just the absence of fighting; it means a place of blessing.

Peace, in a biblical context, is a positive. It means that people are getting along in a good way to accomplish something that they could not do apart. It means to harmonize, to produce something – two or more people who were playing separate tunes decide to play a tune together in which both can equally participate. Something more than the absence of hostility is involved in real biblical peace – a reuniting of relationship and a new teamwork to create a new thing.

joy

This is the Hebrew word *simchah* which means joy, gladness, mirth. It carries with it the idea of internal happiness and fulfillment. Joy always is about lining up in a deeper way with some relationship. The joy comes from the deeper connection with the person in the relationship. It could be God who gives you this new joy as you pursue and secure a new relationship with Him. It could be with your spouse, your children, your job, your friends, or with folks at church; but deeper relationships are so satisfying that it bubbles up a level of pleasure that can only be described as joy.

One of the things that Solomon is pointing out in this proverb is that in order to do evil, someone has to be harmed. That harm will be exposed at some later date. But if instead of doing harm to others you were a counselor of peace, you would have more joy when the relationship lined up for more results. Don't be selfish. Don't be selfish to the level that it is beyond the Ten Commandments because it will require that you set about hiding some truth. Also, you will miss out on the deep joy of harmonizing with the people in your life in a new way.

PROVERBS 12:21 - *No harm befalls the righteous, but the wicked are filled with trouble.*

This is a statement of Solomon's observation. It sounds wrong, but you have to look beneath the surface to see what Solomon is saying. The word *harm* is the Hebrew word *aven* which means vanity, unrighteousness, mischief, sorrow. The word *befalls* is the Hebrew word *anah* which means happen upon, meeting, approach. The key idea in this proverb is that the righteous God protects them from chance evil and harmful difficulties. The wicked, on the other hand, are always around that which is harmful and are constantly bumping into and having chance occurrences with problems, difficulties, and the like.

It is not that the righteous don't have bad things happen to them, but they do not have chance or random evil happen to them. God protects them from those things. The things that God lets into the righteous' life are there for a reason. The life of the wicked has lots of chance destruction that pour into their lives.

Solomon is saying that if you live the righteous life (stay within the Ten Commandments), you will not have all these bad things just happen to you. He is saying that he has watched people live both ways and what he has noted is that the wicked have one tragedy after another slam into their lives unannounced and unwanted. But the righteous are protected from so much. On one hand, it is because they do not constantly live around evil and selfish pursuits. And on the other hand, God keeps the righteous from being impacted by them.

I have heard some people say that they think that they are cursed because all kinds of bad things keep happening to them. Solomon is saying that you are not cursed, you are wicked. There is a level of selfishness in how you are living that has moved you outside of God's moral boundary structure and, therefore, random evil and chance destruction slams into you. Get out of there – repent of your selfishness and run to Jesus for forgiveness and a new start.

PROVERBS 12:22 - *Lying lips are an abomination to the Lord, but those who deal faithfully are His delight.*

lying

This is the Hebrew word *sheqer* which means deception, disappointment, falsehood. Solomon does not pull any punches. To be a liar is clearly a huge thing. Don't think that lying is just a little sin; it is an abomination.

abomination

This is the Hebrew word *toebah* which means abomination, detestable, loathsome. To become a person who twists and distorts the truth to suit your own interest causes the society to lose an essential cohesion. It loses its trust.

faithfully

This is the Hebrew word *emunah* which means firmness, steadfastness, fidelity. The idea is clearly that truthfulness wins out over lies in God's eyes. You want to please God.

delight

This is the Hebrew word *ratson* which means good will, favor, acceptance, will. God takes delight when you tell the truth and are firm about what you pledged to do – even if it will cost you. Never forget this.

Notice that the focus of this proverb is on morality that we are aware of, but the benefit of being moral is not what we typically think a lot about. How do we bring delight to God and how do we become His delight? Isn't this a wonderful concept of being the delight of God? Think of God watching you and just delighting in what you are doing and how you are acting. When we say the truthful thing – even if hurts us or makes life difficult for us – God finds that delightful. I believe that it is because doing the unselfish thing is so contrary to our nature. This is evidence of the spark of God in our lives. Can't you see His saying to one of the angels: "Look over there, Gil is telling the truth even though it will cost him. I delight in that." Think about what it is like to be the delight of God's eyes. Think about the relationship God has with those who are His delight. Think about the blessings that He bestows on those who delight Him. Think about how He protects those who delight Him. Become God's delight and turn away from lying.

PROVERBS 12:23 - *A prudent man conceals knowledge, but the heart of fools proclaims folly.*

prudent

This is the Hebrew word *orma* which means guile, prudence, shrewdness. The idea seems to carry with it the idea of strategy to accomplish a goal. In other words, one needs to know what to share and when to share it so that a righteous goal can be accomplished.

conceals

This is the Hebrew word *kasa* which means to cover, to conceal, to hide. There are many times that the knowledge and even the strategy you are following needs to be hidden in order to accomplish your goals. Solomon is stating that there are times for secrecy of purpose and goal in order to bring about a righteous end.

knowledge

This is the Hebrew word *data* which means knowledge and skill. Not saying all that you know or all that you can do is strategic at various points in your life.

heart

This is the Hebrew word *leb* which is the standard word for the inner part of man or the soul. Notice that the soul of the fool is what proclaims what the person is about – the whole idea of what you think about proclaiming whether you are a fool or not. If you are consumed in your mind with yourself, with what you want, and with your pleasure, then you are a fool.

fools

This is the Hebrew word *kesil* which is a standard Solomonic designation for a selfish, rebellious, impulsive person: the fool.

proclaims

This is the Hebrew word *qara* which means to call out, to call, to recite. The idea is of proclamation or announcement. When you ask fools what they are thinking about, the answer is themselves. They want themselves to win even though others – even lots of others – lose. They do not think of ways to bless others; they think of ways to bless themselves.

folly

This is the Hebrew word *ewili* which means foolish, folly. The whole of folly is that which is selfish. It is what I really want to do with little thought to consequences, to impact, to others. What the fool is thinking about just screams out selfishness.

One of the things that you must learn to do is to focus on benefiting those around you as you are looking to benefiting yourself. Your choices and actions must encompass both or they are not an option. You must also develop an ability to be strategic about the accomplishment of your wise goals. You must also realize that the world does not revolve around you. You have a part to play in God's plan, but you are not the center of His plan for the kingdom.

PROVERBS 12:24 - *The hand of the diligent will rule, but the slack hand will be put to forced labor.*

You either make yourself work hard or someone else will make you work hard. It is your choice, but you will work hard. It is always more pleasant to be your own goad than to have someone else who does not have your best interests at heart do it.

diligent

This is the Hebrew word *harus* which means sharp, diligent, diligence, decisive. There is an idea in this word of acting quickly and decisively. While the translation of the word diligence is not wrong, it does not usually bring to mind a crucial part of this word in the Hebrew which is decisiveness.

One of the things that Solomon is pointing out is that a person who wants to be in charge must not be lazy or slow or procrastinate, but they must be decisive. A person who wants to be in charge must not be afraid to make a decision. If you constantly want to wait until the right decision is obvious to everyone, then you will not be put in charge.

This is one of the problems with the bureaucratic mentality: launch another study instead of making a decision and moving forward. Now wisdom collects as much knowledge as it can and always wants more, but there will be a time when a decision is called for along with the hard work and you must be prepared to make it.

Because the translators chose to use the English word *diligent* instead of *decisive,* one of the crucial insights from this 3,000-year old proverb is missed. It is not how hard you work that will lead to authority but your ability to make critical decisions that will eventually put you in a leadership position.

Do you know how to make the tough decisions? What informs those decisions? Do you have biblical, personal, and professional counselors who can walk you through these kinds of decisions?

rule

This is the Hebrew word *masal* which means rule, have dominion, reign. It clearly means to be a leader, to be in charge here. If you want to ever be in charge, you must develop the ability to be decisive.

slack

This is the Hebrew word *remiya* which means slackening or deceit. This is the word often associated with sloth, slow, loose, less than the best. It is interesting that it is clearly about putting in a two-thirds effort.

But there is also, in this word that Solomon chooses here, the idea of betrayal and deceit which is an interesting play-off of decisiveness. If your decisiveness is selfish and it deceives others or betrays others, then you will be put to forced labor. We are seeing this kind of selfish grasping in the ranks of major business leaders who deceived stockholders, the government, and even its own board to amass great wealth for themselves. They are ending up in prison doing forced labor.

forced labor

This is the Hebrew word *mas* which means taskmasters, forced labor, slave labor. You are not in charge is the idea, and others are making you do things that are not easy or enjoyable.

Laziness and deceit will produce this type of result. It may look like you have a situation where you don't have to work hard or where you can deceive people for your own gain, but it will catch up with you. You will not gain leadership by laziness and deceit.

PROVERBS 12:25 - *Anxiety in a man's heart weighs it down, but a good word makes it glad.*

anxiety

This is the Hebrew word *deagah* which means anxiety, concern, anxious care. If we follow the rest of the Scripture, this is a nervous preoccupation with what is beyond our control. The key to fixing anxiety is action. Do what you can do and leave the rest to God and others. Anxiety gets a grip on our heart because it convinces us that all this worry is really accomplishing something.

In the New Testament it says: *Be anxious for nothing, but in everything by prayer and supplication with thanksgiving let your requests be made known to God.* (Philippians 4:6)

weighs

This is the Hebrew word *shachah* which means to bow down, to bring homage, brings down. The idea here is that this nervous energy and desire to change what you cannot change becomes a weight that wears you down. The opposite of this is faith or action. Anxiety is inaction and a lack of trust.

When we are anxious, we are just sitting still and revving our engines with nothing to do. We need to determine if there is anything we can do and if there is, then we need to do it. If there is not, then we must trust God and pray to Him for what He understands to be the best.

Too many times we cop-out instead of really engaging in actual efforts that we can do. We allow anxiousness to eat us alive because something is out of our control. If it is, then let it be in God's hands where it belongs. If there are things that you need to do, then do them.

but a good word makes it glad

Nervous energy that takes no action or won't trust God is a great weight, but good news about what we are waiting for brings a lightness to the soul. Encouraging words may be just words, but they make all the difference.

There are a few questions that automatically jump out of this proverb:

- Do you worry regularly? Take action in a righteous direction. It is hard to be anxious when you are busy doing good and right things.

- When people see you coming, do they expect you to give them an encouraging word or a negative/critical word?

- Name three people you will run into today. What three positive encouraging things can you say to each of them?

PROVERBS 12:26 - *The righteous is a guide to his neighbor, but the way of the wicked leads them astray.*

Solomon is trying to get us to see that the righteous person is more than just the person who does things right. He is screaming that righteousness is about positive benefit to others. We often see righteousness as Pharisaical obsession with the rules, but this is not the essence of true godly righteousness.

True godly righteousness is about positive benefit being added to the relationships in your life. Look at the two great commandments: *You shall love the Lord your God with all your heart, and with all your soul, and with all your mind. You shall love your neighbor as yourself.* These two commandments which sum up the whole law and the prophets are about positive benefit. With God, it is glorify Him in your actions, words, attitudes, and motives. With all the other relationships, it is the positive benefit of meeting their needs.

See how Solomon is phrasing it here. The righteous person makes sure that his neighbor is guided to the right place, to a beneficial place. It is not okay for a person making a claim to righteousness to not help another person whom they can help. This is Jesus' lesson with the parable of the Good Samaritan. Your neighbor is anyone whose need you see and whose need you're in a position to help.

guide

This is the Hebrew word *tur* which means seek out, explore, investigate, guide. The idea is that the righteous person cares about those around him. He seeks to understand them and what they need.

Are you making a positive difference in each of the ten relationships that surround you: God, Self, Marriage, Family, Church, Work, Money, Society, Friends, Enemies. That is what it means to be righteous. Make sure that you do not limit your understanding of righteousness to a little concept of not making any mistakes.

but the way of the wicked leads them astray

Notice that the wicked person does harm to his neighbor. The wicked person is the one who selfishly seeks his own benefit to the degree that he regularly harms his neighbor to get it.

In other words, if the wicked have to steer a person they know into a bad investment to make a commission, they will. If the wicked have to cover up a faulty aspect of a used car to sell it, they will. If the wicked person can get a better grade by taking a page from the library so that others can't study from that page, the wicked person will do that. If a wicked person needs a dupe to make fun of and to have a good time, he may fake friendship to get someone drunk to make fun of them. If a wicked person wants sexual relations, he may use drugs to date-rape a woman. Remember that the key to moving across the line to wickedness is being willing to harm others to get what you want.

Solomon is trying to get us to move across the righteousness line and look to be benefiting others. Don't slide across the line of wickedness. It is not worth it.

PROVERBS 12:27 *A lazy man does not roast his prey, but the precious possession of a man is diligence.*

lazy

This is the Hebrew word *emiyyah* which means laxness, slackness, laziness, negligent.

Solomon is acting like a life coach to those who need to recognize certain types of people that will come across their path. You do not want to become the partner of a lazy person or become a lazy person yourself. So you need to know the clues that will tip you off to this character flaw in other people or in yourself.

The character flaw that Solomon exposes here is that lazy people skip essential or crucial steps to get what they want. It is not that they don't know the steps; it is that they just skip them. This is a sign of laziness. Eliminate this tendency in yourself and lower your association and/or contracts with partners like this.

roast

This is the Hebrew word *churak* which means scorch, parch, or roast. The idea here seems to be cook in some form. The person who caught a game animal would clean it and then cook it on an open spit which would kill parasites and other bacteria.

The point Solomon is trying to make is that lazy people are unwilling to do basic things. They just want the easy way. They take risks to get to what they want then suffer the consequences for what they have not done.

Solomon is saying that there are clues to the fact that you are dealing with lazy or slack people. The clue is that they skip crucial steps.

precious

This is the Hebrew word *yaqar* which means precious, rare, splendid, weighty. The idea here is that this is rare. It is wonderful to possess personally and to see evidenced in your friends, family, and associates. This quality of diligence is extremely valuable.

possession

This is the Hebrew word *hon* which means wealth, sufficiency, riches, possession. Solomon is separating out character qualities that are worth paying the price to develop. One of them is diligence.

diligence

This is the Hebrew word *charuts* which means sharp, diligent. The idea of staying with it; the idea of doing all the parts of a project and not skipping any just because it is easier; making sure that you are fully prepared for the task at hand.

Is the person prepared? Does he/she take the necessary steps in order to produce the best outcome? Are you skipping steps in order to get what you want?

PROVERBS 12:28 - *In the way of righteousness is life, and in its pathway there is no death.*

This proverb is so profound and significant in that it gives a glimpse of where the life of righteousness leads after separation from the body in this present world. The phrasing in the Hebrew of the second part is very difficult to translate. Some have really liked the NIV translation: *along that path is immortality.*

Solomon explains clearly that it is righteousness that is the requirement for entrance to heaven and immortality. This verse is considered one of the earliest references to immortality in the Old Testament.

righteousness

This is the Hebrew word *sedeq* which means justice or righteousness. It means living within God's moral boundaries and doing positive, loving things within those boundaries. It is our original design to happily stay within God's boundaries, looking to bless and love others; but because of the Devil's and Adam's sin, we now face a world and an inner man that is completely dedicated to selfishness. We must lean against this in-borne selfishness and choose to love and care for others even though at times it does not feel right.

The Apostle Paul picks up this theme in Romans when he says what if those who were not seeking righteousness found the righteousness of God? And what if those seeking it missed it?

life

This is the Hebrew word *haya* which means live, have life, live prosperously. At times this word means just physical life, but at other times it is a quality of existence for which we all strive.

Solomon points out that this quality is connected to righteous living. It feels like real fun and living is out there on the plains of selfishness doing what you want. But it is not.

pathway

Clearly the pathway here refers to the way of life that a righteous person lives. Their life has consequences just as the way of sin does. A quality of life comes from living righteously just as a natural result of living in sin is death – either spiritual, mental, emotional, or physical.

Interestingly enough the Septuagint version is somewhat different and reads in this second phrase: *in the way of malice is death*. The word malice does not appear in the Hebrew.

death

This is the Hebrew word *mawet* which means death, dying. All men are *bene mawet* "sons of death," but this passage is looking at death from a different angle. This verse pierces beyond the veil and encourages us to see that immortality and righteousness are connected.

Physical death for the righteous is just a momentary interruption in the life of connectedness they have been experiencing with an even greater fulfillment on the other side.

Some commentators do not want to see that Solomon jumped beyond the horizontal plane of human existence in this verse. But it is natural for Solomon to project out and show the end of the life of righteousness: immortality.

Being righteous and wise brings ever deepening relationships with those whom we love and who are willing to love us back. This verse declares that the love and depth and joy that are developed here through righteousness and wisdom continue even after the physical separation from the body. God invites us into life at a whole new plane of existence.

About the Author

Gil Stieglitz is a catalyst for positive change both personally and organizationally. He excites, educates, and motivates audiences all over the world through passion, humor, leadership, and wisdom. He has led seminars in China, Europe, Canada, Mexico, and all over the United States.

In 1992, Dr. Gil founded the non-profit ministry *Principles to Live By* to help people and organizations win at life through biblical wisdom. Dr. Gil has been asked to repair, lead, and reinvigorate numerous organizations and individuals. He successfully led a church to 1,400% growth in a disadvantaged area. As a Denominational Superintendent in the Western United States, he led 50 churches and 250 pastors to over 300% growth. As a Superintendent of Schools, he oversaw a school system as it doubled in four years. As an executive pastor at a mega-church, he rebuilt a staff and added over one thousand people to its congregation. He injects dynamic life-change as a professor at universities and graduate schools on the West Coast and through seminars, sermons, and lecture series. He also partners with Courage Worldwide, a ministry that rescues young girls away from forced sexual slavery in America.

He has a B.A. from Biola University, as well as a Master's Degree and a Doctorate in Christian Leadership from Talbot School of Theology. He has authored over two-dozen books, manuals, and development courses, including three best sellers. Dr. Gil's resources are available at Amazon.com as well as at www.ptlb.com.

Gil and his wife, Dana, have enjoyed over twenty-five years of marriage and reside in Roseville, California, where they raised their three precious girls.

Other Resources by Gil Stieglitz

Books

Becoming Courageous

Breakfast with Solomon Volume 1

Breakfast with Solomon Volume 2

Breakfast with Solomon Volume 3

Breaking Satanic Bondage

Deep Happiness: The Eight Secrets

Delighting in God

Delighting in Jesus

Developing a Christian Worldview

God's Radical Plan for Husbands

God's Radical Plan for Wives

Going Deep In Prayer: 40 Days of In-Depth Prayer

Leading a Thriving Ministry

Marital Intelligence

Mission Possible: Winning the Battle Over Temptation

Proverbs: A Devotional Commentary Volume 1

Satan and The Origin of Sin

Secrets of God's Armor

Spiritual Disciplines of a C.H.R.I.S.T.I.A.N

The Schemes of Satan

They Laughed When I Wrote Another Book About Prayer,
Then They Read It

Touching the Face of God: 40 Days of Adoring God

Why There Has to Be a Hell

Podcasts

Becoming a Godly Parent

Biblical Meditation: The Keys of Transformation

Everyday Spiritual Warfare Series

God's Guide to Handling Money

Spiritual War Surrounding Money

The Four Keys to a Great Family

The Ten Commandments

If you would be interested in having Gil Stieglitz speak to your group, you can contact him through the website, www.ptlb.com.